The
Genetic, Metabolic and Developmental Aspects
of
Mental Retardation

The
Genetic, Metabolic and Developmental Aspects
of
Mental Retardation

Edited by

ROBERT F. MURRAY, JR, M.D., F.A.C.P.

Associate Professor, Departments of Pediatrics and Medicine; Chief, Genetics Unit, Department of Pediatrics, Howard University College of Medicine; Attending Physician, Freedmen's Hospital, Washington, D.C.

and

PEARL LOCKHART ROSSER, M.D., F.A.A.P.

Associate Professor, Department of Pediatrics; Medical Director, Child Development Center, Department of Pediatrics, Howard University College of Medicine; Attending Physician, Freedmen's Hospital, Washington, D.C.

With a Foreword by

Roland B. Scott, M.D.

Professor and Chairman, Department of Pediatrics and Child Health, Howard University College of Medicine, Washington, D.C.

CHARLES C THOMAS · PUBLISHER
Springfield · Illinois · U.S.A.

Published and Distributed Throughout the World by

CHARLES C THOMAS • PUBLISHER

BANNERSTONE HOUSE

301-327 East Lawrence Avenue, Springfield, Illinois, U.S.A.

With THOMAS BOOKS *careful attention is given to all details of manufacturing and design. It is the Publisher's desire to present books that are satisfactory as to their physical qualities and artistic possibilities and appropriate for their particular use.* THOMAS BOOKS *will be true to those laws of quality that assure a good name and good will.*

Printed in the United States of America

C-1

CONTRIBUTORS

WILLIAM W. BARR, B.A., M.S.W.

Deputy Director for Youth Services
Department of Human Resources
Government of the District of Columbia
Washington, D.C.

BARBARA D. BATEMAN, Ph.D.

Professor of Education
Department of Special Education
University of Oregon
Eugene, Oregon

E. PAUL BENOIT, Ph.D.

Professor of Psychology
Université du Québec á Trois-Riviéres
Trois-Riviéres, Québec

HARRIE R. CHAMBERLIN, M.D.

Director, Division for Disorders of Development and Learning
Child Development Institute
University of North Carolina
Professor of Pediatrics
University of North Carolina School of Medicine
Chapel Hill, North Carolina

MARY B. COLEMAN, M.D.

Associate Director, Clinical Research Center
Children's Hospital of D.C.
Washington, D.C.

LOIS-ELLIN DATTA, Ph.D.

Acting Chief, Evaluation Branch, Research and Evaluation
Office of Child Development
Department of Health, Education and Welfare
Washington, D.C.

LEON EISENBERG, M.D.

Professor of Psychiatry
Harvard University School of Medicine
Chief of Psychiatry
Massachusetts General Hospital
Boston, Massachusetts

MURRAY FEINGOLD, M.D.

Director, Center for Genetic Counseling and
Birth Defects Evaluation
Boston Floating Hospital
Boston, Massachusetts

C.B. FERSTER, Ph.D.

Professor and Chairman
Department of Psychology
The American University
Washington, D.C.

MAURICE H. FOURACRE, Ph.D.

Director
St. John's Child Development Center
Washington, D.C.

WILFRED Y. FUJIMOTO, M.D.

Assistant Professor of Medicine
Division of Endocrinology
Department of Medicine
University of Washington School of Medicine
Seattle, Washington

HOSSEIN GHADIMI, M.D., F.A.A.P.

Professor of Pediatrics
Downstate Medical Center
State University of New York
Brooklyn, New York

EDWARD GLASSMAN, Ph.D.

Professor of Biochemistry and Genetics
Division of Chemical Neurobiology
Department of Biochemistry
Director of the Neurobiology Program
University of North Carolina Medical School
Chapel Hill, North Carolina

JACOB D. GOERING, Ph.D.

Associate Professor of Education
Institute for Child Study
University of Maryland
College Park, Maryland

I. IGNACY GOLDBERG, Ed.D.

Professor of Education
Columbia University
New York, New York

EDMUND W. GORDON, Ed.D.

Chairman and Professor
Department of Guidance
Teacher's College
Columbia University
New York, New York

FREDERICK HECHT, M.D.

Associate Professor of Pediatrics and Medical Genetics
Co-Director, Genetics Clinic
University of Oregon Medical School
Portland, Oregon

CLIFTON R. JONES, Ph.D.

Professor and Chairman
Department of Sociology and Anthropology
Howard University
Washington, D.C.

JENNY W. KLEIN, Ed.D.

Senior Education Specialist
Project Head Start
Office of Child Development
Washington, D.C.

ROBERT F. MURRAY, JR., M.D., M.S.

Associate Professor
Departments of Pediatrics and Medicine
Chief, Medical Genetics Unit
Howard University College of Medicine
Washington, D.C.

JOHN S. O'BRIEN, M.D.

Professor and Chairman of Neurosciences
Department of Neurosciences
University of California School of Medicine
San Diego, California

WRETHA K. PETERSEN, Ed.D.

Program Director
Children's Achievement Center
Falls Church, Virginia

C. RONALD SCOTT, M.D.

Associate Professor
Department of Pediatrics
University of Washington School of Medicine
Seattle, Washington

J. PHILIP WELCH, M.D., Ch.B., Ph.D.

Assistant Professor of Paediatrics
Department of Paediatrics
Dalhousie University
Halifax, Nova Scotia, Canada

JOHN E. WILSON, Ph.D.

Professor of Biochemistry and Genetics
Division of Chemical Neurobiology
Department of Biochemistry
Associate Director of the Neurobiology Program
University of North Carolina Medical School
Chapel Hill, North Carolina

CARL J. WITKOP, JR., D.D.S., M.S.

Chairman, Division of Human and Oral Genetics
School of Dentistry
University of Minnesota
Minneapolis, Minnesota

To Our Families

FOREWORD

THE contents of this book originated from presentations made by participants in a seminar entitled "The Genetic, Metabolic and Developmental Aspects of Mental Retardation" held at the Howard University College of Medicine in 1969. This seminar was developed and organized cooperatively by the Medical Genetics Unit and the Child Development Center of this University. The main objective of the seminar was to provide an opportunity for physicians, educators, sociologists, social workers, psychologists, nurses and other professionals to review the advances in, and application of, newer knowledge in the area of genetics and child development in the everyday practice of child care.

The large attendance at the seminar and the enthusiastic reception of the program by the people from many disciplines encouraged the editors to compile this publication. Manuscripts were updated and revised for publication by individual authors prior to compilation and printing. This book is particularly timely in that it reflects the team or multidisciplinary approach which is receiving wide acceptance at present in the delivery of comprehensive medical care to healthy as well as retarded children. The book should be of interest and value to all persons who play a role in the professional care of children both average and exceptional.

ROLAND B. SCOTT

PREFACE

THE seminar on the "Genetic, Metabolic and Developmental Aspects of Mental Retardation," of which this book is an outgrowth, brought together many persons of varying backgrounds and specialties, all united in a common bond of interest, namely brain function at the biochemical genetic level, the developmental level and the behavioral level.

The common denominator used was that of mental retardation. The fundamental interest was in child and human development. The common goal was to relate behavior and development to brain function, and brain function to biochemical, genetic and environmental factors. Though this seems an impossible task at this point in time, progress is evident and continuing communication is essential.

It is a well-established fact that genetic and environmental factors work together to produce the complex world of living matter. It is an equally important fact that even after living matter has been established, typically or atypically, an infinite number of interactions between exogenous and environmental forces modify its basic pattern of development and level of function.

Homo sapiens is distinguished from the remainder of the animal kingdom by virtue of his superior intellectual development. The distinctive cerebral functions by which man has achieved his fantastic evolutionary success are also the most susceptible to malfunction and to damage from exogenous forces. This is not surprising since it is those most sensitive and complex mechanical and/or biological mechanisms that have the greatest chance of breaking down. That this is true is seen not only in the high frequency of mental retardation found in Western society, but also in the much higher frequency of cerebral dysfunctions and mental illness that is found.

Biological scientists have been able to gain considerable insight into the mechanisms that underlie the functions of most of the major organs of the body, but they are still essentially in the dark about the way the human brain functions to receive, interpret, store and integrate information as well as the multitude of stimuli it receives from the internal and the outside world.

Elucidating the basic biochemical or chromosomal defects responsible for some forms of mental retardation has provided further evidence of the complexity of cerebral function without unlocking the doors hiding the secrets of brain function.

These secrets of function are much more likely to yield to a multifaceted rather than a unilateral approach. In other words, the unified understanding of the function of a single brain may well result from study by many brains with different kinds of special input and biased perceptions. When the brain (or mind) is studied from only one perspective it can only be understood in part. Even more than the study of other organs, it is clear that the study of brain function must be an interdisciplinary effort.

Many questions about mental function remain unanswered.

1. What are the biochemical activities that are responsible for mental function?
2. How do these relate to the reception, interpretation and storage of external (and internal) stimuli?
3. What are the components of learning process?
4. How is learning affected by the environment and the emotions?
5. What can be done to enhance the learning process?
6. What are the best ways to evaluate mental function?

Success in remediation of disturbances in brain function (gross or subtle) frequently depends heavily on early identification. Because of the complexity of the problem the need for a multidisciplinary approach to diagnosis, treatment and research cannot be overemphasized. Not only does this approach provide a more complete understanding of brain function and dysfunction, but it affords the patient the benefit of the most valid diagnosis and the most effective therapy—medical, psychosocial and educational. It requires only humility to acknowledge that any one professional discipline is less than omnipotent.

Conferences such as the one on which this book is based, as well as books such as this one, have as their prime purpose the improvement of communications between members of different disciplines and the fostering of meaningful functioning relationships between the disciplines which aid in keeping members of one area aware of expertise and advances in other areas. If this volume does nothing more than this, it will have been well worth the effort that went into its preparation.

ROBERT F. MURRAY, JR.
PEARL L. ROSSER

ACKNOWLEDGMENTS

THE editors wish to express sincere appreciation to the contributors to this volume who devoted valuable time in preparation of the original manuscript as well as updating these presentations for publication. We are especially grateful to the support received from the United States Children's Bureau, Maternal and Child Health, Department of Health, Education and Welfare (Special Projects 414 and 429), the Johnson and Johnson Institute for Pediatric Service, and the Committee on Continuing Medical Education, Howard University College of Medicine for the presentation of the seminar from which this publication is a result.

We are especially indebted to Mrs. Mary O. Lofton and Mrs. Sue-Anne Wall for their skilled secretarial work; and to Mrs. Zoë Page for library assistance.

Finally, we wish to thank the staff of Charles C Thomas, Publisher, for all consideration, assistance and cooperation.

CONTENTS

Page

Foreword—*Roland B. Scott* xii

Preface xv

Acknowledgments xix

PART I

GENETIC AND METABOLIC ASPECTS OF MENTAL RETARDATION

Chapter

I. HUMAN CHROMOSOME ABERRATIONS: CORRELATIONS WITH MENTAL AND GROWTH RETARDATION—*Frederick Hecht* . 5

II. 5-HYDROXYTRYPTOPHAN ADMINISTRATION IN DOWN'S SYNDROME—*Mary B. Coleman* 26

III. BEHAVIORAL AND COGNITIVE ASPECTS OF THE XYY CONDITION—*J. Philip Welch* 30

IV. AMINOACIDOPATHIES AND MENTAL RETARDATION—*Hossein Ghadimi* 45

V. MENTAL RETARDATION AND SELF-DESTRUCTIVE BEHAVIOR (CLINICAL AND BIOCHEMICAL FEATURES OF THE LESCH-NYHAN SYNDROME)—*Wilfred Y. Fujimoto* 58

VI. MOLECULAR DEFECT AND MENTAL RETARDATION (GENERALIZED GANGLIOSIDOSIS)—*John S. O'Brien* 75

VII. THE MUCOPOLYSACCHARIDOSES (RECOGNITION AND DIAGNOSIS)—*C. Ronald Scott* 93

VIII. HISTIDINEMIC-LIKE BEHAVIOR IN CHILDREN RECOVERED FROM KWASHIORKOR—*Carl J. Witkop, Jr.* 108

IX. POSSIBLE BIOCHEMICAL APPLICATIONS IN THE TRAINING OF THE MENTALLY RETARDED—*Edward Glassman and John E. Wilson* 138

X. HAND ABNORMALITIES IN MALFORMATION SYNDROMES ASSOCIATED WITH MENTAL RETARDATION—*Murray Feingold* 151

XI. "SIMPLE" MENTAL RETARDATION—*Robert F. Murray, Jr.* 159

xxi

Part II

DEVELOPMENTAL ASPECTS OF MENTAL RETARDATION

Chapter   *Page*

XII. PERINATAL FACTORS IN THE PRODUCTION OF CEREBRAL
DEFICIT—*Harrie R. Chamberlin* 173

XIII. CASTE, CLASS AND INTELLIGENCE—*Leon Eisenberg* . . 185

XIV. THE DISADVANTAGED CHILD: HIS CULTURAL MILIEU AND
EDUCATION—*Clifton R. Jones* 199

XV. SOME EDUCATIONAL APPROACHES AND TECHNIQUES FOR
CHILDREN FROM SOCIALLY DISADVANTAGED BACKGROUNDS—
Edmund W. Gordon 215

XVI. THE AMELIORATION OF MENTAL DEFICIENCY—*Barbara D.
Bateman* 228

XVII. THE MULTIDIMENSIONAL PROBLEMS AND ISSUES OF EDUCAT-
ING RETARDED CHILDREN, YOUTH AND ADULTS—*I. Ignacy
Goldberg* 238

XVIII. THE USE OF LEARNING PRINCIPLES IN THE EDUCATION AND
MANAGEMENT OF RETARDED CHILDREN—*C. B. Ferster* . 262

XIX. DIAGNOSTIC TEACHING OF THE RETARDED PRESCHOOL
CHILD—*Jenny W. Klein* 274

XX. EARLY EDUCATION OF MODERATELY MENTALLY RETARDED
CHILDREN—*Maurice H. Fouracre* 279

XXI. A THEORETICAL LOOK AT LEARNING IN THE MENTALLY
RETARDED—*E. Paul Benoit* 288

XXII. DEVELOPMENTAL-ENVIRONMENTAL VARIABLES ASSOCIATED
WITH MENTAL RETARDATION—*Jacob D. Goering* . . . 295

XXIII. SOME FINDINGS ON THE IMPACT OF EARLY STIMULATION
PROGRAMS ON ASPECTS OF COGNITIVE AND SOCIAL-EMO-
TIONAL DEVELOPMENT—*Lois-ellin Datta* 304

XXIV. PROBLEMS OF DELINQUENCY IN THE MILDLY RETARDED
CHILD—*William W. Barr* 316

XXV. THE IMPORTANCE OF AN EARLY DEFINITIVE EDUCATIONAL
EVALUATION OF THE CHILD WITH LEARNING DISABILITIES—
Wretha K. Petersen 324

Glossary 329
Index 335

The
Genetic, Metabolic and Developmental Aspects
of
Mental Retardation

Part I

GENETIC AND METABOLIC ASPECTS OF MENTAL RETARDATION

Chapter I

HUMAN CHROMOSOME ABERRATIONS: CORRELATIONS WITH MENTAL AND GROWTH RETARDATION

FREDERICK HECHT

AUTOSOMES AND INTELLIGENCE

THE first illustration (Fig. I-1) shows a pair of nonidentical twins. One youngster has Down's syndrome whereas her nonidentical twin sister does not. Many of the stigmata of Down's syndrome (mongolism) can be recognized, such as epicanthal folds. The findings that a) dizygotic twins were concordant for Down's syndrome, and b) approximately half the children born

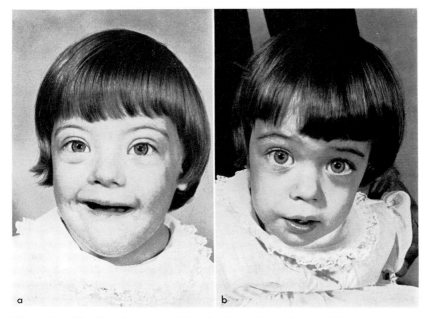

Figure I-1. Nonidentical twins. One has Down's syndrome. The other is normal. Such twin sets are historically important in having suggested the chromosomal basis of Down's syndrome before chromosomal studies were possible in man.

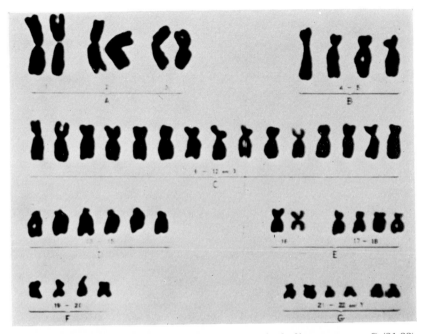

Figure I-2. Karyotype showing 47 chromosomes including an extra G (21-22) chromosome, characteristic of Down's syndrome.

to mothers with Down's syndrome were themselves affected, hinted in the prechromosomal era at the genetic basis of Down's syndrome. The chromosome studies in Down's syndrome published by Lejeune and co-workers in 1959 ushered in the era of medical cytogenetics in man. The historical development of human cytogenetics is described by Turpin and Lejeune in their now classical book.[1]

The karyotype in Figure I-2 comes from the medical genetics file at Howard University. It shows the extra chromosome which is found in a large majority of children with Down's syndrome. There is an extra chromosome in the G group which includes pairs 21 and 22. The extra chromosome has been agreed upon as chromosome 21. This chromosome is now easily distinguished from chromosome 22 by quinicrine fluorescent or by modified Giemsa staining methods. Figure I-3 shows a partial karyotype. At the top are the usual chromosome findings in mongolism: an extra chromosome 21. On the bottom line is one of the other types of chromosomal configurations found in Down's syndrome: a translocation in which the extra chromosome has been broken and has been attached to one of the other chromosomes, in this case, from the D (13-15) group. Autoradiographic studies[2] indicate these translocations commonly involved chromosome 14, less commonly chromosome 15 and only rarely to date chromosome 13. Translocations are potentially heritable types of chromosome abnormality. The recurrence risks are not predictable on theoretical grounds alone. They can only be based upon data that has been collected from family studies,[3] which incidentally is why segregation data on translocations should be published to add to our collective experience. Each translocation appears to follow its own set of rules in the risk it offers to the offspring.

Down's syndrome exemplifies one type of evidence connecting chromosomal abnormalities with mental retardation. It is a syndrome that was previously known to involve mental retardation and was then discovered to have a chromosomal etiology. There are other examples of this line of evidence. Figure

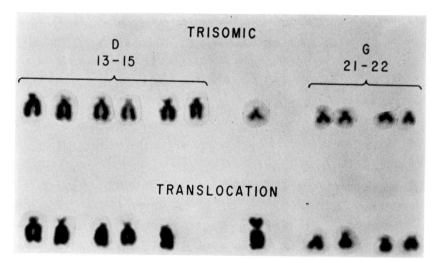

Figure I-3. The top line shows trisomy 21, which is the common chromosomal hallmark of Down's syndrome. The bottom line shows a D/21 translocation capable of producing Down's syndrome.

1-4A shows a youngster with the 13 or D_1 trisomy syndrome with cleft lip and palate, polydactyly and other anomalies. Figure I-4B-E shows the same youngster and demonstrates the facial configurations with sloping forehead, poor development of the supraorbital ridges, typical nasal configuration, low-set malformed ears, and so on. The syndrome is due to an extra D (13) chromosome. It is comparable to Down's syndrome in that it was known in the 1800's to be associated consistently with mental retardation and then in 1960 was found to have a chromosomal basis.

The opposite process has occurred in some instances: a chromosomal abnormality has been described and then the patients with it recognized to have a consistent set of findings, a syndrome including mental retardation. An example of this is the trisomy 18 syndrome (Fig. I-5). Figure I-5 shows several of the typical malformations, especially the low-set, malformed ears. (This shaped ear is called elfin by some people. By using some mythologic terms, we make ourselves feel that the youngsters

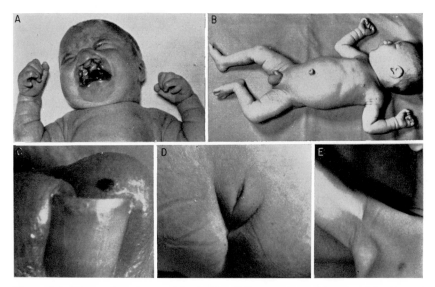

Figure I-4. Views of patients with the D_1 (13) trisomy syndrome with (A and B) cleft lip-palate, sloping forehead, hypoplastic supraorbital ridges, low-set ears, (C) abortive polydactyly, (D) deep pilonidal groove and (E) web across the axillary fossa. (From reference 12, reproduced by permission of the *Alabama Journal of Medical Science.*)

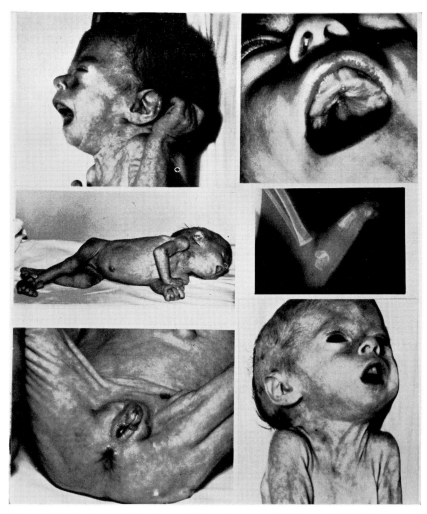

Figure I-5. Patients with trisomy 18 syndrome with low-set "elfin" ears and other typical features. (From reference 13, reproduced by permission of the *Journal of Pediatrics*.)

are from another world and are perhaps less malformed than they are.) Figure I-6 shows one of the hand configurations in trisomy 18 with malrotation of the digits and tightly clenched hands. Figure I-7 shows the usual karyotype found in these patients: an extra chromosome in the number 18 position. The

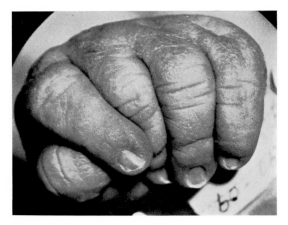

Figure I-6. Typical hand configuration in trisomy 18 syndrome. (From reference 13, reproduced by permission of the *Journal of Pediatrics*.)

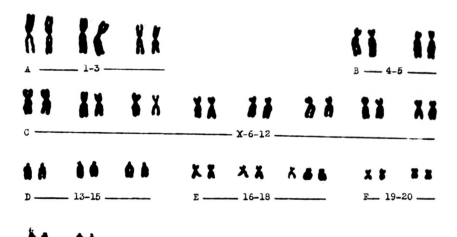

Figure I-7. Karyotype showing 47 chromosomes including an extra chromosome No. 18, characteristic of most patients with trisomy 18 syndrome. Minority groups in this syndrome have mosaicism or translocations. (With minor changes from reference 13, reproduced by permission of the *Journal of Pediatrics*.)

infant mortality[4, 5] with trisomy 18 and trisomy 13 is very high; approximately 70 per cent of the youngsters are dead at three months of age; about 90 per cent by one year of age. There are other examples of this phenomenon. These include the cat-cry syndrome (cri-du-chat syndrome) which is due to absence of a part of the short arm of chromosome 5 (5p-), and other syndromes due to partial deletion of various other chromosomes. In all these instances the correlation with mental retardation was made after the discovery of the chromosome abnormality.

One can ask how much of the total mass of mental retardation is occupied by chromosomal abnormalities? To get some estimate about this, one has to design a study in a somewhat different way. This approach is exemplified by a paper which was published by Robert L. Summitt.[6] Table I-I shows data from Dr. Summitt's study. Dr. Summitt took normal controls, individuals who had no minor physical anomalies and no mental retardation, and studied them chromosomally using lymphocyte cultures. The test group consisted of individuals with mental retardation plus at least three anomalies. The anomalies could be minor in degree. The reason for taking three or more anomalies was derived from the fact that approximately 13 per cent of normal newborns have one minor anomaly, a preauricular sinus, a pilonidal dimple, or something of the sort, whereas only a small percentage (approximately 0.05%) of newborns have three or more anomalies. The test population was also defined as having no recognizable syndrome. Individuals with Down's syndrome, for example, were excluded. The slides were coded and then read. Dr. Summitt has now studied 250 normal controls and 250 test patients. The paper[6] gives the methodology of the study

TABLE I-I

CONTROLLED CHROMOSOME STUDY

Group	No. Studied	No. and Type Anomaly
Normal controls	50	0 (0%)
Mental retarded with 3 or more anomalies of unknown origin	50	4 (8%)

Note: Data from Summitt.[6]

plus results on the first fifty from each group. Among the normal controls none were found to have chromosomal abnormalities. Among the first fifty individuals in the test group four had chromosomal abnormalities, i.e. 8 per cent were chromosomally abnormal. One of these individuals had a translocation between chromosomes two and three, one had trisomy 18 (and incidentally, had not been recognized prior to the chromosomal studies, suggesting that some individuals with syndromes such as trisomy 18 are not easily recognized), and one had partial deletion of the long arm of chromosome 18 (18q-).

SEX CHROMOSOMES AND INTELLIGENCE

It appears that sex chromosomal abnormalities are connected with mental retardation. The evidence concerning this association is more subtle. The approach in general, therefore, had to be made relative to populations, very similar to Dr. Summitt's approach that was just detailed. Studies in this instance have been greatly facilitated because of the presence of the X chromatin body. X chromatin bodies are darkly staining structures just adjacent to the nuclear membrane. They occur in interphase nuclei and are highly coiled, relatively inactive chromosomes. The usual rule is that there is one less X chromatin body than the number of X chromosomes. This permits the screening of large numbers of individuals for aberrant numbers of X chromosomes. Table I-II shows the results of X chromatin surveys of males.[7] From among the normal population of newborn males, 34 of 16,000 (0.2%) were found to be X chromatin positive. Thus, one in every five hundred newborn males has two or more X chromosomes. Similar studies of re-

TABLE I-II

SEX CHROMATIN SURVEYS OF MALES

Population	Number in Survey	Chromatin Positive No.	%
Normal	16,463	34	(0.21)
Retarded at home	3,409	30	(0.88)
Institution	11,613	98	(0.84)

Note: Compiled from data compiled by Ferguson-Smith.[7]

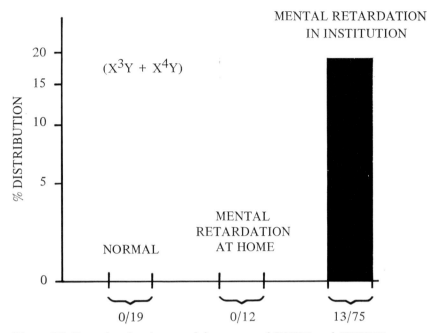

Figure I-8. Data showing increased frequency of XXXY and XXXXY among male institutionalized retardates, indicating that more X chromosomes apparently make for more severe mental retardation. Data taken from reference 7.

tarded males at home and in institutions give fourfold that percentage. This is slightly less than 1 per cent, so that if one has a clinic for mentally retarded youngsters and is screening males, one might expect slightly less than one out of one hundred of them to be chromatin positive.

This presents a paradox. Retarded boys, who are at home and are therefore presumably more mildly affected, and those in institutions, have a similar percentage of chromatin positivity. Figure I-8 provides a partial explanation. It shows the results of chromosome studies of males who were found to be chromatin positive. None of nineteen chromatin positive, normal males were found to have more than two X chromosomes. The same was true for twelve chromatin positive retarded males, who were at home. Whereas, from seventy-five youngsters, who were detected as being chromatin positive males in institutions, thirteen (approximately 17%) showed triplo-XY or tetra-XY, suggesting very strongly that the greater the number of X chromosomes, the greater is the degree of mental retardation.

SEX CHROMOSOMES AND GROWTH

Figure I-9 depicts a youngster with typical stigmata of XO Turner's syndrome. Individuals with XO Turner's syndrome end up almost always between 50 and 60 inches in height as adults. It is also known that they tend to be short at birth. Youngsters with Turner's syndrome lack the normal adolescent growth spurt (Fig. I-10), whether they are given estrogen therapy or not. Although they should be given estrogens for other reasons, it does not increase their height.

Figure I-11 presents further interesting data.[8] The open circles represent height of normal siblings in a family. The closed circles (the darkened circles) represent the height of a youngster in that sibship with Turner's syndrome. Along the X-axis are given the mean parental heights. Along the Y-axis are given the prod-

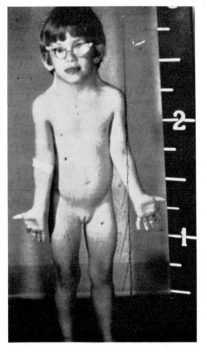

Figure I-9. Patient with XO Turner's syndrome.

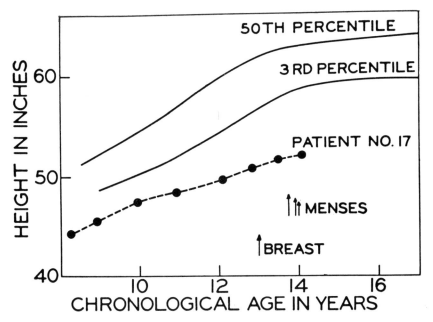

Figure I-10. Linear growth of patient before and during adolescence compared to the normal taken from data compiled by the Iowa Child Welfare Research Station. Note the lack of an adolescent growth spurt. (From reference 8, reproduced by permission of L. Lemi and D.W. Smith and the *Journal of Pediatrics*.)

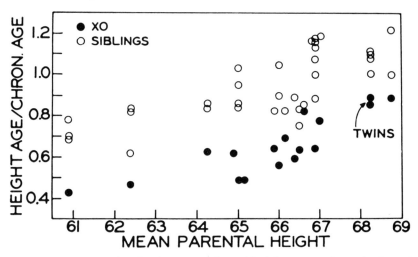

Figure I-11. Relative height (as proportion of height age to chronologic age) of 17 XO patients and 34 of their sibs, all younger than 15 years, versus mean height of their parents. Note the marked positive correlation (+0.84) in height between Turner's syndrome patients and their sibs and parents. (From reference 8, reproduced by permission of L. Lemli and D.W. Smith and the *Journal of Pediatrics*.)

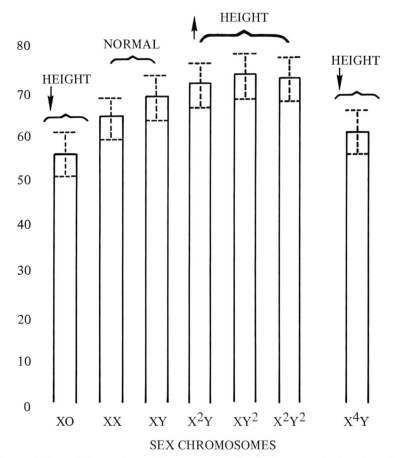

Figure I-12. Height and sex chromosomes. Crude bar graph showing that height increases with more sex chromosomes until XXXXY which causes severe growth retardation.

uct of the height age of the patient with Turner's syndrome divided by their chronologic age. The conclusion is that when the parents and the siblings tend to be tall, the individuals with Turner's syndrome tend to be on the tall side. The overall conclusion is that the genetic background does make a difference in the phenotype even in the face of an overwhelming chromosomal insult such as XO Turner's syndrome. The correlation coefficient is +0.84 for the XO patients. The next illustration (Fig. I-12) represents a crude attempt to generalize. As mentioned, the mean height of individuals with XO Turner's syndrome is between 50 and 60 inches. For normal females, it is considerably taller. Normal males are taller than females. Individuals with Klinefelter's syndrome are associated with unusually tall stature. Individuals who have two X's and two Y's tend to be even taller. The conclusion, presumably, is that with increasing numbers of X and Y chromosomes there is increasing height. This holds to a certain point, after which there seems to be a drop off with XXXXY in which there is growth retardation.

AUTOSOMES AND GROWTH

With trisomy 21 the mean height for males is 5 feet plus or minus 5 inches. For females the mean height is less. There is

AUTOSOMES AND GROWTH

CHROMOSOME	No. 13	No. 18	No. 21
RELATIVE REAL SIZE	 (chromosome figure)	 (chromosome figure)	 (chromosome figure)
% OF HAPLOID GENOME	3.6%	2.7%	1.9%
EFFECT OF TRISOMY ON GROWTH	+	+++	++
EFFECTIVE SIZE RELATIVE TO GROWTH FACTORS	 (chromosome figure)	 (chromosome figure)	 (chromosome figure)

Figure I-13. Growth or, more properly, anti-growth effects of different autosomal trisomies. These comparisons indicate trisomy 18 may eventually provide keys to understanding growth.

greater growth retardation with the trisomy 18 syndrome. In fact, very striking growth retardation, whereas with the trisomy 13 syndrome there is relatively little growth retardation. Figure I-13 represents the relative sizes of these three chromosomes; chromosome 13, relatively large; chromosome 18, medium size; and chromosome 21, relatively small. If one adjusts for the effect of trisomy on height, one gets quite a different picture of things because trisomy 18 results in striking growth retardation, trisomy 21 in moderate, and trisomy 13 in relatively little growth retardation. If one were to diagram the chromosomes in relationship to their anti-growth equivalents, one would get quite a different picture. Chromosome 18 in terms of anti-growth equivalents would be depicted as quite large and chromosome 21 as moderate in size relative to chromosome 13.

CHROMOSOMES AND INTRA-UTERINE GROWTH

A number of chromosomal abnormalities interfere with growth and development in such a severe fashion that they eventuate in abortions.[9] Approximately a quarter of early trimester abortions that occur spontaneously are due to chromosomal abnormalities. The relative contributions are shown in Figure I-14. A large percentage are due to unusual trisomies, which are not found in living individuals (Fig. I-15). A surprising percentage is due to XO. Likewise, a large percentage is due to triploidy or tetraploidy (Fig. I-16). Individuals who either have entirely triploid or tetraploid cells are apparently unable to survive during the process of intra-uterine growth and differentiation.

CHROMOSOME BREAKAGE, INTELLIGENCE AND GROWTH

Several syndromes, which involve chromosome breakage, also interfere with the patient's growth.[10] Figure I-17 shows an individual with ataxia-telangiectasia.[10] This individual is now twenty-two years old. He has severe progressive cerebellar ataxia. Figure I-18 shows the dilated vessels in his sclerae. Table I-III compares this syndrome with two other syndromes which in many ways are quite analogous: Fanconi's syndrome of pancytopenia with skeletal anomalies and Bloom's syndrome of dwarfism and telangiectatic skin eruption. All three syndromes are genetical in origin and are autosomal recessive diseases. The parents are carriers. A quarter of their offspring are affected. All three syn-

TABLE I-III

DISEASES WITH INCREASED CHROMOSOME BREAKAGE

Disease	Autosomal Recessive	Growth Retardation	Mental Retardation	Tendency to malig.
Ataxia-telangiectasia	+	+	+/−*	+
Fanconi's pancytopenia	+	+	+/−	+
Bloom's syndrome	+	+	+	+

*Where +/− = sometimes present (variable).

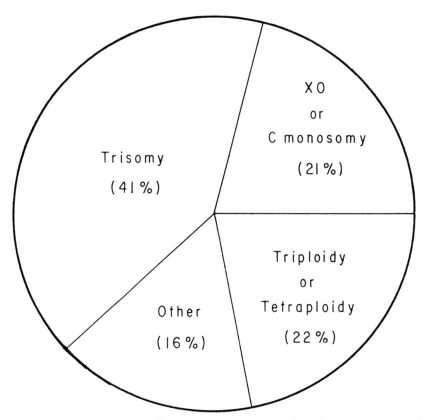

Figure I-14. Pie diagram indicating relative frequencies of different types of chromosome aberrations among chromosomally abnormal unselected abortuses. Based on data in reference 9.

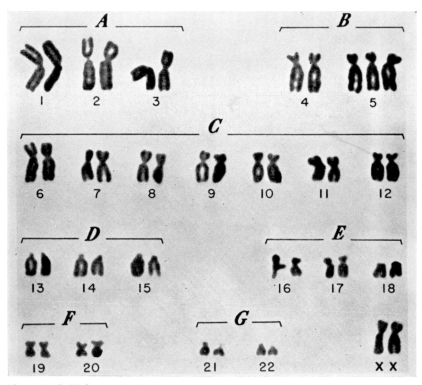

Figure I-15. Trisomy B (4-5) found in a spontaneous abortion. This type of complete trisomy has never been found in a living person (from reference 9, reproduced by permission of D.H. Carr and *Obstetrics and Gynecology*).

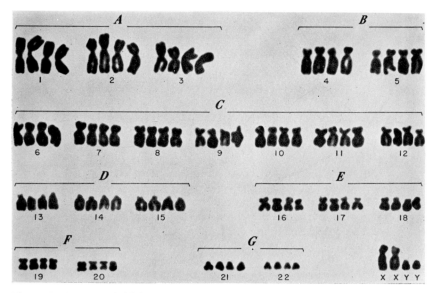

Figure I-16. Tetraploid karyotype from an abortus. (From reference 9 reproduced by permission of D.H. Carr and *Obstetrics and Gynecology*.)

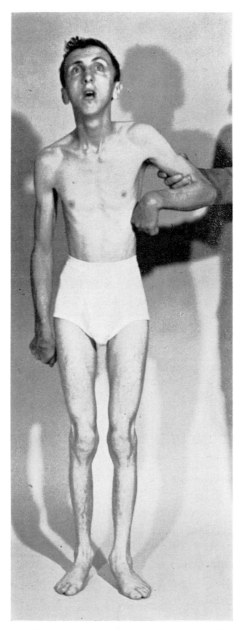

Figure I-17. Patient with ataxia-telangiectasia syndrome, 2 of whose sibs were affected and died with acute lymphocytic leukemia.[10] He has increased chromosome breakage.

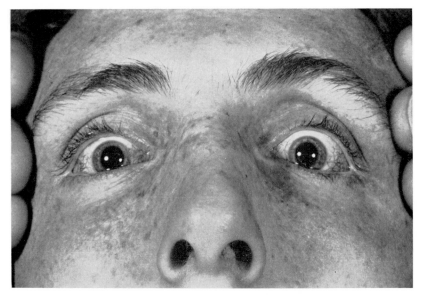

Figure I-18. Same patient with ataxia-telangiectasia showing bulbar telangiectases.

dromes involve growth retardation and variable mental retardation. All three are associated with a significantly increased risk of malignancy. As mentioned, the chromosomal common denominator is the association with markedly increased chromosome breakage.

CHROMOSOME VARIATIONS AND NORMALITY

There are some chromosomal variations which are found in normal individuals and which are really quite interesting. They may include abnormalities of chromosome number, abnormalities of chromosome structure of a major and minor degree. In a sense, the finding that trisomy 21 was the basis of Down's syndrome has retarded our understanding of normal chromosomal variation in man. Normal variations are just now coming in for careful, methodical study.

SEX CHROMOSOMES AND MENTAL DISORDER

In a useful publication Professor Polani[11] reviewed a number of relevant matters, many of which are not yet widely recognized. Among his points are the following:

1. A small but probably excessive proportion of (XO) subjects are found with an IQ in the educationally subnormal range.
2. The data suggest "that there is no tendency for (XO) women to be admitted to subnormality hospitals." Apparently when mental retardation does occur with XO, it is no more often of a degree requiring institutionalization than with the chromosomally normal population.
3. There may be a "true excess" of women with XO mosaicism in institutions for the retarded. The notion that chromosomal mosaics may be *more* severely damaged than individuals all of whose cells show the chromosomal abnormality is a new one.
4. The XXX chromosome abnormality clearly predisposes to significant mental retardation, since its prevalence in institutions for the retarded is approximately 1 in 245 individuals, five times the incidence at birth.
5. The tendency to bizarre and deviant psychological functioning is probably not limited to XYY, but is found more often than would be expected by chance in XXY Klinefelter's syndrome. Likewise in females there is evidence that XXX may predispose to "schizophrenia" since its frequency in such women is approximately five times its frequency in newborns in the general population.

The correlation between chromosomal abnormality and mental disorder is not dealt with in this chapter in detail. However, it is clearly a similar problem. First, there was the need to establish the fact that some association existed between chromosomal abnormalities and mental disorder. This association now appears to be rather well established. The extent of this association, however, as regards both the types of chromosomal abnormalities and the types of mental disorder involved, is as yet unknown. Establishing the degree to which chromosomal abnormalities contribute to the total pool of mental illness is an additional, important task ahead for human population cytogenetics.

SPECULATIONS

By the study of chromosomal abnormalities and their effect upon the individual one can get some idea as to what one might

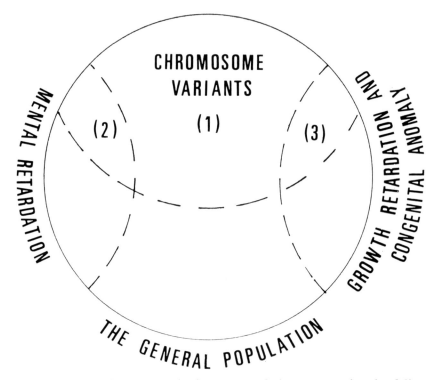

Figure I-19. A major problem for human population cytogenetics: the delineation of the extent of a) chromosome variation in the normal population; b) the contribution by chromosome abnormality to mental retardation; and c) the contribution by chromosome abnormality to growth retardation. The dashed lines represent current uncertainty.

call anti-growth and anti-intellectual equivalents. When a particular piece of chromosome material is triplicated or is deleted, what does this do to growth and to intellectual development?

The entire population of human beings is represented in the accompanying diagram (Fig. I-19). A subgroup has one or another chromosome abnormality. A second subgroup has mental retardation. A third subgroup has growth retardation. This can be represented by a Boolian diagram. The vast majority of individuals with chromosome abnormalities are probably normal. Some, however, do have mental retardation; some have growth retardation; and some have both. The relative sizes of these three areas and their overlap are not yet fully known. One of the tasks of human population cytogenetics is to define the numbers and types of chromosomal variation in the general population and their contribution to mental retardation and to somatic anomalies, such as growth retardation.

REFERENCES

1. Turpin, R. and Lejeune, J.: Les Chromosomes Humains (karyotype normal et variations pathologiques), Gautier-Villars, 1965, translated as Human Afflictions and Chromosomal Aberrations. Long Island City, New York, Pergamon Press, 1969.
2. Hecht, F., Case, M.P., Lovrien, E.W., Thuline, H.C. and Melnyk, J.: Non-randomness of translocations in man: Preferential entry of chromosome 14 into 13-15/21 translocation. *Science,* 161:371, 1968.
3. Punnett, Hope J. and Mellman, W.J.: Familial chromosome translocations. In *Endocrine and Genetic Diseases of Childhood,* Gardener, Lytt I. (Ed.). Philadelphia, W.B. Saunders Co., 1969.
4. Weber, W.: Survival and the sex ratio in trisomy 17-18. *Am J Human Genet,* 19:369, 1967.
5. Magenis, R.E., Hecht, F. and Milham, S., Jr.: Trisomy 13 (D) syndrome: Studies on parental age, sex ratio, and survival. *J Pediatr,* 73:222, 1968.
6. Summitt, R.L.: Cytogenetics in mentally defective children with anomalies: A controlled study. *J Pediatr,* 74:58, 1969.
7. Ferguson-Smith, M.A.: Sex chromatin, Klinefelter's syndrome and mental deficiency in *The Sex Chromatin,* Moore, Keith L. (Ed.). Philadelphia, W.B. Saunders, 1966.
8. Lemli, L. and Smith, D.W.: The XO syndrome: A study of the differentiated phenotype. *J Pediatr,* 63:577, 1963.
9. Carr, D.: Chromosome studies in spontaneous abortions. *Obstet Gynec,* 26:308, 1965.
10. Hecht, F., Koler, R.D., Rigas, D.A., Dahnke, G.S., Case, M.P. and Tisdale, V.: Leukaemia and lymphocytes in ataxia-telangiectasia. *Lancet,* 2:1193, 1966.
11. Polani, P.E.: Abnormal sex chromosomes and mental disorder. *Nature,* 223:680, 1969.
12. Hecht, F.: Phenotypic differentiation of autosomal chromosomal abnormalities. Anomalies on the gross, radiologic, autopsy, cellular and molecular levels in the D_1 (13-15) trisomy syndrome. *Ala J Med Sci,* 3:489, 1966.
13. Hecht, F., Bryant, J.S., Motulsky, A.G., and Giblett, E.R.: The No. 17-18 (E) trisomy syndrome. *J Pediatr,* 63:605, 1963.

Chapter II

5-HYDROXYTRYPTOPHAN ADMINISTRATION IN DOWN'S SYNDROME

Mary B. Coleman

SINCE 1960, a large number of investigators have reported that variations in the concentrations of metabolites of tryptophan occur in patients with Down's syndrome.[1-5] Tryptophan is an amino acid which is hydroxylated in the liver, kidney, mast cells and intestines, to 5-hydroxytryptophan (5-HTP). This compound is then in turn decarboxylated in almost all tissues in the body to serotonin or 5-hydroxytryptamine (5-HT). The major depots of serotonin in the body are in the gastrointestinal tract, in the central nervous system and in the platelets (which contain 99 per cent of 5-HT found in whole blood).

SIGNIFICANCE OF REDUCED 5-HT LEVELS

Studies carried out at Children's Hospital of the District of Columbia, since 1965, have demonstrated a depression of whole blood 5-HT in patients with Down's syndrome due to trisomy 21.[6-9] Since the initial report, two other investigators[10, 11] have also found low levels of 5-HT in the whole blood of patients with Down's syndrome.

The depression of 5-HT in patients with Down's syndrome is of particular interest because there are a number of other syndromes with retardation associated with abnormalities of serotonin. These include phenylketonuria,[12] histidinemia,[13] infantile spasm syndrome,[14] infantile hypothyroidism,[15] Pare's high serotonin syndrome[16] and primary infantile autism.[17] In phenylketonuria and histidinemia, correction of the metabolic abnormality by dietary or chemical methods is correlated with a simultaneous rise of whole blood 5-HT into the normal range. These treatments also result in reduced severity of mental retardation in some patients.

26

THERAPY WITH 5-HTP

Starting in December of 1965, we began administering the D,L type of 5-hydroxytryptophan (5-HTP), the 5-HT precursor, to neonatal patients with Down's syndrome.[18] Most patients were begun on 5-HTP in the first 7 to 10 days of neonatal life. Three patients ranged from one to three months of age. The dose for each patient varied and ranged from 0.30 to 2.10 mg of 5 HTP per kilogram of body weight per day given in two or three portions.

In small infants we noted improvement of hypotonia or floppiness, and better activity levels. Patients usually had a normal Landau posture after 1 to 7 weeks of 5-HTP administration. As the children grew older, it was noted that most spoke single words between the first and second birthdays, and by four years of age the majority were putting words together, although speech often was difficult to understand. Dosage regulation was based on the neurological examination and whole blood 5-HT levels. Clinical criteria for increasing the dose were as follows:

1. Hypotonia and hyporeflexia.
2. Depression of infantile reflexes (as appropriate for age).
3. Sluggish activity level and vacant stare, e.g. too easy to take care of.
4. Tongue visibility—thick in appearance, visible or protruded. Rare—darting or pointed tongue.
5. Constipation not improving.

Clinical criteria for decreasing the dose or signs of toxicity were as follows:

1. Hypertonus, opisthotonus, hyperreflexia.
2. Hyperactivity, motor restlessness, irritability.
3. Tongue reappearance after successful suppression, usually darting or pointed.
4. Diarrhea (no vomiting).
5. Hypertension (very rare).
6. Infant turns over too soon or too frequently for age.
7. Emotional withdrawal from parents.
8. Seizure phenomenon—staring spells, blankly staring at one

outstretched immobile hand, flexion spasms, EEG abnormal at later stage.[14]

The results in the fifteen oldest patients are as follows:

Age of Walking (months)	Best Speech to Date	Home or School Status
18	Sentences	Normal kindergarten
15	Sentences	Retarded nursery school
25	Sentences	Normal nursery school
15	Paragraphs	Normal nursery school
18	Paragraphs	Normal nursery school
48	Single words	Not in school
24	Sentences	Not in school
23	Paragraphs	Normal nursery school
21	Sentences	Normal nursery school
17	Sentences (rare)	Retarded nursery school
22	Sentences	Not in school
23	Sentences	Normal nursery school
17	Sentences	Normal nursery school
36	Single words	Institutionalized
17	Sentences (rare)	Retarded nursery school

The last patient in this list has the mosaic form of Down's syndrome, which sometimes is a less severe form of this disease entity. No improvement in head size was noted when compared to a control population in England.[19] The results in these oldest patients in our series suggest that 5-HTP administration, as given by our method, is not sufficient in itself to bring these patients' level of central nervous system functioning into the completely normal range. Whether it is of some value cannot definitely be settled until we have completed a double-blind study now in progress. The development of an infantile-spasm syndrome (without EEG changes) in two of the patients is of concern.

The mechanism by which 5-HTP administration operates to improve muscle tone in Down's syndrome patients is unknown. It might be due to changes in cerebral 5-HT, but this compound is present in the spinal cord as well as autonomic ganglia in significant quantities.

REFERENCES

1. McCoy, E. and Chung, S.: The excretion of tryptophan metabolites following deoxypyridoxine administration in mongoloid and non-mongoloid patients. *J Pediatr*, 64:277, 1964.
2. O'Brien, D. and Groshek, A.: The abnormality of tryptophan metabolism in children with mongolism. *Arch Dis Childhood*, 37:17, 1962.

3. Perry, T.: Urinary excretion of amines in phenylketonuria and mongolism. *Science,* 136:879, 1962.
4. Jerome, H., Lejeune, J. and Turpin, R.: Study of the urinary excretion of some tryptophan metabolites in mongoloid children. *C R Acad Sci (Paris),* 251:474, 1960.
5. Gershoff, S., Hegsted, D. and Trulson, M.: Metabolic studies of mongoloids. *Am J Clin Nutr,* 9:526, 1958.
6. Rosner, F., Ong, B., Paine, R. and Mahanand, D.: Biochemical differentiation of trisomic Down's Syndrome (mongolism) from that due to translocation. *N Engl J Med,* 273:1356, 1965.
7. Rosner, F., Ong, B., Paine, R. and Mahanand, D.: Blood serotonin activity in trisomic and translocation Down's syndrome. *Lancet,* 1:1191, 1965.
8. Bazelon, M.: Serotonin metabolism in Down's syndrome. *Clin Proc Child Hosp (Washington),* 23:58, 1967.
9. Boullin, D., Coleman, M. and O'Brien, R.: Defective binding of 5-HT by platelets in children with trisomy 21. *Br J Physiol,* 204:128P, 1969.
10. Tu, J. and Zellweger, H.: Blood serotonin deficiency in Down's syndrome. *Lancet,* 2:715, 1965.
11. Berman, J.: Blood serotonin in Down's syndrome. *Lancet,* 1:730, 1967.
12. Pare, C., Sandler, M. and Stacey, R.: 5-hydroxytryptamine deficiency in phenylketonuria. *Lancet,* 1:551, 1957.
13. Corner, B., Holton, J., Norman, R. and Williams, R.: A case of histidinemia controlled with a low histidine diet. *Pediatrics,* 41:1074, 1968.
14. Coleman, M.: Infantile spasms induced by 5-hydroxytryptophan in patients with Down's syndrome. *Neurology,* in press.
15. Coleman, M.: Serotonin levels in infant hypothyroidism. *Lancet,* 2:365, 1970.
16. Coleman, M. and Barnet, A.: Parachlorophenylalanine administration to a retarded patient and high blood serotonin levels. *Trans Am Neurol Assoc,* 95:224, 1970.
17. Boullin, D., Coleman, M. and O'Brien, R.: Abnormalities in platelet 5-hydroxytryptamine efflux in patients with infantile autism. *Nature,* 226:371, 1970.
18. Bazelon, M., Paine, R., Cowie, V., Hunt, P., Houck, J. and Mahanand, D.: Reversal of hypotonia in infants with Down's syndrome by administration of 5-hydroxytryptophan. *Lancet,* 1:1130, 1967.
19. Cowie, V.: *A Study of the Early Development of Mongols.* Long Island City, New York, Pergamon Press Ltd., 1970.

Chapter III

BEHAVIORAL AND COGNITIVE ASPECTS OF THE XYY CONDITION

J. Philip Welch

BACKGROUND AND CHARACTERISTIC FINDINGS

THIS chapter concerns males with an extra Y chromosome, the so-called XYY syndrome. A representative karyotype of this condition is shown in Figure III-1. In this chromosome disorder there are 47 chromosomes instead of the normal complement of 46, and in a high proportion of cases the two Y chromo-

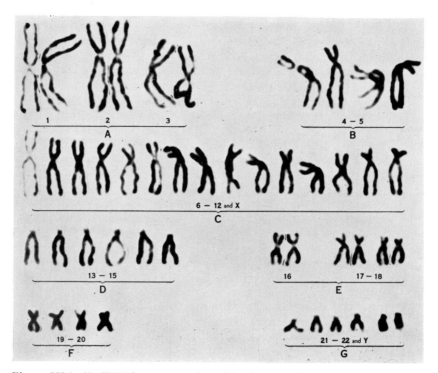

Figure III-1. 47, XYY karyotype of a tall prisoner. The two Y chromosomes are easily distinguishable from other members of the G group.

somes can be distinguished from the others in the G group, as in the case shown here. This condition is quite different from that of males with an extra X chromosome, the more familiar Klinefelter's syndrome. The Y chromosome is the sex-determining or male chromosome; in other words, persons with a Y chromosome have, in general, a male external appearance, whereas those without a Y chromosome have a female appearance.

The XYY condition first came to prominence late in 1965, when Jacobs and her colleagues surveyed men in an institution for dangerous, violent or aggressive criminals and found that 7 of the 196 examined had an extra Y chromosome, i.e. there were XYY males.[1] Predictably, this caused a flurry of interest, since it suggested the possibility of an association between a particular kind of behavior and a particular chromosome abnormality. Also predictably, this finding and subsequent related investigations have been reported in many newspaper articles and popular magazines, often accompanied by poorly informed comment and premature or frankly unjustified conclusions. This is unfortunate, and, from the scientific viewpoint, undesirable.

Jacobs' study and subsequent similar investigations have given rise to two main questions, and these are the subject of this chapter. First, is the proportion of XYY males greater among inmates of correctional institutions than in other populations? Second, are men with an extra Y chromosome behaviorally different in some way from XY males; and, if so, in what way are they different?

One of the interesting findings in Jacobs' study was that the XYY males were of above-average height; in fact, most of them were over 6 feet tall. In consequence, many subsequent surveys have been restricted to tall criminals; the findings of which are summarized in the accompanying table. Among the mentally "normal" tall criminals, most of whom were over 6 feet tall, there was little variation in the frequency of XYY males. The table shows that 27 XYY males were found among 681 such tall people in correctional institutions, a frequency very close to 4 per cent. To estimate the relative frequency of XYY males in the whole inmate population of these institutions, it is necessary to know the proportion of inmates who are over 6 feet tall and the

TABLE III-I

FREQUENCY OF XYY MALES AMONG TALL PRISONERS

Source and Comment	Height	Mentally Subnormal	Mentally Ill	Mentally "Normal"
Casey et al.[25]	≧ 72 in.	12/50	4/50	2/24
Hunter[26]	Youths ≧ 90th percentile			3/29
Welch et al.[4]	≧ 72 in.	0/10		1/35
Goodman et al.[27]	≧ 73 in.			2/100
Jacobs et al.[13]	≧ 72 in.	5/21		
Wiener et al.[28] Mode of ascertainment not clearly stated	≧ 69 in.			4/34
Telfer et al.[29]	≧ 71 in.	0/30	2/50	3/49
Nielsen et al.[30]	> 180 cm.		2/37	
Court Brown[2]	≧ 72 in.			1/106
Marinello[11]	≧ 72 in.			2/86
Knox and Nevin[31]	≧ 72 in.			0/5
Melnyk and Derencsenyi[32]	≧ 72 in.		2/121	7/79*
Daly[33]	≧ 72 in.		10/210	
Griffiths et al.[19]	≧ 72 in.			2/34
Fattig[34] Negroes	> 72 in.			0/100

* Males with "personality disorders."

corresponding proportion of males in the general population. Using the rough estimate of Court Brown[2] that about 50 per cent of XYY males are over 6 feet tall, and the statistics for 1960-62 that approximately 12 per cent of American males are over 6 feet tall,[3] we may expect the frequency of XYY males in correctional institutions for mentally "normal" males to be about $4/100 \times 12/100 \times 2 = 9.6 \times 10^{-4}$, or about 1 per cent. It should be borne in mind, however, that Court Brown's estimate was only approximate, and that, even if correct for British XYY males, this figure may be inappropriate for American XYY males. Furthermore, it is not known whether the height distribution of males in correctional institutions corresponds to that of males in the general population. In the Patuxent Institution in Maryland, some 20 per cent of males are over 6 feet tall.[4] If this is the case in other institutions also, then the frequency of XYY males in such institutions might be expected to be substantially greater than the 1 per cent estimated as above.

FREQUENCY OF THE XYY CONDITION

To determine whether there is a real increase in the frequency of XYY males in these institutional populations we need to compare the above estimate of 1 per cent with the frequency in the general population.

In their first report on this subject, Jacobs and colleagues estimated the probable frequency of XYY males in the general population as about 1 in 2000, or 0.05 per cent: this figure also was an indirect estimate from several surveys and involved a number of assumptions. Since then, there have been at least four direct estimates of the frequency in the general population —one by Lubs and Ruddle,[5] who found three XYY males in 4400 consecutive newborn males, another by Turner and Wald,[6] who found two among 1000 randomly ascertained newborn; and two in which higher frequencies were noted. Thus, Sergovich *et al.*[7] detected four XYY males among 1200 male neonates and Ratcliffe *et al.*[8] found five XYY males in 3500 consecutive liveborn males. The overall frequency in these studies is approximately 0.14 per cent. Taking this figure as the frequency in the general population, comparison with the estimated 1.0 per cent of XYY males in correctional institutions suggests that the frequency of the XYY condition is some seven times greater among the male institutional inmates.

ANTISOCIAL BEHAVIOR: ROLE OF THE ENVIRONMENT

At this point it is useful to look at the problem another way. Are the XYY males in institutions different in some other way from their XY peers in institutions? More appropriately, are they different in terms of the behavior which resulted in their imprisonment in the first place? Answers to these questions may indicate whether XYY males have any predisposition to some kind of asocial behavior.

Two lines of investigation have indicated that there are such differences. The first concerns the age of the offender at the time of first conviction. In one study in Scotland[9] this occurred at an average age of eighteen years in XY males and slightly over thirteen years in XYY males, suggesting that whatever the activity that results in imprisonment the XYY males seem to start it earlier. Second, the frequency of familial crime—that is, how often other family members have been in trouble with the law. One examination of the background of siblings of males in institutions[9] revealed that twelve of sixty-three sibs of XY males had themselves been convicted of some crime, whereas only one of thirty-one sibs of XYY males had been convicted. These data strongly suggest that the XYY male behaves differently from the rest of his family.

This evidence suggests that there is some kind of predisposition to antisocial behavior on the part of XYY males. Are these people, then, predestined to antisocial behavior? Does this mean that if you have a boy with an extra Y chromosome, he will end up sooner or later in some kind of correctional institution? I think not. There are two reasons for this belief. First, several investigators, including myself, have seen some XYY males in the general population who have not been in trouble with the law. Furthermore, according to the now generally accepted frequency of XYY males among neonates, there are probably about 100,000 adults with this condition in the United States alone; however, the investigations in United States correctional institutions clearly indicate that the majority of these men are not resident there.

Secondly, and somewhat more interestingly, many of the XYY males seen in institutions seem to be the product of broken homes, by which I mean that there has been a long-standing divorce, parental separation, or other severe disruption of the home environment. This was a feature of both cases ascertained from the Patuxent Institution, and also of an XYY male I subsequently ascertained in a Canadian correctional institution,[10] and also of all four patients studied by Marinello *et al.*[11]

Although Price and Whatmore[12] stated that there was "no predisposing family environment" in the case of nine XYY males studied by them at a Scottish maximum-security hospital, closer study suggests that this statement might not be entirely warranted. A year later, Jacobs *et al.*[13] gave some further information on these nine men. In case 122/65 the proband's mother died when he was six years old and his father when he was fourteen; the authors stated that after the death of his mother the boy was brought up by his stepmother and sisters. In case 123/65 the parents were separated when the proband was seven years of age; the patient continued to live with his mother. The father, it was noted, drank excessively and was unable to keep steady employment. In case 142/65 the proband was illegitimate and was subsequently adopted by a maternal aunt and her husband; and in case 150/65 the proband's father died when the boy was fourteen years old. Further study of the home environment of these Scottish XYY males would probably be of interest.

These observations suggest to me that there is a substantial environmental component to behavioral changes in XYY males. Such a finding should not occasion surprise, for whether we are studying mongolism, diabetes, phenylketonuria, or any other observable condition, the phenotype is always the result of two factors—the genotype, or genetic endowment, and the environment. The XYY male appears to be no exception to this general rule.

MENTAL AND EMOTIONAL CHARACTERISTICS

In seeking other attributes of the XYY state, Jacobs' study appeared to provide a valuable clue. She found 3.5 per cent of males in the institution studied to be XYY, whereas most other investigators have found rather less, but there was a qualitative difference in that the men she studied were both mentally subnormal and labeled as aggressive, violent and dangerous. Could these two features constitute a predisposing factor? In other words, perhaps XYY males tend to be mentally subnormal and aggressive. Since we are dealing with Y chromosomes, and males are supposedly more aggressive than females, the second possibility seemed at first to be particularly attractive.

We attempted to investigate the first possibility, namely, tallness in association with subnormal mentality, by examining a group of Patuxent inmates who satisfied these criteria. None of the ten males examined had an XYY constitution.[4] This is in contrast to the findings of Jacobs and colleagues (1965) in a similar group, in which about half were XYY males—a difference which is statistically significant.[4] Further evidence suggests that XYY males are not necessarily mentally retarded. In the institution in which we had ascertained the ten mentally subnormal tall XY males, we later found two XYY males[14] who were mentally "normal" and had, therefore, not been included in the earlier group. In other words, they were not tall *and* mentally retarded. At least three other XYY males are now known who have superior intelligence, with IQ's of 114, 118, and 125.[10, 15, 16] Since an IQ of 119 or more includes only about 10 per cent of the general population, the ascertainment of even two or three XYY individuals with IQs in this range, among the fifty or so reported XYY males whose IQ data are given, strongly suggests that there is *no* particular association with mental subnormality. Finally, this suggestion is further supported by two of three studies which compared intelligence levels of XYY males and of chromosomally normal males in the same institution and found no significant difference.[17, 18, 19]

If this is the case, you may question why this condition is included in a discussion of genetic forms of mental retardation. The answer, in part, is that there do seem to be subtle changes in the abilities of these individuals. Psychologists commonly di-

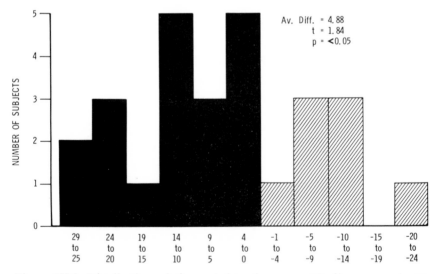

Figure III-2. Distribution of the verbal/performance IQ discrepancy in 27 XYY males. The black area indicates subjects in whom performance IQ was greater than verbal IQ and includes one male whose scores on both subtests were equal.

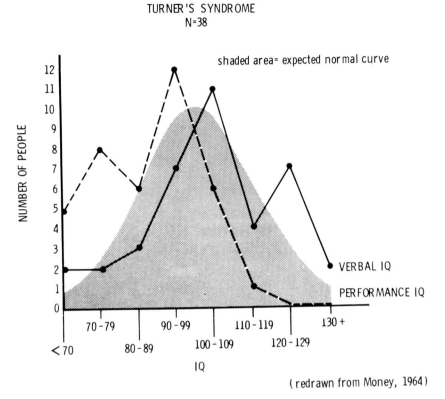

TURNER'S SYNDROME
N=38

(redrawn from Money, 1964)

Figure III-3. Distribution of scores of verbal and performance IQ subtests in 38 females with Turner's syndrome.

vide measurable intelligence into two subsets, termed "performance" and "verbal" components. The tests are constructed so that for most people there is a roughly equal chance that their score for verbal IQ will be greater than that for performance IQ and *vice versa*. In the case of XYY males, it seems that most have a performance IQ greater than verbal IQ (Fig. III-2). These findings are significantly different from an expectation that the higher of the two components is a random event.

Curiously, there is a similar subtle change in ability in another chromosome disorder;[20, 21] this is Turner's syndrome, or the XO condition—females who have only one X chromosome. As shown in Figure III-3, the *verbal* IQ of these people is greater than their performance IQ, and again the difference is statistically significant (t = 7.24, p < 0.001). This is not the case for all chromosome abnormalities, however, since males with an extra X chromosome (Klinefelter's syndrome) appear to show no significant difference between verbal IQ and performance IQ.[21] These findings suggest that in the field of mental retardation, the time has come to look at all aspects much more closely than we have become accustomed to do.

I come now to the second point, the suggestion that XYY males are unduly aggressive. The important consideration here is the definition of aggression. It seems to me that the word "aggressive," used in this context and applied to an individual, implies that this person is more likely than the average to do some other individual a personal injury. In our Maryland study,[4] we looked for XYY males among ten tall men who were chosen by the institution's custodians as being particularly dangerous, aggressive and violent: none was an XYY male. However, as I have mentioned, we *did* find XYY males in other groups, selected by different criteria, in the same institution. In other words, we could find no evidence of an association between aggression and the XYY condition.

Subsequent studies in Scotland[12] appear to confirm the impression we obtained from our studies. The Scottish investigators examined the proportion of crimes committed "against the person" by XYY males and by normal males. In a control group consisting of XY criminal males, seventeen of the eighteen had been convicted at some time for a crime against the person, whereas only four of the nine XYY males had been similarly convicted. This difference is statistically significant (p < 0.05), suggesting that if crimes against people, rather than crimes involving property, can be correlated with aggression, XYY males are *less* aggressive than their institutional peers.

To summarize thus far, although it appears likely that some behavioral difference is linked with the XYY condition, it is doubtful whether XYY males, as a group, are either mentally retarded or aggressive. What then might these presumed behavioral differences be?

BEHAVIORAL CHARACTERISTICS

In attempting to answer this, we have investigated two aspects of behavior among XYY and other males. First I shall discuss the question of anxiety. It seemed reasonable to consider this factor, since it is generally believed that people in correctional institutions such as the Patuxent Institution tend to be overly anxious.[22] Therefore, we compared XYY males (not all of whom were in Patuxent) with XY males in Patuxent. The latter were matched for race and were relatively tall. Each man was asked to complete the test forms of the Taylor Manifest Anxiety Scale.[23] The scores for the two groups are shown in Figure III-4. Statistical analysis by the Student t test produced a t value of 3.93 ($p < 0.005$) indicating that the XYY males were significantly more anxious than their institutional peers—a finding which, incidentally, appears to be corroborated clinically by an impression that a considerable proportion of these men are chronic nail-biters.

Another behavioral feature which seemed worthy of investigation was the degree of impulsiveness shown by these unusual males. The history of some of them, including the circumstances which resulted in their imprisonment, and also their general behavior within the institution, suggested to me that perhaps they were more impulsive than other individuals. Again, inmates of such institutions as Patuxent are characteristically described as impulsive or as persons who find it difficult to resist their impulses.[22] It seemed pertinent, therefore, to compare the XYY males with other males in a correctional institution rather than with normal males; hence tall, white, mentally "normal" male inmates were chosen as a control group. A psychological measure of the degree of impulsiveness has been developed by Barratt,[24] who very kindly supplied some test forms and the scoring procedure. The results of this test are shown in Figure III-5. Although there was no significant difference ($0.10 < p < 0.25$) in the level of impulsiveness in these two groups there was possibly a trend toward greater impulsiveness in the XYY group. All we can reasonably conclude from these data is that more information is needed for elucidation of this question.

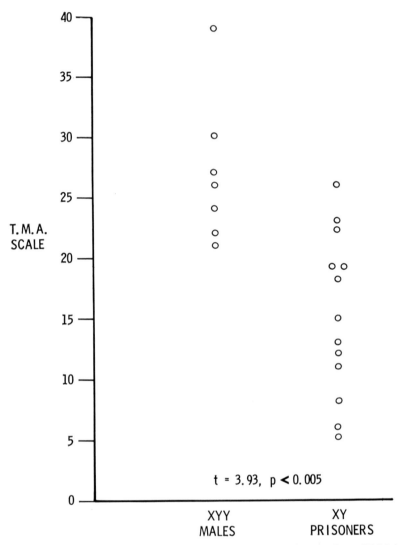

Figure III-4. Distribution of scores on the Taylor Manifest-anxiety (T.M.A.) Scale by 7 XYY males and 13 white criminal XY males (inmates of Patuxent Institution, Maryland), all of whom were $\geq$ 6 feet tall.

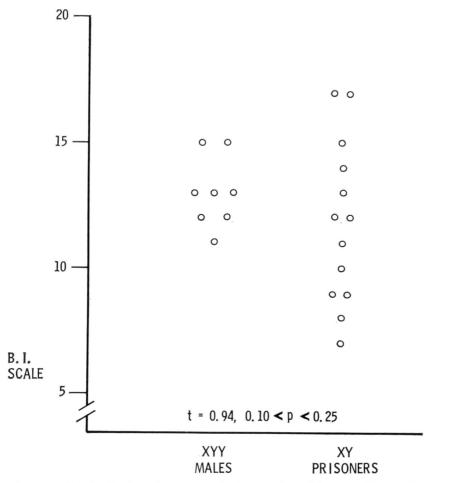

Figure III-5. Distribution of scores on the Barratt Impulsiveness (B.I.) Scale by 8 XYY males and 13 white criminal males (inmates of Patuxent Institution, Maryland), all of whom were $\geq$ 6 feet tall.

In summary, I have attempted to review the current state of knowledge concerning the XYY male and to indicate which way the evidence seems to point at present. The evidence does suggest that there is a greater frequency of XYY males in correctional institutions than in the general population, but the magnitude of this difference remains in doubt (Table III-I). There does seem to be some variation in frequency of XYY males between correctional institutions; at the moment it seems tempting to relate this to the operation of the legal systems in different areas rather than to any other factor.

Behavioral data on XYY males suggest that there is a real predisposition towards what we, as a society, call "antisocial" behavior; in other words, these people do not fit into our notions of what is socially acceptable behavior. The weight of evidence suggests that these men are not mentally retarded to any significant degree, but there is evidence of a more covert change in their abilities which is of considerable interest. There is no evidence that they are overly aggressive or violent—indeed, taken as a group they seem to be *less* aggressive or violent than their criminal confrères. There is evidence indicating that they are overanxious; and, finally, just a suggestion that their behavior may be unduly impulsive.

ACKNOWLEDGMENTS

The skilled technical assistance of Miss H.M. Herr (Johns Hopkins Hospital) and of Mrs. S.K. Vethamany (Dalhousie University) is gratefully acknowledged.

This work was supported, in part, by the Medical Research Council of Canada (grant MA-3346). Thanks are extended for assistance in various phases of this study to Dr. V.A. McKusick and Dr. D.S. Borgaonkar, Department of Medicine, Johns Hopkins Hospital, Baltimore, Maryland and Dr. R.M. Bannerman, Department of Medicine, State University of New York at Buffalo. Also, I am grateful to Dr. L.F. Jarvik, Department of Psychiatry, Columbia University, New York and to Dr. M.D. Casey, Department of Genetics, Sheffield University, England, who kindly allowed me to use their unpublished data; and Dr. H.M. Boslow and the staff of the Patuxent Institution, Maryland for their cooperation at all times.

REFERENCES

1. Jacobs, P.A., Brunton, M., Melville, M.M., Brittain, R.P. and McClemont, W.F.: Aggressive behavior, mental sub-normality, and the *XYY* male. *Nature,* 208:1351, 1965.
2. Court Brown, W.M.: Males with an XYY sex chromosome complement. *J Med Genet,* 5:341, 1968.

3. U.S. Dept. of Health, Education and Welfare: National Center for Health Statistics. Weight by Height and Age of Adults; United States —1960-62. Public Health Service Publication No. 1000, Series 11, No. 14. Washington, D.C., U.S. Govt. Printing Office, 1966.

4. Welch, J.P., Borgaonkar, D.S. and Herr, H.M.: Psychopathy, mental deficiency, aggressiveness and the *XYY* syndrome. *Nature,* 214:500, 1967.

5. Lubs, H.A. and Ruddle, F.H.: Chromosomal abnormalities in the human population: Estimation of rates based on New Haven newborn study. *Science,* 169:495, 1970.

6. Turner, J.H. and Wald, N.: Chromosome patterns in a general neonatal population. In Jacobs, P.A., Price, W.H. and Law, P. (Eds.): *Human Population Cytogenetics.* Baltimore, Williams and Wilkins, 1970, Pfizer Med. Monograph No. 5, pp. 153-158.

7. Sergovich, F., Valentine, G.H., Chen, A.T.L., Kinch, R.A.H. and Smout, M.S.: Chromosome aberrations in 2159 consecutive newborn babies. *N Engl J Med,* 280:851, 1969.

8. Ratcliffe, S.G., Stewart, A.L., Melville, M.M., Jacobs, P.A. and Keay, A.J.: Chromosome studies on 3500 newborn male infants. *Lancet,* 1:121, 1970.

9. Price, W.H. and Whatmore, P.B.: Criminal behaviour and the XYY male. *Nature,* 213:815, 1967 (a) .

10. Welch, J.P.: Unpublished observations.

11. Marinello, M.J., Berkson, R.A., Edwards, J.A. and Bannerman, R.M.: A study of the XYY syndrome in tall men and juvenile delinquents. *JAMA,* 208:321, 1969.

12. Price, W.H. and Whatmore, P.B.: Behaviour disorders and pattern of crime among XYY males identified at a maximum security hospital. *Br Med J,* 1:533, 1967 (b) .

13. Jacobs, P.A., Price, W.H., Court Brown, W.M., Brittain, R.P. and Whatmore, P.B.: Chromosome studies on men in a maximum security hospital. *Ann Hum Genet,* Lond, 31:339, 1968.

14. Welch, J.P.: The XYY syndrome—A genetic determinant of behavior. *Birth Defects: Orig Art Ser,* 5 (5) :10, 1969.

15. Borgaonkar, D.S., Murdoch, J.L., McKusick, V.A., Borkowf, S.P., Money, J.W. and Robinson, B.W.: The YY syndrome. *Lancet,* 2:461, 1968.

16. Leff, J.P. and Scott, P.D.: XYY and intelligence. *Lancet,* 1:645, 1968.

17. Hope, K., Philip, A.E. and Loughran, J.M.: Psychological characteristics associated with XYY sex-chromosome complement in a state mental hospital. *Br J Psychiat,* 113:495, 1967.

18. Bartlett, D.J., Hurley, W.P., Brand, C.R. and Poole, E.W.: Chromosomes of male patients in a security prison. *Nature,* 219:351, 1968.

19. Griffiths, A.W., Richards, B.W., Zaremba, J., Abramowicz, T. and Stewart, A.: Psychological and sociological investigation of XYY prisoners. *Nature,* 227:290, 1970.

20. Shaffer, J.W.: A specific cognitive deficit observed in gonadal aplasia (Turner's syndrome). *J Clin Psychol,* 18:403, 1962.
21. Money, J.: Two cytogenetic syndromes: psychologic comparisons. 1. Intelligence and specific-factor quotients. *J Psychiat Res,* 2:223, 1964.
22. Boslow, H.M., Rosenthal, D., Kandel, A. and Manne, S.H.: Methods and experiences in group treatment of defective delinquents in Maryland. *J Soc Ther,* 7 (2) :65, 1961.
23. Taylor, J.A.: A personality scale of manifest anxiety. *J Abnorm Soc Psychol,* 48:285, 1953.
24. Barratt, E.S.: Factor analysis of some psychometric measures of impulsiveness and anxiety. *Psychol Rep,* 16:547, 1965.
25. Casey, M.D., Blank, C.E., Street, D.R.K., Segall, L.J., McDougall, J.H., McGrath, P.J. and Skinner, J.L.: YY chromosomes and antisocial behaviour. *Lancet,* 2:859, 1966.
26. Hunter, H.: YY chromosomes and Klinefelter's syndrome. *Lancet,* 1:984, 1966.
27. Goodman, R.M., Smith, W.S. and Migeon, C.J.: Sex chromosome abnormalities. *Nature,* 216:942, 1967.
28. Wiener, S., Sutherland, G., Bartholomew, A.A., and Hudson, B.: XYY males in a Melbourne prison. *Lancet,* 1:150, 1968.
29. Telfer, M.A., Baker, D., Clark, G.R. and Richardson, C.E.: Incidence of gross chromosomal errors among tall criminal American males. *Science,* 159:1249, 1968.
30. Nielsen, J., Tsuboi, T., Stürup, G. and Romano, D.: XYY chromosomal constitution in criminal psychopaths. *Lancet,* 2:576, 1968.
31. Knox, S.J. and Nevin, N.C.: XYY chromosomal constitution in prison populations. *Nature,* 222:596, 1969.
32. Melnyk, J., Derencsenyi, A., Vanasek, F., Rucci, A. J. and Thompson, H.: XYY survey on an institution for sex offenders and the mentally ill. *Nature,* 224:369, 1969.
33. Daly, R.F.: Neurological abnormalities in XYY males. *Nature,* 221:472, 1969.
34. Fattig, W.D.: An XYY survey in a Negro prison population. *J Hered,* 61: 10, 1970.

Chapter IV

AMINOACIDOPATHIES AND MENTAL RETARDATION

HOSSEIN GHADIMI

GENETIC engineering is imminent. Bacterial and viral diseases are being eradicated. Organ transplantation is a reality. Surgery, utilizing the great advances in the physical sciences, is helping to safeguard life even before birth. The very definition of death has been changed. Yet, our knowledge of the biochemistry of the brain, the causes of mental retardation and the physiopathology of mental diseases has remained almost as primitive as the instruments the Egyptians used for opening the skull several thousand years ago. The brain has remained sheltered in the fortress of the skull immune to the advances of sciences. We pay dearly for our ignorance.

THE SCOPE OF RETARDATION

According to one estimation, there are 5,000,000 retarded individuals in the United States. Perhaps the significance of this figure can be better understood in view of the fact that there are in the world today sixty-three countries with populations less than 5,000,000. Assuming that only 10 per cent of retarded individuals require institutional care because of gross retardation, the cost of lifetime care for these people comes to 125 billion dollars. This staggering figure does not take into consideration the losses from unrealized gains. That is, if these individuals had been able to lead normal lives, they would have added value to the lives of others as well as themselves. Ignorance is more expensive than any other waste.

For obvious reasons, therefore, in recent years great emphasis has been placed on advancing our understanding of the biochemical causes of mental retardation. There are about two hundred known causes of mental retardation. In practice, however,

45

the etiology of mental retardation in most instances remains unknown.

THE DEFICIT INDEX

Fifty-three molecular diseases are associated with mental retardation; yet, the specific biochemical sequences leading to mental retardation in these instances are not well understood. The simple truth is that we are still appallingly ignorant of biochemical aspects of learning; therefore, the mechanism leading to inability to learn remains obscure. There are no satisfactory means by which to characterize or measure mental ability. Probably the conventional approach to the estimation of IQ is too crude to bring to light minor differences in mental ability. The newly introduced neuropsychological Deficit Index offers a better possibility of the detection of the degree of learning ability or deficit.[1] Administration of a battery of 17 tests and 106 subtests takes three hours. The information obtained is converted into standard scores by a computer and then compared with mean scores for the patient's age. The percentage of scores falling more than two standard deviations below the mean is the Deficit Index. This index is, therefore, a measure of the degree of brain damage. Scores between 0 and 9 are considered normal, between 10 and 18 are indicative of mild brain damage and those between 19 and 27 suggest a moderate degree of brain damage.

HISTIDINEMIA AND THE DEFICIT INDEX

To cite an example of the sensitivity of the Deficit Index, a brief discussion of the patients with histidinemia reported by Gatfield *et al.*[2] is in order. After discovery of the index patient who was severely retarded, the entire family consisting of the parents and six children were screened for histidinemia. Three siblings, in addition to the index case, were found affected. Two children were normal. The index case and a nineteen-month-old sibling could not be tested for the Deficit Index because of the profound degree of retardation of the first and the young age of the second. The tests on the four remaining siblings showed scores of 6 for each of the two normal siblings and scores of 23 and 17 for the two histidinemics. The corresponding WISC scores for the last two patients (histidinemics) were 107 and 88. The conventional IQ tests, therefore, failed to

TABLE IV-I

PKU	Hydroxyprolinemia
Tyrosinemia	Lysinemia
Hyperammonemia	Dopa-Uria
Citrullinemia	Hartnup's Syndrome
Argininosuccinic	Oast-House Disease
aciduria	Maple Syrup Urine Disease
Homocystinuria	Certain Types of Goitrous Cretinism
Cystathioninemia	
Histidinemia	

reveal the neuropsychological deficits of the two patients with biochemical evidence of histidinemia.

The mother was aware of the mental limitations of these two children in spite of their normal IQs. When she was informed that some of her other children were also histidinemic, she correctly identified these last two. She states that they did poorly in school, had very bad tempers and "flighty attitudes," and were somehow different from the others. One wonders if the temper tantrums, difficulty in getting along with peers, failures in school which were also seen in our original patient with histidinemia, are a psychological consequence of the biochemical aberration in histidinemia.

A cause-and-effect relation is tacitly implied in all instances where a biochemical anomaly is associated with mental retardation or a behavioral problem. Aminoacidopathies associated with mental retardation, therefore, offer new opportunities to investigate the biochemical causes of mental retardation.

Approximately 50 per cent of the aminoacidopathies described thus far are associated with mild to gross degrees of mental retardation. These are listed in Table IV-I.

In a single presentation, a comprehensive discussion of aminoacidopathies is, obviously, impossible. Discussion will therefore be limited to a consideration of screening for, and diagnosis of, aminoacidopathies and the relationship of biochemical anomalies to mental retardation.

SCREENING AND DIAGNOSIS

The importance of screening cannot be overemphasized, since early diagnosis is prerequisite to successful treatment. Even though much of our knowledge of biochemical aberrations in relation to mental retardation is superficial, prevention of retardation is possible in an increasing number of inborn errors.

At present, blood samples of newborns in many states are tested for phenylketonuria. Simple screening tests can be used to detect other inborn errors. In all instances where screening tests are positive, quantitative analysis of biological fluids for the incriminated amino acid and its metabolites is carried out. Further work-up may involve studies on the patient's response to a loading dose of the amino acid. Loading tests are usually carried out by oral administration of 100 to 200 mg amino acid per kg body weight. The plasma level of the substance following administration of the load and the proportion of the dose excreted in the twenty-four-hour urine are then determined.

Final confirmation of the diagnosis is usually made through enzymic tests on tissue samples obtained from the patient. Since liver specimens are not easily obtainable, blood and skin specimens may be substituted whenever they contain the necessary enzyme.

LIMITATIONS OF SCREENING TECHNIQUES

The diagnostic process, therefore, starts with a positive screening test. However, there are inherent shortcomings in this approach. In practice, only gross and persistent increases in the concentration of an amino acid in biological fluids are considered abnormal. Such deviations from the norm generally result from a block in an *early step* of the *major* catabolic pathway of an essential amino acid. A disturbance in the metabolism of a nonessential amino acid, on the other hand, may not affect the concentration of that substance in the blood. For all these reasons, if there is a block in a minor, yet vital, metabolic pathway of the substance, the present screening technique would fail to disclose it. Less than 1 per cent of histidine, for example, is decarboxylated to histamine. A complete absence of histidine decarboxylase would not substantially affect the blood histidine concentration. Similarly, lack of the tyrosinase system, resulting in the conspicuous feature of albinism, hardly affects the blood tyrosine level. Albinism could not be diagnosed through blood screening tests for amino acids.

Metabolic blocks proximal to the amino acid may result in increased blood levels of the amino acid, and thereby be detectable by screening. On the other hand, a block distal to the amino acid may have no effect on the blood concentration of the amino acid, and therefore, escape detection by the present approach.

In screening for aminoacidopathies, persistently *high* blood values are considered significant. *Low* levels of an amino acid are not generally sought, since increased breakdown or decreased synthesis of body proteins presumably maintains the blood concentration within approximately the normal range.

Finally, unlike other substances in the body, the normal range of amino acid concentrations is wide (for most amino acids 1 to 4 mg per 100 ml). Therefore, persistently small deviations from normal are hard to evaluate.

Considering the numerous metabolic pathways of each amino acid and the possibility of an enzymic block for each step, it is logical to assume that a great number of aminoacidopathies still await recognition. However, it is unlikely that this will be accomplished with present screening tests, even if the widely used semiquantitative techniques are substituted by quantitative methods.

Clinical signs do not provide a practical diagnostic means for most aminoacidopathies. With the exception of Maple Syrup Urine Disease, albinism and alcaptonuria, the clinical manifestations of aminoacidopathies are nonspecific or suggestive, at best. In any case, biochemical diagnosis should precede full development of symptoms, if treatment is to meet with success.

A most promising aspect of investigations on inborn errors of metabolism is the growing understanding of the biochemistry of brain development (Chap. IX). Equally fascinating is the relation between the biochemical anomaly and the clinical manifestations of the disease.

Once this relationship is defined, the rational approach to therapy of prevention would follow.

BIOCHEMICAL BASIS FOR CLINICAL ABNORMALITIES

To illustrate the relationship of biochemical anomaly to clinical manifestation, to explain the natural history of the disease on the basis of brain development and biochemical anomaly, to exploit the presently available knowledge for selection of the right approach in the management of the disease, I shall briefly review both clinical and biochemical aspects of a recently described disease, namely, Lesch-Nyhan Disease. The condition is a disorder of purine *de novo* synthesis; nevertheless, it is a good example of an inborn error of metabolism showing the host of biochemical anomalies resulting from an enzymic defect. Moreover, as can be seen in Figure IV-1, the amino acids glutamine, glycine and aspartic acid are needed for formation of the uric acid.[3]

A syndrome marked by a combination of conspicuous neurological disturbances, such as self-mutilation, spasticity and choreoathetoid movements, and mental retardation was first described in 1964 by Lesch and Nyhan.[4] Two brothers described by these investigators had chewed away their fingers and lips and had high concentrations of uric acid in their blood. By the use of ^{14}C-glycine, a precursor of uric acid, Lesch and Nyhan proved that the hyperuricemia in these two patients was distinctly different from that in adult gout. In gout, the rate of incorporation of glycine into uric acid is two to three times that of normal, whereas in the two siblings the rate was found to be twenty times greater than that of controls.

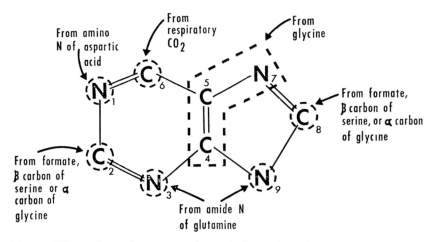

Figure IV-1. Schematic presentation of the uric acid molecule, showing sources of C and N atoms.

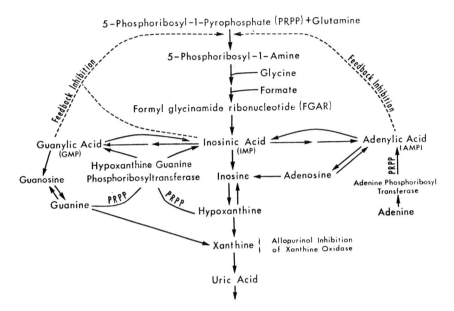

Figure IV-2. Pathway of the *de novo* purine synthesis.

Subsequent to the original publication, over twenty-five additional cases have been reported. In 1967, Seegmiller and his co-workers[5] identified the enzymic defect in this syndrome and laid the foundation for interpreting the clinical manifestations of the disease in terms of biochemical anomalies.

Hyperuricemia is the most widely-recognized biochemical anomaly in Lesch-Nyhan Disease. To understand the sequence of events leading to hyperuricemia, it is necessary to review the key steps in *de novo* purine synthesis (Fig. IV-2). The initial steps in this pathway involve reaction of PRPP with various substrates including glutamine, aspartic acid and glycine, resulting in the synthesis of inosinic acid (IMP). IMP in this particular pathway proceeds to hypoxanthine, which is further oxidized to xanthine and, finally, to uric acid by xanthine oxidase.

If this was the entire story of *de novo* purine formation, excessive purine synthesis would primarily mean a sheer waste of valuable nutritional substances, such as glutamine, glycine and aspartic acid. Obviously, the survival of homo sapiens required that a conserving mechanism be added, and our diagram illustrates how this mechanism for "reclaiming" important metabolites operates. The enzyme, hypoxanthine guanine phosphoribosyl-transferase (HG-PRTase) functions to salvage some hypoxanthine by converting it back to IMP.

IMP is also converted to guanylic acid (GMP) and adenylic acid (AMP). It is most important to bear in mind that the presence of GMP and AMP together act as a governor, by feedback inhibition, of the first step of purine biosynthesis by inhibiting the enzyme phosphoribosyl amino transferase. Another source of GMP is the phosphorylation of guanine by HG-PRTase. In any case, absence of HG-PRTase results in deficiency of GMP. With no feedback inhibition, acceleration of purine synthesis results. The twenty-fold increase in the formation of uric acid from glycine observed in Lesch-Nyhan disease has already been mentioned. In this condition, the tissues lack HG-PRTase activity.

The salient biochemical abnormalities observed in Lesch-Nyhan Disease to date can be summarized as follows:

1. Hyperuricemia, resulting in excessive output of uric acid.
2. Increased concentration of oxypurine (hypoxanthine and xanthine).[6]
3. Increased concentration of adenylic acid in red cells as a "compensatory mechanism."
4. Lack of HG-PRTase activity, usually demonstrated in red cells.[5]
5. Increased levels of PRPP.[7]
6. Relative decrease in plasma glutamine values.[8]

What is the connection between hyperuricemia and neurological impairment? At first, it was difficult even to hypothesize an answer. But the discovery that basal ganglia of normal persons are particularly rich in HG-PRTase and the fact that basal ganglia control the coordination of movement shed new light on the relation between biochemical anomaly and neurological manifestations.

Rosenbloom and co-workers[6] examined basal ganglia, frontal lobe, cerebellum, spinal cord, ovary, liver, spleen, kidney, muscle, pancreas, jejunum and adrenal tissues from controls and found that basal ganglia had the highest activity of HG-PRTase.

Basal ganglia of one patient with Lesch-Nyhan Disease tested by the same technique did not show any activity.

The natural history of the disease is fully consistent with the biochemical findings. During the first year of life, patients with Lesch-Nyhan Disease do not show any of the typical neurological manifestations of the disease. Indeed, in some respects the early clinical manifestations are in contrast to the late, more typical findings. The patients in the first year of life are hypotonic; feeding difficulties followed by failure to sit without support are common early manifestations. At one year of age, our patient could not sit without support or transfer objects with forefinger and thumb. He was below the third percentile for height and in approximately the twenty-fifth percentile for weight. Except for hypotonia, physical retardation and small stature, no other abnormality was observed. The typical clinical manifestations of Lesch-Nyhan Disease developed in this patient in the latter part of the second year. The patient became increasingly hypertonic, developed scissoring, opisthotonus and finger-biting.

This pattern of development of neurological manifestations is understandable since basal ganglia are not fully developed at birth. The potential abnormalities of the basal ganglia would not manifest themselves in early infancy.

Patients with Lesch-Nyhan Disease are generally malnourished. Sixteen out of twenty-three reported cases were below the third percentile for weight; four were at the third percentile, and three were between the third and tenth percentile. Our patient at $3\frac{1}{2}$ years of age before the initiation of therapy consumed less than 10 gm of protein per day and less than 1,000 calories daily. He was thirsty, repeatedly asking for juice. One wonders if hyperuricemia in a way similar to hyperglycemia may not be responsible for excessive thirst.

Obviously, with increasing knowledge of the biochemical aspects of Lesch-Nyhan Disease better understanding of the relationship between clinical manifestation and underlying biochemical processes will be forthcoming. Nevertheless, even the limited knowledge of the biochemical processes we have allows a deductive analysis of possible avenues of treatment.

The ideal goal of therapy would be the introduction of missing enzymes into specific cells, at the proper time and in the correct concentration. Since achievement of this aim is still remote, the logical alternative is the correction of the host of biochemical defects resulting from enzymic deficiency. Hyperuricemia, the easiest biochemical anomaly to recognize, was the first on the list to be corrected. By erroneous analogy with adult gout, where the patient is generally overweight from overeating, a low protein diet was tried in an attempt to reduce the hyperuricemia. In nine malnourished children in whom this dietary regimen was tried, the hyperuricemia did not respond.

Among uricosuric agents used in the attempt to control hyperuricemia, allopurinol is the favorite choice. The drug inhibits the enzyme xanthine oxidase. Its effect on hyperuricemia in conventional doses is dramatic. Nevertheless, the wisdom of employing allopurinol in Lesch-Nyhan Disease seems questionable, since the decrease in uric acid is obtained at the expense of increasing oxypurines which are already abnormally high in this disease. As far as renal lithiasis is concerned, all three substances (xanthine, hypoxanthine and uric acid) are known precursors of renal calculi. In any case, the control of blood uric acid levels does not bring about improvement in the patient's clinical condition. The initial reports on guanylic acid therapy are also disappointing.[9] It is doubtful whether this substance reaches the proper cells in active form.

The already malnourished patient with Lesch-Nyhan Disease continues excessive uric acid formation in spite of drastically low protein intake. Obviously, the amino acids used as precursors for uric acid must come from breakdown of some bodily proteins or failure to synthesize others. Based on this hypothesis, as well as our inability to control accelerated purine synthesis, the obvious choice was to supply abundant precursors and to try to rectify deficiencies. This involved administration of a high protein diet. The only way our patient could be induced to accept the high protein diet was through the addition of 10 gm monosodium glutamate (MSG) to his daily food. MSG may have specific therapeutic value since 2 molecules of glutamine are needed for formation of each molecule of uric acid. The rationale for MSG therapy can be summarized as follows:

1. The patient's relatively low plasma glutamine concentration.
2. Exaggerated *de novo* purine synthesis requiring large amounts of amino acid precursors.
3. History of malnutrition in patients with Lesch-Nyhan Disease.
4. Clinical manifestations of malnutrition evidenced by height and weight mostly below the 10th percentile.
5. The fact that, in rats, gluconeogenesis following starvation is accompanied by a marked reduction in the intracellular glutamine concentration in liver.[10]

MSG therapy and the high protein diet, as reported elsewhere,[8] resulted in dramatic improvement in the patient's condition. Self-mutilation virtually disappeared.

In short, the clinical manifestations of an inborn error may be related to deficiencies in certain metabolites, excesses in the concentrations of others or the presence of alien substances. In most cases, deficiencies have not received proper attention. Excesses are always most conspicuous and, on occasion, have completely monopolized the thoughts of investigators. The presence of alien substances, sometimes the metabolites of alternative pathways, is always looked upon with suspicion. In any case, a deficiency, excess, or alien substance, individually or in any combination may disturb anabolic processes. For instance, in phenylketonuria, melanin formation is partially inhibited, probably due to high phenylalanine levels. Low serotonin levels in the same disease may have a similar etiology.

In the example of Lesch-Nyhan Disease, emphasis was placed on a deficiency. It is interesting to note that in many inborn errors of metabolism associated with mental retardation, there is reason to suspect glutamine deficiency. In Maple Syrup Urine Disease, glutamine, glutarate and γ-aminobutyric acid are markedly decreased in brain tissue.[11] In histidinemia, the endogenous source of glutamic acid from the major catabolic pathway of histidine is blocked. With the absence of histidase, histidine cannot be deaminated to urocanic acid, which proceeds through imidasolone-propionic acid to glutamic acid.

In phenylketonuria, glutamine conjugates with phenylacetic acid (a metabolite of the subsidiary pathway of phenylalanine) and is eliminated in excessive amounts via urine. Thus, in addition to the hyperphenylalaninemia, there is a drain of glutamine from the body. The daily urinary output of the latter is 5 to 10 times normal.[12, 13]

In a recent article, Perry *et al.*[14] reported quantitative data on plasma-free amino acids in two patients with untreated phenylketonuria with normal intelligence, patients with phenylketonuria under dietary control, control groups and retarded patients with untreated phenylketonuria. The first three groups showed glutamine values within the normal range. In contrast, the glutamine values of retarded patients with untreated phenylketonuria showed a statistically significant decrease from normal.

There is experimental evidence that glutamine deficiency results in convulsions.[15] Methionine sulfoximine, which inhibits glutamine synthetase[16, 17, 18] results in lowered glutamine concentrations in the brain.[16, 19] Large doses of glutamine or asparagine protect mice from methionine sulfaximine toxicity.[19] This kind of exidence suggests that glutamine plays an essential role in brain metabolism in addition to its function in protein structure.

One might conclude that generally in any metabolic abnormality there is a host of biochemical anomalies and a variety of clinical manifestations. To pick one biochemical aberration because of its conspicuousness and try to explain the complex of signs and symptoms on that basis is most unrewarding and may be misleading.

REFERENCES

1. Knight, R. and Watson, P.: The use of computerized test profiles in neuropsychological assessment. *J Learn Disab*, 1:696, 1968.
2. Gatfield, P., Knight, R., Devereaux, M. and Pozsonyi, J.: Histidinemia: Report of 4 new cases in one family and the effects of low histidine diets. *Can Assoc J*, 101:465, 1969.
3. Gutman, A. and Yu, T.: The uric acid metabolism in normal man and in primary gout. *N Engl J Med*, 273:252, 1965.
4. Lesch, M. and Nyhan, W.: A familial disorder of uric acid metabolism and central nervous system function. *Am J Med*, 36:561, 1964.
5. Seegmiller, J., Rosenbloom, F. and Kelley, W.: Enzymic defect associated with a sex-linked human neurological disorder and excessive purine synthesis. *Science*, 155:1682, 1967.
6. Rosenbloom, F., Kelley, W., Miller, J., Henderson, J. and Seegmiller, J.: Inherited disorder of purine metabolism. *JAMA*, 202:175, 1967.

7. Rosenbloom, F., Henderson, J., Caldwell, I., Kelley, W. and Seegmiller, J.: Biochemical basis of accelerated purine biosynthesis de novo in human fibroblasts lacking hypoxanthine-guanine phosphoribosyltransferase. *J Biol Chem,* 243:1166, 1968.

8. Ghadimi, H., Bhalla, C. and Kirschenbaum, D.: The significance of the deficiency state in Lesch-Nyhan disease. *Acta Paed Scand,* 59:233, 1970.

9. Rosenberg, D., Monnet, P., Mamelle, J., Colombel, M., Salle, B. and Bovier-Lapierre, M.: Encephalopathie avec troubles du metabolisme des purines: Observation familiale. *La Press Medicale,* 76:2333, 1968.

10. Paleologos, G., Muntwylen, E. and Kesner, L.: Alanine and glutamine levels in rat liver tissue: A direct relationship to gluconeogenic state. *Proc Soc Exp Biol Med,* 132:210, 1969.

11. Prensky, A. and Moser, H.: Brain lipids, proteolipids and free amino acids in Maple Syrup Urine Disease. *J Neurochem,* 13:863, 1966.

12. Stein, W., Paladini, A., Hirs, C. and Moore, S.: Phenylacetylglutamine as a constituent of normal human urine. *J Am Chem Soc,* 76:2848, 1954.

13. Woolf, L.: Excretion of conjugated phenylacetic acid in phenylketonuria. *Biochem J,* 49:IX, 1951.

14. Perry, T., Hansen, S., Feschler, B., Bunting, R. and Diamond, S.: Glutamine depletion in phenylketonuria: Possible cause of mental defect. *N Engl J Med,* 282:761, 1970.

15. Proler, M. and Kellaway, P.: The methionine sulfoximine syndrome in the cat. *Epilepsia,* 3:117, 1962.

16. Kolousek, J. and Juracek, V.: The nitrogen metabolism of the rat brain and liver after administration of methionine sulfoximine. *J Neurochem,* 4:178, 1959.

17. Pace, J. and McDermott, E.: Methionine sulfoximine and some enzyme systems involving glutamine. *Nature,* 169:415, 1952.

18. Gershenovich, Z., Krichevskaya, A. and Koloagek, J.: The effect of raised oxygen pressure and of methionine sulfoximine on the glutamine synthetase activity of rat brain. *J Neurochem,* 10:79, 1963.

19. Peters, E. and Tower, D.: Glutamic acid and glutamine metabolism in cerebral cortex after seizures induced by methionine sulfoximine. *J Neurochem,* 5:80, 1959.

Chapter V

MENTAL RETARDATION AND
SELF-DESTRUCTIVE BEHAVIOR

Clinical and Biochemical Features of the Lesch-Nyhan Syndrome

WILFRED Y. FUJIMOTO

BACKGROUND AND CLINICAL FEATURES
OF THE SYNDROME

IN 1964, Lesch and Nyhan[1] described in two brothers a disorder consisting of hyperuricemia, spastic cerebral palsy, developmental retardation, choreoathetosis and bizarre, self-mutilating, aggressive behavior manifest in biting of their own lips and fingers. The metabolic abnormality of hyperuricemia in these children was demonstrated to be due to an excessive production of purines *de novo*. This disorder is now commonly called the Lesch-Nyhan syndrome. The behavior of this trait in all pedigrees studied to date has been consistent with an X-linked recessive mode of inheritance.[2-5]

In 1967, Seegmiller and co-workers[6] found markedly reduced activity of the enzyme hypoxanthine-guanine phosphoribosyltransferase, or PRT, in cells from such patients. Thus, a specific enzyme defect, resulting in the metabolic abnormality of uric acid overproduction, was associated with a distinctive and bizarre behavioral pattern, psychomotor retardation, and neurological abnormalities.

> This thirteen-year-old boy had been hospitalized elsewhere at the time he was referred to the National Institutes of Health. He was fairly well-developed and was adequately nourished. He had been known to be mentally retarded from early childhood. Choreoathetotic movements were noted at about one year of age, he had never walked, and had delayed speech development. The diagnosis of cerebral palsy was made. At 2½ years of age, he began to bite his fingers (Fig. V-1) ; however, he has never bitten his lips. At about five years of age, he passed a urinary calculus. Subsequently, many urate crystals have been noted in his urine. Serum uric acids have been normal or only slightly elevat-

58

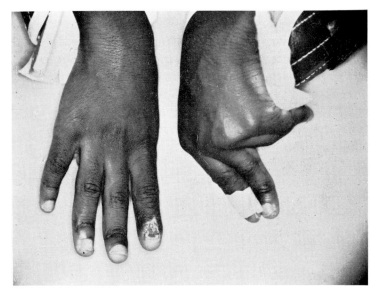

Figure V-1. Mutilated finger.

ed. Large renal calculi were also found and these have decreased significantly in size on allopurinol therapy. Although these children are mentally retarded, it has been the impression of those who have been associated with this patient's care that his intelligence is greater than first appearances suggest. The patient is usually pleasant, and self-mutilation has become less of a problem during his hospitalization. However, he still attempts to strike out at individuals or objects within reach. Speech is characterized by an athetoid dysarthria. Frequent vomiting of food has also been a problem. The diagnosis in this case was confirmed by demonstrating absence of PRT activity.

This boy illustrates the cardinal features of the Lesch-Nyhan syndrome: a) hyperuricosuria secondary to overproduction of purines *de novo,* b) absence of activity of PRT, c) psychomotor retardation, d) neurological abnormalities and e) self-mutilatory and aggressive behavior. In addition, this patient's family history is positive since two maternal uncles died early in childhood with a history of "infantile paralysis," mental retardation and self-mutilation, consistent with an X-linked mode of inheritance.

Hyperuricemia is usually present in these children, but sometimes, as in this case, serum uric acids have been normal or only slightly elevated despite hyperuricosuria and marked overproduction of purines *de novo*. Overproduction of uric acid may be quantitated in several ways. One of these is to measure the uric acid excretion in a twenty-four-hour period on a standard, purine-free diet. Uric acid excretion in this disorder is in the range of 30 to 50 mg/kg/day, and in some cases even higher; this is about 5 to 6 times greater than in controls.[1, 4, 7] Even simpler is to obtain a random urine specimen and to measure the uric acid to creatinine ratio; normally this is less than 1.0, while in these children the ratio is in the range of 2 to 5.[8] Overproduction of purines *de novo* may be measured by an isotopic method. The child is given glycine-1-^{14}C orally or intravenously and its incorporation into urinary uric acid is measured. Glycine is chosen because it is incorporated into the 4, 5 and 7 positions of uric acid. These children incorporate about twenty times as much glycine into uric acid as normals.[1, 4, 7] This overproduction of uric acid leads to uric acid renal stones, renal damage and progressive renal insufficiency if untreated. Treatment consists of high fluid intake and administration of allopurinol. This drug inhibits the enzyme xanthine-oxidase and thus blocks the formation of uric acid from xanthine. Urinary alkalinization may also be added to this regimen. During infancy, mothers of such children may report the presence of orange uric acid crystals on diapers, a clue to this disorder that may be picked up by the alert physician.

The diagnosis is established conclusively by demonstrating the absence of activity of erythrocyte PRT. This enzyme catalyzes the reaction of hypoxanthine or guanine with 5-phosphoribosyl-1-pyrophosphate, or PRPP, to form inosinic acid or guanylic acid, respectively. The original assay method for this enzyme involved the incubation of dialyzed erythrocyte lysate with the appropriate incubation mixture containing either hypoxanthine-8-^{14}C or guanine-8-^{14}C and PRPP as substrate.[6] Incorporation of these isotopes into inosinic acid or guanylic acid after electrophoretic separation of the reaction products was measured. By this method, such patients have less than 0.01% activity as measured with hypoxanthine-8-^{14}C as substrate, and less than 0.004% activity with guanine-8-^{14}C as substrate (Table V-I).[9]

TABLE V-I

Subjects	PRT Activity (mμmoles/mg Protein per Hour)	
	Hypoxanthine Mean ± S.D.	Guanine Mean ± S.D.
Normal (32) *	103 ± 18	103 ± 21
Lesch-Nyhan (9) *	<0.01	<0.004

* Number of subjects studied.

We have recently reported a simplified assay method which measures the same reaction products but which does not require venous blood.[10] Instead, blood taken by fingerstick or heelstick is spotted onto a piece of filter paper, dried and sent to a laboratory equipped to do the assay. Uniform-sized discs are cut out of the blood spots, and these are incubated with the reaction mixture. We have found that these samples are quite stable, even when sent through the mail. Samples from normal individuals retain 40 to 60 per cent of their original activity even if they are stored at room temperature for forty days. If stored in the freezer, nearly all the activity is retained. Affected children have been found to have essentially zero activity by this assay technique.

The neurological signs of this condition usually begin to appear in the second half of the first year of life. In a few cases neurological abnormalities have been noted from birth, while in others they have been less pronounced. Neurological abnormalities consist of spasticity, choreoathetosis, dysarthria, dysphagia and frequent vomiting. Mental retardation is variable, and at times it appears that these children are a good deal brighter than one initially takes them to be. Their facial expression may even appear extremely alert. Growth is also retarded in these children. Height and weight are below the third percentile, usually with a greater retardation in weight than in height.

Less consistent is the finding of aggressive and self-mutilatory behavior, although this is one of the most distinctive and dramatic features of this syndrome. This sign generally does not appear until later in life. This bizarre behavior is not only self-directed, as is the case with biting of the lips and fingers, head-

banging and catching their fingers in the spokes of their wheel-
chair, but is also directed at others. Aggression toward others is
also expressed in blasphemous language. Self-mutilation will occur with or without an audience. These children feel pain, and
plead with you to keep them from biting themselves. Arm
braces placed on these children prevent them from getting their
fingers to their mouths. If these braces are removed, the child
becomes extremely apprehensive and agitated.

METABOLIC DEFECT

How does deficiency of PRT cause overproduction of uric
acid? The enzyme PRT catalyzes the transfer of ribose-5-phos-
phate from PRPP to the free purine bases, hypoxanthine and
guanine, forming their respective ribonucleotides, iosinic acid
and guanylic acid (Fig. V-2). These products are effective feedback inhibitors of purine synthesis *de novo* at the rate-limiting
step, PRPP amidotransferase, the first step in this purine pathway. The overproduction of uric acid is believed to be due
either to the release of feedback inhibition or to an increased
amount of PRPP available for this first step of purine synthesis,

HYPOXANTHINE-GUANINE PHOSPHORIBOSYLTRANSFERASE

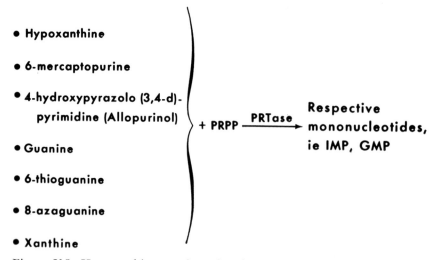

Figure V-2. Hypoxanthine-guanine phosphoribosyltransferase (PRT) reaction.

both of which could result from absence of **PRT**. Increased amounts of intracellular **PRPP** have been reported in erythrocytes[11] and in cultured fibroblasts from such patients.[12] Another possible mechanism for increased purine synthesis *de novo* is a decreased sensitivity of **PRPP** amidotransferase to feedback inhibition.

WHAT CAUSES THE SYMPTOMS?

Why the deficiency of this enzyme leads to the behavioral, neurological and developmental abnormalities in this disorder is not known. It is known, however, that under normal conditions, the specific activity of **PRT** in normal tissues is highest in the brain, and that the basal ganglia have the highest levels.[13] These areas showed no **PRT** activity in brain tissue from a patient with this disorder. Hence, there is good evidence that the deficiency of this enzyme leads in some way to the neurological and mental abnormalities.

When cerebrospinal fluid (CSF) oxypurines (hypoxanthine and xanthine) are measured, it has been found that the level of CSF oxypurines in these patients is increased three to four times their normal level in the CSF.[13, 14] Plasma oxypurines and CSF uric acid in these patients are identical with those in normals. Furthermore, the increase in CSF oxypurines is due entirely to an increase in hypoxanthine, the levels of xanthine being equal in patients and controls. These data may be interpreted to indicate that oxypurines are produced in the central nervous system rather than entering the cerebrospinal fluid from the blood. The normal levels of xanthine and uric acid in the cerebrospinal fluid indicate that they probably have no causative role in the production of the neurological symptoms. When allopurinol is given these patients, there is a two to three-fold increase in CSF oxypurines, and a five to twelve-fold increase in plasma oxypurines; the increase in plasma oxypurines is probably the source of the increased cerebrospinal fluid oxypurines when allopurinol is given.[13, 14] Since the increase in hypoxanthine could be responsible for the neurological dysfunction, the administration of allopurinol might be expected to worsen neurological signs. This is not the case since allopurinol administration to these patients over extended periods has not caused an increase in neurological dysfunction. From these findings, it seems more likely that a decrease in some necessary purine nucleotide such as guanine ribonucleotide might be responsible for neurological damage, rather than the increase in oxypurine. If PRT is necessary to maintain the normal guanine ribonucleotide levels required for RNA synthesis, then decreased guanine ribonucleotide might lead to impaired cell function. Furthermore, guanine ribonucleotides are also required as cofactors for protein synthesis. Another way in which accelerated purine biosynthesis *de novo* might lead to impaired cell function is through the depletion of one or more of the substrates for this pathway, such as glutamine, PRPP, glycine and one-carbon units. At this time, these mechanisms are all speculative.

INHERITANCE AND CARRIER DETECTION

The mode of inheritance of the Lesch-Nyhan syndrome is X-linked recessive, that is, the locus for the gene coding for PRT is on the X chromosome and transmission of the deficiency is through an asymptomatic carrier female to an affected male. This is illustrated in the pedigree in Figure V-3. The successful detection of carrier females is of paramount importance for effective genetic counseling in this disorder. This is especially true since the successful use of cultured amniotic fluid cells for antenatal diagnosis in this disorder.[15, 16]

In 1961, Mary Lyon[17] proposed that early in embryonic development one of the two X chromosomes becomes inactivated as a random process, but once the choice is made, it is maintained in all descendants of that cell. Hence, the female would have either an active paternal X chromosome or an active maternal X chromosome in each somatic cell, and would therefore be chromosomally and genetically mosaic. If one of these chromosomes carries a mutant gene, such a female would be a mosaic for that mutation, with some of her cells being normal and others being deficient. If a cellular marker is available, then it should be possible to detect this mosaicism in such a carrier.

The erythrocyte PRT assay, previously mentioned, is extremely useful in the detection of mutant hemizygotes, but not for the detection of carriers. Carrier females usually have normal levels

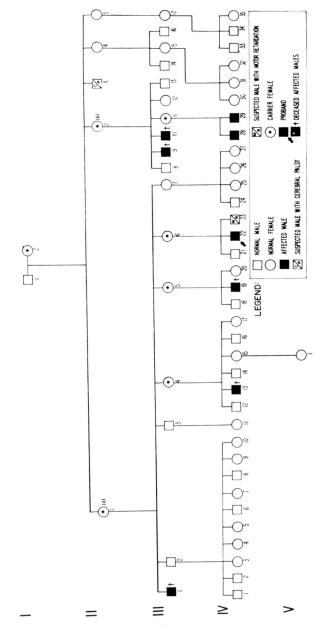

Figure V-3. Pedigree showing X-linked recessive inheritance of PRT deficiency (reproduced with permission of authors[3]).

of erythrocyte PRT activity, rather than the intermediate levels one would expect from the Lyon hypothesis.[9] Mosaicism is also absent in heterozygote lymphocytes since all such cells appear to be normal.[22, 23] At the present time, cultured fibroblasts seem to provide the only method for detection of carriers for this disorder.

Fibroblast cultures are established from minced skin biopsies. Such fibroblasts when obtained from normal subjects are able to incorporate radioactive hypoxanthine and guanine (hypoxanthine-³H or guanine-³H) into nucleic acids, a process requiring PRT. Such incorporation can be shown by a radioautographic

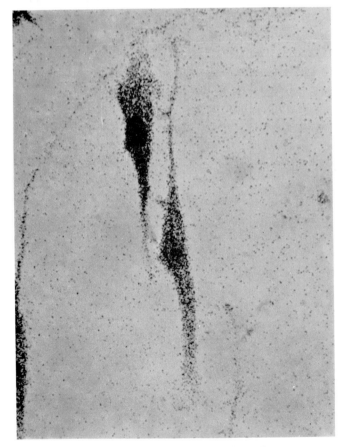

Figure V-4. Normal cultured fibroblast.

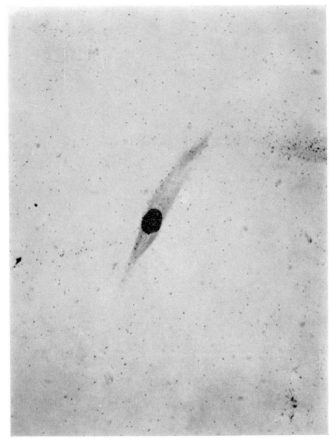

Figure V-5. Mutant cultured fibroblast.

technique. Fibroblasts are grown on slides in medium containing one of these isotopes. After twenty-four hours, the slides are washed, fixed, treated with cold 5% trichloroacetic acid, dried, and coated with photographic emulsion. After exposure to the emulsion for three to five days, the preparations are developed and treated with Giemsa stain. Normal fibroblasts show dense silver granules overlying the cells (Fig. V-4). Fibroblasts obtained from patients with the Lesch-Nyhan syndrome are unable to incorporate the isotope into nucleic acids and no silver granules develop over the cells (Fig. V-5). Carrier females show mosaicism in their cultured fibroblasts. Some cells show incor-

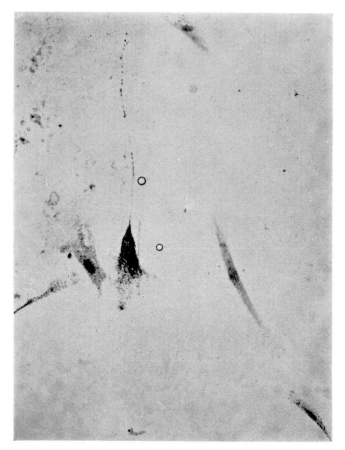

Figure V-6. Heterozygote cultured fibroblasts.

poration of the isotope while other cells are devoid of such in-corporation (Fig. V-6).[24] In some cells there are intermediate de-grees of isotope incorporation which is probably due to meta-bolic cooperation.[21] In addition, cellular clones with and with-out PRT activity have been isolated from fibroblast cultures from carrier females.[25, 26]

GENETIC COUNSELING AND THE ROLE OF AMNIOCENTESIS

Once a child afflicted with this serious metabolic disorder ap-pears in a family, any subsequent pregnancy exposes the parents to a one-in-four risk of producing another affected child. Stated more precisely, each son of a carrier female has a one-in-two risk of being affected. It is not surprising, therefore, that parents, when faced with this grim prospect would often choose not to take the risk and instead stop having children. The use of the techniques of amniocentesis and amniotic fluid cell cultures allows the parents confronted with this high risk situation to ensure the birth of normal children.

Amniocentesis is the process of obtaining amniotic fluid by a needle puncture of the pregnant uterus. The needle is inserted by the transabdominal approach, using local anesthesia. The optimum time for obtaining fluid is between sixteen and eighteen weeks of fetal gestation.

It has been previously found that amniotic fluid cells obtained by amniocentesis were of value in the prediction of fetal sex.[27-31] In X-linked disorders like the Lesch-Nyhan syndrome, such studies are of limited usefulness, since the fetus will not be affected if a female but has a one-in-two chance of being affected if a male.

Another possibility in such a pregnancy at risk would be to directly assay the amniotic fluid uric acid concentration. As noted previously, the urinary uric acid excretion of patients with the Lesch-Nyhan syndrome is greatly elevated. There is little doubt that fetal urine contributes significantly to the amniotic

TABLE V-II

ENZYMES DEMONSTRATED IN CULTURES OF AMNIOTIC FLUID CELLS

Acid phosphatase[34]
Alkaline phosphatase[34]
α-glucosidase[34]
α-keto-isocaproate decarboxylase[35]
β-glucuronidase[34]
Cystathionine synthase[35]
Galactose-l-phosphate uridyl transferase[34]
Glucocerebrosidase[35]
Glucose-6-phosphate dehydrogenase[34]
Hypoxanthine-guanine phosphoribosyltransferase[35]
Lactate dehydrogenase[34]
Phytanic acid α-hydroxylase[35]
6-phosphogluconic dehydrogenase[34]
Sphingomyelinase[35]
Valine transaminase[36]

fluid.[32] Hence, it might be expected that the amniotic fluid uric acid concentration of a fetus with the Lesch-Nyhan syndrome would be significantly elevated above the amniotic fluid uric acid levels found in other pregnancies.[33, 34] This has not yet been confirmed.

Recently, Steele and Breg[35] and Jacobson and Barter[36] showed that it was possible to cultivate amniotic fluid cells and use such cultures for chromosomal analysis. Even more recently, a large number of enzymes, known to be associated with specific hereditary metabolic disorders, were found to be normally active in amniotic fluid cell cultures (Table V-II). In addition, several other metabolic disorders are now diagnosable in amniotic fluid cell cultures without actual enzyme assays, e.g. mucopolysaccharidosis[40] and cystinosis.[41] Among the enzymes active in amniotic fluid cell cultures is PRT. In six normal amniotic fluids taken from infants of nine to thirty-two weeks fetal gestation, the cultivated cells showed levels of PRT activity comparable to those found in normal cultured fibroblasts (Table V-III).[42] Those cells that are serially cultured from amniotic fluid have the morphologic appearance of fibroblasts. These findings suggested that the determination of PRT activity in amniotic fluid cell cultures from women heterozygous for the gene determining the Lesch-Nyhan syndrome would be helpful in making the antenatal diagnosis in affected males.

A twenty-four-year-old housewife who was the first cousin of an affected male wanted to investigate her carrier status (related through the mothers). During her thirteenth gestational week, a

TABLE V-III

NORMAL PRT ACTIVITY IN CULTURED HUMAN FIBROBLASTS
AND AMNIOTIC FLUID CELL CULTURES

	Number	Age	Specific Activity*
Fibroblast 11		Adult	81.0 ± 24.9 (Average ± S.D.)
Amniotic Fluid 6		9 Wks. to 33 Wks.	66.86 ± 8.08 (Average ± S.D.)

* Specific activity of PRT represents the mμmoles of hypoxanthine-8-^{14}C converted to inosinic acid and inosine per mg cell extract protein per hour at 25° C.

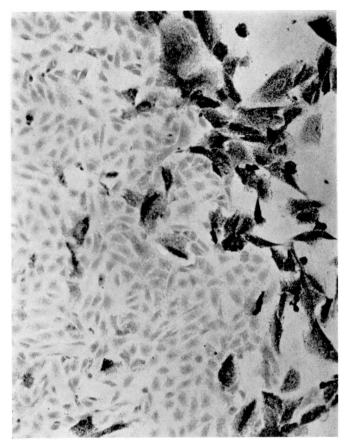

Figure V-7. Amniotic fluid cell culture indicating carrier status of fetus.

skin biopsy was obtained and fibroblast cultures studied by the radioautographic procedure previously described confirmed her carrier status. During her seventeenth gestational week, a transabdominal amniocentesis was performed. A sample of the amniotic fluid cells obtained were 30 per cent sex chromatin positive, consistent with a female fetus. This was later confirmed by chromosome studies which showed a 46/XX karyotype. The cultured amniotic fluid cells studied for PRT activity were shown to be of two cell types; one normal and the other mutant, consistent with the fetus being a carrier female (Fig. V-7). This demonstrates the way in which this technique can help in antenatal diagnosis in this disorder.[15] Subsequently, DeMars and co-workers[16] have made a successful antepartum diagnosis of the complete defect.

By utilizing the techniques described here in any high risk pregnancy, the physician is now potentially able to inform the parents during pregnancy whether they will have an affected or a normal child. This will allow genetic counseling to be very precise. If therapeutic interruption of pregnancy is acceptable, then the fear of having a child with the Lesch-Nyhan syndrome no longer becomes an obstacle to pregnancy. This is particularly pertinent at this time since, although there had been a few encouraging preliminary reports of the possible therapeutic benefits from adenine and folic acid,[18] there is probably no adequate therapy that will prevent or reverse the bizarre neurological aspects of this distressing disorder.[19, 20]

REFERENCES

1. Lesch, M. and Nyhan, W.L.: A familial disorder of uric acid metabolism and central nervous system function. *Am J Med,* 36:561, 1964.
2. Hoefnagel, D., Andrew, E.D., Mireault, N.G. and Berndt, W.O.: Hereditary choreoathetosis, self-mutilation and hyperuricemia in young males. *N Engl J Med,* 273:130, 1965.
3. Shapiro, S.L., Sheppard, B.L., Jr., Dreifuss, F.E. and Newcombe, D.S.: X-linked recessive inheritance of a syndrome of mental retardation with hyperuricemia. *Proc Soc Exp Biol Med,* 122:609, 1966.
4. Nyhan, W.L., Pesek, J., Sweetman, L., Carpenter, D.G. and Carter, C.H.: Genetics of an X-linked disorder of uric acid metabolism and cerebral function. *Pediatr Res,* 1:5, 1967.
5. Henderson, J.F., Kelley, W.N., Rosenbloom, F.M. and Seegmiller, J.E.: Inheritance of purine phosphoribosyltransferase in man. *Am J Hum Genet,* 21:61, 1969.
6. Seegmiller, J.E., Rosenbloom, F.M. and Kelley, W.N.: An enzyme defect associated with a sex-linked human neurological disorder and excessive purine synthesis. *Science,* 155:1682, 1967.
7. Nyhan, W.L., Oliver, W.J. and Lesch, M.: A familial disorder of uric acid metabolism and central nervous system function. II. *J Pediatr,* 67:257, 1965.
8. Kaufman, J.M., Greene, M.L. and Seegmiller, J.E.: Urine uric acid to creatinine ratio—a screening test for inherited disorders of purine metabolism. *J Pediatr,* 73:583, 1968.
9. Kelley, W.N.: Hypoxanthine-guanine phosphoribosyltransferase deficiency in the Lesch-Nyhan syndrome and gout. *Fed Proc,* 27:1047, 1968.

10. Fujimoto, W.Y., Greene, M.L. and Seegmiller, J.E.: X-linked uric aciduria with neurological disease and self-mutilation: diagnostic test for the enzyme defect. *J Pediatr,* 73:920, 1968.
11. Greene, M.L., Boyle, J.A. and Seegmiller, J.E.: Substrate stabilization: Genetically controlled reciprocal relationship of two human enzymes. *Science,* 167:887, 1970.
12. Rosenbloom, F.M., Henderson, J.F., Kelley, W.N. and Seegmiller, J.E.: Accelerated purine biosynthesis *de novo* in skin fibroblasts deficient in hypoxanthine-guanine phosphoribosyltransferase. *Biochem Biophys Acta,* 166:258, 1968.
13. Rosenbloom, F.J., Kelley, W.N., Miller, J., Henderson, J.F. and Seegmiller, J.E.: Inherited disorder of purine metabolism. Correlation between central nervous system dysfunction and biochemical defects. *JAMA,* 202:175, 1967.
14. Sweetman, L.: Urinary and cerebrospinal fluid oxypurine levels and allopurinol metabolism in the Lesch-Nyhan syndrome. *Fed Proc,* 27: 1055, 1968.
15. Fujimoto, W.Y., Seegmiller, J.E., Uhlendorf, B.W. and Jacobson, C.B.: Biochemical diagnosis of an X-linked disease in utero. *Lancet,* 2:511, 1968.
16. De Mars, R., Sarto, G., Felix, J.S. and Benke, P.: Lesch-Nyhan mutation: prenatal detection with amniotic fluid cells. *Science,* 164:1303, 1969.
17. Lyon, M.F.: Gene action in the X-chromosome of the mouse *(Mus musculus L.). Nature,* 190:372, 1961.
18. Felix, J.S. and De Mars, R.: Purine requirement of cells cultured from humans affected with Lesch-Nyhan syndrome (hypoxanthine-guanine phosphoribosyltransferase deficiency). *PNAS,* 62:536, 1969.
19. Marks, J.F., Baum, J., Keele, D.K., Kay, J.L. and MacFarlen, A.: Lesch-Nyhan syndrome treated from the early neonatal period. *Pediatr,* 42: 357, 1968.
20. Schulman, J.D., Greene, M.L., Fujimoto, W.Y. and Seegmiller, J.E.: Unpublished data.
21. Fujimoto, W.Y. and Seegmiller, J.E.: Hypoxanthine-guanine phosphoribosyltransferase deficiency: Activity in normal, mutant, and heterozygote cultured human skin fibroblasts. *PNAS,* 65:577, 1970.
22. Dancis, J., Berman, P.H., Jansen, V. and Balis, M.E.: Absence of mosaicism in the lymphocyte in X-linked congenital hyperuricosuria. *Life Sciences,* 7 (part II):587, 1968.
23. Fujimoto, W.Y. and Seegmiller, J.E.: Unpublished observations.
24. Rosenbloom, F.M., Kelley, W.N., Henderson, J.F. and Seegmiller, J.E.: Lyon hypothesis and X-linked disease. *Lancet,* 2:305, 1967.
25. Migeon, B.R., Der Kaloustian, V.M., Nyhan, W.L., Young, W.J. and Childs, B.: X-linked hypoxanthine-guanine phosphoribosyltransferase deficiency: heterozygote has two clonal populations. *Science,* 160:425, 1968.

26. Salzmann, J., De Mars, R. and Benke, P.: Single allele expression at an X-linked hyperuricemia locus in heterozygous human cells. *PNAS,* 60: 545, 1968.

27. Fuchs, F. and Riis, P.: Antenatal sex determination. *Nature,* 177:330, 1956.

28. Makowski, E.L., Prem, K.A. and Kaiser, I.H.: Detection of sex of fetuses by the incidence of sex chromatin body in nuclei of cells in amniotic fluid. *Science,* 123:542, 1956.

29. Serr, D.M., Sachs, L. and Danon, M.: Diagnosis of sex before birth using cells from the amniotic fluid. *Bull Res Counc Israel,* 58:137, 1955.

30. Shettles, L.B.: Nuclear morphology of cells in human amniotic fluid in relation to sex of infant. *Am J Obstet Gynec,* 71:834, 1956.

31. Dewhurst, C.J.: Diagnosis of sex before birth. *Lancet,* 1:471, 1956.

32. Pitkin, R.M., Reynolds, W.A. and Burchell, R.C.: Fetal contribution to amniotic fluid. *Am J Obstet Gynec,* 100:834, 1968.

33. Bonsnes, R.W.: Composition of amniotic fluid. *Clin Obstet Gynec,* 9:440, 1966.

34. Marks, J.F., Baum, J., Kay, J.L., Taylor, W. and Curry, L.: Amniotic fluid concentrations of uric acid. *Pediatrics,* 42:359, 1968.

35. Steele, M.W. and Breg, W.R., Jr.: Chromosome analysis of human amniotic fluid cells. *Lancet,* 1:383, 1966.

36. Jacobson, C.B. and Barter, R.H.: Intrauterine diagnosis and management of genetic defects. *Am J Obstet Gynec,* 99:796, 1967.

37. Nadler, H.L.: Pattern of enzyme development using cultivated human fetal cells from amniotic fluid. *Biochem Genet,* 2:119, 1968.

38. Uhlendorf, B.W., Jacobson, C.B., Sloan, H.R., Mudd, S.H., Herndon, J.H., Brady, R.P., Seegmiller, J.E. and Fujimoto, W.: Cell cultures derived from human amniotic fluid: their possible application in the intrauterine diagnosis of heritable metabolic disease. *In vitro,* 4:158, 1969.

39. Dancis, J.: The antepartum diagnosis of genetic diseases. *J Pediatr,* 72: 301, 1968.

40. Fratantoni, J.C., Neufeld, E.F., Uhlendorf, B.W. and Jacobson, C.B.: Intrauterine diagnosis of the Hurler and Hunter syndromes. *N Engl J Med,* 280:686, 1969.

41. Schulman, J.D., Fujimoto, W.Y., Bradley, K.H. and Seegmiller, J.E.: Identification of heterozygous genotype for cystinosis *in utero* by a new pulse-labelling technic. *J Pediatr,* in press.

42. Uhlendorf, B.W., Fujimoto, W.Y., Jacobson, C.B. and Seegmiller, J.E.: Unpublished data.

43. van der Zee, S.P.M., Schretlen, E.D.A.M. and Monnens, L.A.H.: Megaloblastic anemia in the Lesch-Nyhan syndrome. *Lancet,* 2:1427, 1968.

Chapter VI

MOLECULAR DEFECT AND MENTAL RETARDATION

Generalized Gangliosidosis

JOHN S. O'BRIEN

IT has been estimated that each one of us carries six lethal genes in his genetic material. You might wonder which six you carry. Carriers for many lethal genes have been detected. Carriers have lower than normal levels of the enzymes which are produced by the specific mutant gene they carry. One can envision a brave new world in which we might carry an IBM card punched for each of our lethal genes. Before we marry, we would match IBM cards with our future spouse. By family planning, we hope to prevent the conception of children who would otherwise die with a fatal genetic disease. Let me tell you about one of these genetic diseases; one that I have been intimately involved in studying, named generalized gangliosidosis.

CLINICAL MANIFESTATIONS

The infant with generalized gangliosidosis is usually floppy and hypotonic from birth. He has edema of the face and of the extremities. He fails to thrive and has a weak cry. His face is quite peculiar, with coarsening of facial features, frontal bossing, facial hirsutism, especially of the forehead and the neck, hypertelorism, a flattened bridge of the nose, mild macroglossia, and hyperplasia of the gums.

Figure VI-1 depicts a boy with generalized gangliosidosis. This picture, taken at seven months of age, shows the coarse facial features that are evident in these patients early in life. Other important physical findings include a claw-hand deformity, cherry red spots on the retina (in one-half of the patients), and a gib-

Note: This work was supported in part by Grants HE 08429 and NB 08682 from the National Institutes of Health.

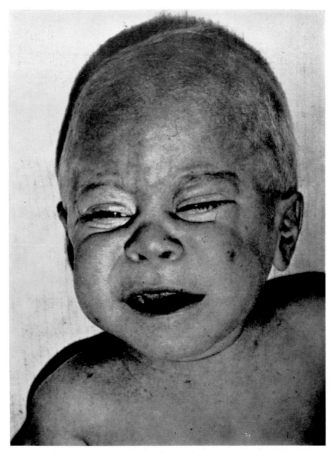

Figure VI-1. Child at 7 months of age with generalized gangliosidosis.

bus deformity of the lumbar spine. All of the patients described
have moderate hepatomegaly, and about 70 per cent have splenomegaly.

The infant is usually flaccid and hypotonic early in life and
later in the course of the disease has clonic-tonic seizures, spasticity and a generalized hyperreflexia syndrome. Developmental
milestones are very slowly achieved. The infant often does not
sit up, does not crawl or stand, and is out of contact with his surroundings most of the time.

In contradistinction to children with the Hurler's syndrome

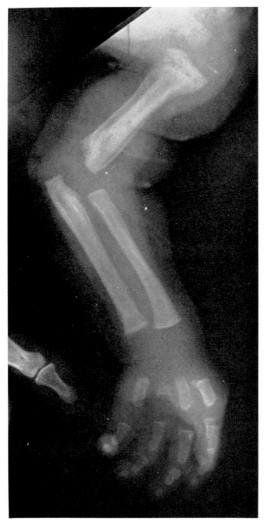

Figure VI-2. Upper extremity at 2 months of age. Note the hypoplastic appearance, midshaft widening, periosteal cloaking and pinching off of the ends of the humerus (courtesy of G. Mitchell and A. Berne, Syracuse Memorial Hospital).

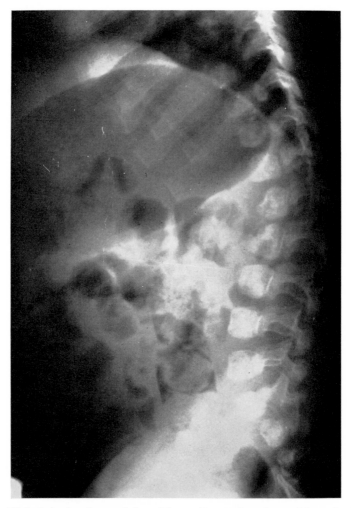

Figure VI-3. Spinal column deformities at 7 months of age. Note the hypoplastic vertebral bodies, the beaking of L_1 and L_2 and the lumbar kyphosis
(courtesy of G. Mitchell and A. Berne, Syracuse Memorial Hospital) .

(Mucopolysaccharidosis (MPS) type 1) the infant with generalized
gangliosidosis does not usually have corneal clouding and the clinical course is much more rapid. In eighteen cases reported, death
has occurred by age two, usually due to intercurrent infections.[1]

RADIOLOGIC FINDINGS

The skeletal deformities are characteristic and the radiologist often makes the diagnosis.[2] One such deformity occurs in the humerus which is often larger in midshaft than at the ends. There is a tapering off of the ends both proximally and distally giving a "pinched-off" appearance. The cortex is hypoplastic and has a "reamed out" appearance. Periosteal "cloaking" of the humerus and of other long bones is present. The humeral deformity and the periosteal cloaking are two of the most diagnostic radiological signs in this disorder (Fig. VI-2).

The vertebral bodies in the spinal column are markedly hypoplastic with inferior beaking of the lumbar vertebrae. A markedly hypoplastic vertebral body is usually present at or near the site of a well-defined dorsolumbar kyphosis. Various degrees of retarded bone development occur in most of the bones (Fig. VI-3).

GENETICS

There appears to be no particular ethnic predilection. Thus far, affected Algerian, Negro, Mexican, Northern European, and Jewish children have been described. Fourteen sibships are either known to me or reported in the literature. Four of these have involved more than one affected child. Males and females have been affected with about equal frequency (11 boys, 7 girls). Although large numbers of patients have not been reported, examination of the inheritance patterns in families, the high consanguinity rate, and adjustment of family data by ascertainment by truncate selection suggests that the disorder is transmitted in an autosomal recessive manner.

PATHOLOGIC MANIFESTATIONS

Generalized gangliosidosis was first classified as a lipid storage disease and is now considered to be a mucopolysaccharidosis as well.

Figure VI-4 illustrates the cytoplasmic vacuolation seen in splenic histiocytes. Involved cells stain periodic acid Schiff (PAS) positive are weakly sudanophilic and weakly metachromatic.

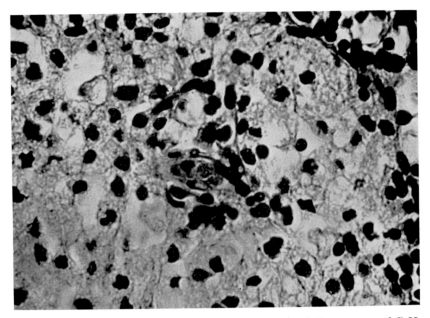

Figure VI-4. Vacuolation of splenic histiocytes (H and E; courtesy of B.H. Landing, Childrens Hospital, Los Angeles) .

Landing *et al.*[2] found that the substance in the histiocytes was a glycolipid, probably a ganglioside.

The neurons are ballooned, the nucleus is displaced and the cytoplasm is filled with lipid material. These cells look very similar to those seen in Tay-Sach's disease. By electron microscopy Gonatas and Gonatas[2] have demonstrated membranous lipid bodies in the cytoplasm, similar to those seen in Tay-Sach's disease (Fig. VI-5).

There is also a characteristic renal lesion in generalized gangliosidosis. The epithelial cells in the glomerulus are ballooned and their cytoplasm is filled with vacuolated material.[2] The diagnosis of generalized gangliosidosis can be made by renal biopsy (Fig. VI-6).

Scott and co-workers[4] have made an electron microscopic study of the glomerular lesion in this disease. They have shown that the renal glomerular lesion involves epithelial cells which are loaded with vacuolated (empty) bodies. During fixation, what-

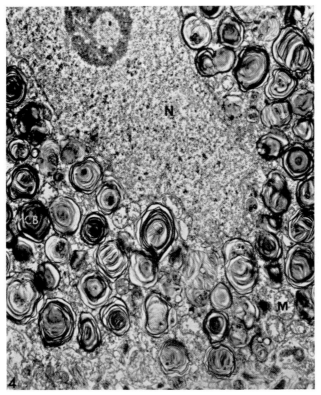

Figure VI-5. Cytoplasmic membranous bodies in neurons (from Gonatas, N.K. and Gonatas, J., reference 3 with permission of authors and publishers).

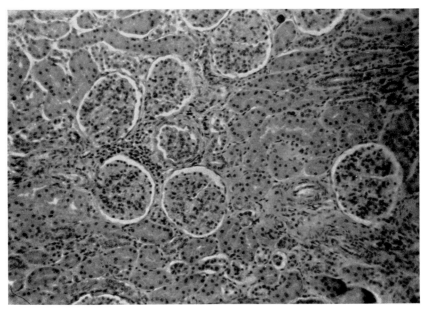

Figure VI-6. Cytoplasmic ballooning of renal glomerular epithelial cells (periodic acid-Schiff stain).

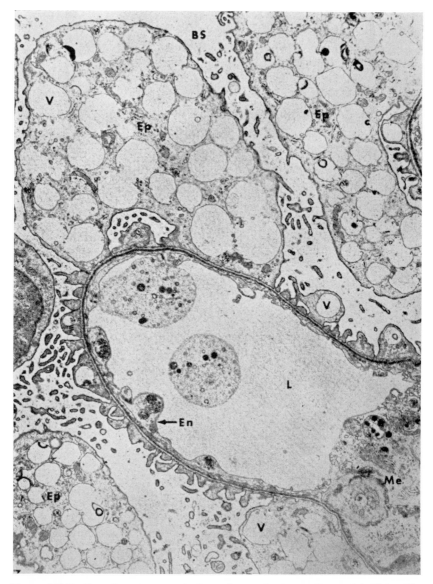

Figure VI-7. Cytoplasmic vacuolation of renal glomerular epithelial cells. BS = Bowmans space, L = capillary lumen, V = vacuole ($\times$23,000) (from Scott *et al.,* reference 4 with permission of authors and publishers) .

ever was in these bodies had dissolved out indicating that they contain a rather soluble material (Fig. VI-7).

Occasionally one can see evidences of osmiophilic bodies in cells of visceral organs. These osmiophilic lamellated bodies have the morphological characteristics of polar lipids. However, most of the storage material in these cells is probably not lipid, but mucopolysaccharide.

CHEMICAL FINDINGS

Let us now discuss the ganglioside storage. Figure VI-8 is a thin-layer chromatogram of gangliosides isolated from the brain of a normal child, a child with Tay-Sach's disease and a patient who expired with generalized gangliosidosis. Lane N shows the normal pattern of brain gangliosides. Normally there are seven different gangliosides present, the major ones being GM_1, GD_{1a} and GT_1.

In gray matter from the patient with generalized gangliosidosis

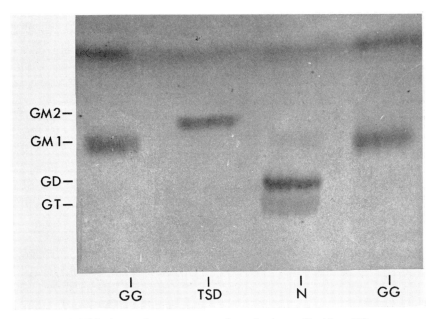

Figure VI-8. Thin layer chromatogram of cerebral gangliosides. GG = two patients with generalized gangliosidosis, N = normal subject, TSD = patient with Tay-Sach's Disease.

there is a large accumulation of a single ganglioside; ganglioside GM_1.[5] This ganglioside differs from that stored in Tay-Sach's disease, ganglioside GM_2.

In order to prove that the ganglioside was GM_1, it was isolated and its structure was examined, including its sugar content and composition, its fatty acid composition and the sequence and linkages of each sugar.[6] The structure of the ganglioside in generalized gangliosidosis is the same as GM_1. We then analyzed the liver and the spleen and found ganglioside GM_1 accumulating in both of these organs.[5] The structure of the stored compound is   [galactosyl-(1→3)-N-acetyl-galactosaminyl-(1→4)-[(2→3)-N-acetyl-neuraminyl]-galactosyl-(1 → 4)-glucosyl-(1 → 4)-glucosyl-(1 → 1)-[2-N-acyl]sphingosine].

ENZYMIC DEFECT

Once the structure of the ganglioside which accumulates was known it became possible to think about mechanisms which could lead to its accumulation. Increased synthesis or decreased degradation were obvious possibilities. Brady and co-workers[7] at the National Institutes of Health had shown that specific lysosomal hydrolases, i.e. cerebrosidase and sphingomyelinase, are deficient in other lipid storage diseases such as Gaucher's disease and Niemann-Pick disease. Therefore, a likely possibility was a ganglioside GM_1 B-galactosidase deficiency in generalized gangliosidosis. This enzyme, which has been shown by Gatt and co-workers[8] to be normally present in brain, cleaves the terminal galactose from GM_1. Subsequently, other enzymes, working in sequence (galactosaminidase, another galactosidase, and a glucosidase), catabolize the molecule to ceramide. Each of these steps appear to involve lysosomal enzymes.

Dr. Okada and the author[9] initially set out to look at beta galactosidase activity in the tissues from two children with generalized gangliosidosis. The B-galactosidase assay that we used is a rather simple one in which p-nitrophenyl-B-D-galactopyranoside serves as substrate. This is the assay that Jacob and Monod used in their work on the molecular genetics of the lac operon in *E. coli* for which they won the Nobel prize. Beta galactosidase converts p-nitrophenyl-B-D-galactopyranoside, which is colorless

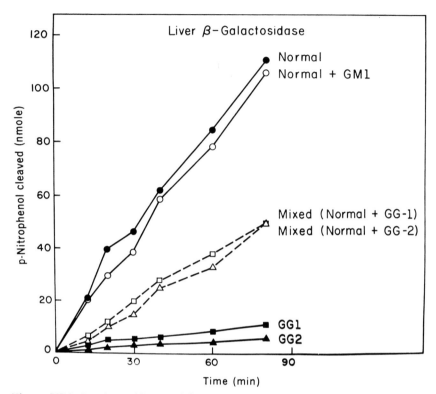

Figure VI-9. B-galactosidase activity in liver. Normal = liver tissue of a boy who died at 2 days of age from meconium peritonitis; Normal + GM_1 = ganglioside GM_1 added to give a concentration of 0.5 per cent of the wet weight; GG_1 = 8-month-old patient with generalized gangliosidosis; GG_2 = 2-year-old patient with generalized gangliosidosis; Mixed = mixtures of equal proportions of normal and patients' homogenates (from Okada, S. and O'Brien, J.S., *Science,* 160:1002, with permission of the publishers. Copyright 1968 by the American Association for the Advancement of Science).

before cleavage, to paranitrophenol (which has a nice yellow color) and free galactose.

Figure VI-9 shows the cleavage of p-nitrophenyl-galactopyranoside in normal liver and in livers from two patients with generalized gangliosidosis.[9] The activity of the enzyme in the patients' tissues was about one twentieth of normal.

We were concerned that the B-galactosidase deficiency might be due to inhibitors in the tissues, especially ganglioside GM_1.

We added to the normal homogenate the same amount of GM_1 that accumulated in the livers of the two patients and assayed B-galactosidase in this preparation. There was a slight depression of activity in the GM_1-enriched homogenate, but the inhibition of activity was small and did not approach the very low levels that were found in the disease. We then mixed the normal and the patients' homogenates in equal proportions and assayed enzyme activity. In the mixed tissue the rate of hydrolysis was very close to the average of the two initial rates, again indicating absence of an endogenous inhibitor for the enzyme (Fig. V-9). We then assayed B-galactosidase activity in a variety of patients to show that the deficiency was specific for generalized gangliosidosis.

Table VI-I shows the B-galactosidase activity in the cerebral gray matter of the brains of patients with a variety of disorders. In-

TABLE VI-I

B-GALACTOSIDASE ACTIVITY OF CEREBRAL GRAY MATER

Age	Diagnosis	Enzyme Activity
2 mo.	Sudden death syndrome	103
3 yr.	Cardiac anomaly	146
6 yr.	Auto accident	211
59 yr.	Adenocarcinoma of lung	120
81 yr.	Myocardial infection	162
3 yr.	Tay-Sach's disease	327
3 yr.	Tay-Sach's disease	278
2 yr.	Tay-Sach's disease	216
2 yr.	Tay-Sach's disease	278
6 yr.	Late infantile amaurotic idiocy	93
5 yr.	Late infantile amaurotic idiocy	105
15 mo.	Infantile cerebral Gaucher's disease	164
7 mo.	Infantile cerebral Gaucher's disease	125
5 yr.	Metachromatic leukodystrophy	151
11 yr.	Metachromatic leukodystrophy	122
3 yr.	Niemann-Pick disease	151
13 mo.	Kinky hair disease	169
11 yr.	Cystic fibrosis	138
4 yr.	Cerebellar hypoplasia	111
2 yr.	Generalized gangliosidosis	18

Note: Enzyme units: muM of p-nitrophenol released per 100 mg of tissue per hour. Assay conditions given in reference 9. In the first five assays, ganglioside GM_1 was added to the homogenate in concentrations equivalent to those found in generalized gangliosidosis (0.5% of the wet weight) .

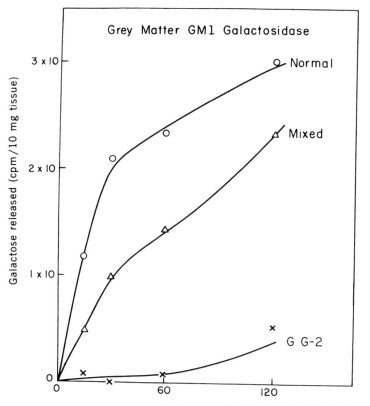

Figure VI-10. B-galactosidase activity for ganglioside GM_1 in the brain. Normal = 32-month-old boy who died from chronic renal disease; GG_2 = 2-year-old patient with generalized gangliosidosis; Mixed = mixture of equal proportions of the normal and patients' enzyme preparations (from Okada, S. and O'Brien, J.S., *Science*, 160:1002, 1968, by permission of the publishers. Copyright 1968 by the American Association for the Advancement of Science).

cluded are patients with Tay-Sach's disease, Jansky-Bielschowsky late infantile amaurotic idiocy, Gaucher's disease, metachromatic leukodystrophy and Niemann-Pick's disease. The patient with generalized gangliosidosis has a tenfold deficiency of beta galactosidase in the brain.

Since P-nitrophenyl-galactoside is an unnatural derivative, ganglioside GM_1 should be tested to show that the tissues are also unable to cleave it. In order to do this experiment we made ganglioside GM_1 with radioactivity in the terminal galactose. Dr. Okada[9] did this by isolating ganglioside GM_2 from the brain of a child who died from Tay-Sach's disease. GM_2 was then incubated in the presence of an enzyme in chick embryos which adds galactose to the end of the carbohydrate chain, a GM_2-GM_1 UDP-galactosyltransferase. He obtained UDP-galactose-C^{14}, and some fertile eggs, prepared the transferase, added GM_2 and carried out the incubation. After many incubations and much purification, Dr. Okada obtained radioactive GM_1 with the label in the terminal galactose and a very high specific activity. He then used this compound to test for galactose cleavage in tissue from the generalized gangliosidosis patients.

Figure VI-10 shows the GM_1 cleavage in the brain. Once again, a twenty- to thirtyfold lower rate is found in generalized gangliosidosis, and the rate in the mixed homogenate is the average of the normal and diseased rates. A similar deficiency was demonstrated in the liver.[9]

The activity of a number of other acid hydrolases were assayed, including acid phosphatase, beta glucosidase and beta-glucosaminidase. The activities of all these enzymes were increased in generalized gangliosidosis, indicating that the deficiency of the beta galactosidase was specific and, that other lysosomal enzymes were neither inhibited nor defective.

To summarize, the ganglioside accumulation in generalized gangliosidosis appears to be due to a diminished degradation of GM_1 due to the deficiency of GM^1 G-galactosidase. This enzyme is an acid hydrolase (pH 5.0) normally present in lysosomes. The metabolic block is shown in Figure VI-11.

Suzuki has shown[10] that a galactose-containing mucopolysaccharide also accumulates which is structurally similar to keratosulfate, a sulfated mucopolysaccharide containing both galactose and N-acetyl-glucosamine. We wondered whether B-galactosidase might cleave both compounds and whether its deficiency could lead to the accumulation of both. In order to test this possibility Dr. Monica MacBrinn in our laboratory isolated "keratosulfate" from the liver of a patient with generalized gangliosidosis and then tested the cleavage of galactose from this compound by nor-

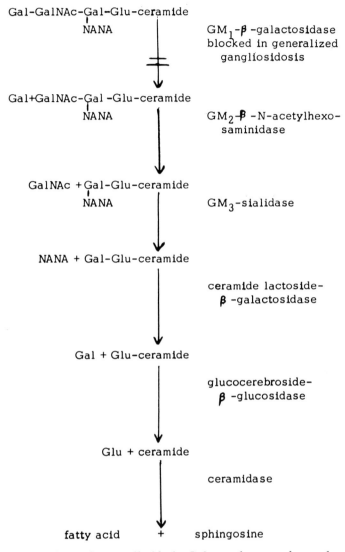

Figure VI-11. Scheme for gangliosidosis. Gal = galactose; glu = glucose; gal NAc = N-acetyl-galactosamine; NANA = N-acetyl-neuraminic acid.

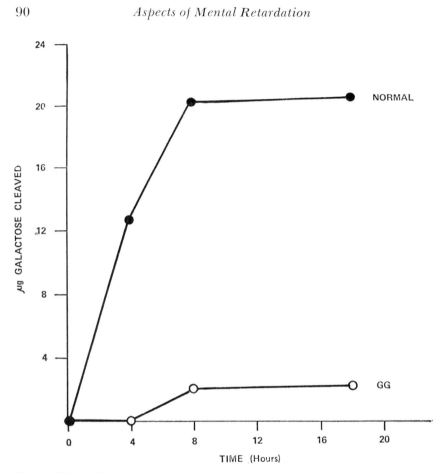

Figure VI-12. Cleavage of galactose from keratosulfate by B-galactosidase prepared from equivalent amounts of normal (N) and generalized gangliosidosis (GG) liver tissue (from MacBrinn, M.D., Okada, S., Ho, M.W., Hu, C.C. and O'Brien, J.S., *Science*, 163:946, 1969, by permission of the publishers. Copyright 1968 by the American Association for the Advancement of Science).

mal and generalized gangliosidosis livers. MacBrinn *et al.*[11] found a tenfold lower rate of cleavage of galactose from the mucopolysaccharide in generalized gangliosidosis (Fig. VI-12).

DIAGNOSIS

The diagnosis of this disease can be made by taking a biopsy of the brain, liver or spleen and examining for the presence of storage products. Less traumatic and equally effective is assay for B-galactosidase in urine, leukocytes or skin. Dr. George Thomas at the Johns Hopkins University has developed a urinary assay for the enzyme and he has detected a profound deficiency of this enzyme in urine in one patient with generalized gangliosidosis.[12]

THERAPY

At this writing, no specific or effective therapy for generalized gangliosidosis is available. Supportive therapy includes prompt use of antibiotics to combat infections, attentive long-term bed care to prevent skin lesions and aspiration pneumonia; tube feeding to allay malnutrition, and anticonvulsants to suppress tonic-clonic convulsions. Even with careful management, patients with generalized gangliosidosis die by two years of age.

PREVENTION

Carriers of the gene for generalized gangliosidosis can be detected by B-galactosidase assay of leucocytes. Affected children can be diagnosed soon after birth by assay of B-galactosidase in urine, skin or leukocytes. Genetic counseling of the family can begin at this point so that conception of other affected children can be prevented. Prenatal diagnosis of generalized gangliosidosis is also possible. B-galactosidase is normally present in fetal fibroblasts[13] and amniocentesis, fetal cell culture and enzyme assay should make possible the detection of the disease in utero soon enough to provide the parents with the option of a therapeutic abortion.

In this way both the conception and birth of children afflicted with this fatal disease may be prevented.

REFERENCES

1. O'Brien, J.S.: Generalized gangliosidosis. *J Pediatr,* 75:167, 1969.
2. Landing, B.H., Silverman, F.N., Craig, J.M., Jacoby, M.D., Lahey, M.E. and Chadwick, D.L.: Familial neurovisceral lipidosis. *Am J Dis Child,* 108:503, 1964.
3. Gonatas, N.K. and Gonatas, J.: Ultrastructural and biochemical observations on a case of systemic late infantile lipidosis and its relationship to Tay-Sachs disease and gargoylism. *J Neuropathol Exp Neurol,* 24: 318, 1965.

4. Scott, C.R., Lagunoff, D. and Trump, B.F.: Familial neurovisceral lipidosis. *J Pediatr,* 71:357, 1967.
5. O'Brien, J.S., Stern, M.B., Landing, B.H., O'Brien, J.K. and Donnell, G.N.: Generalized gangliosidosis. *Am J Dis Child,* 109:338, 1965.
6. Ledeen, R., Salsman, K., Gonatas, J. and Taghavy, A.: Structure comparison of the major monosialogangliosides from brains of normal human, gargoylism and late infantile system lipidosis. *J Neuropathol Exp Neurol,* 24:341, 1965.
7. Brady, R.O.: Enzymatic abnormalities in diseases of sphingolipid metabolism. *Clin Chem,* 13:565, 1967.
8. Gatt, S.: Enzymatic hydrolysis of sphingolipids. V. Hydrolysis of monosialoganglioside and hexosylceramides by rat brain B-galactosidase. *Biochem et Biophys Acta,* 137:192, 1967.
9. Okada, S. and O'Brien, J.S.: Generalized gangliosidosis, B-galactosidase deficiency. *Science,* 160:1002, 1968.
10. Suzuki, K.: Cerebral GM_1 gangliosidosis: Chemical pathology of visceral organs. *Science,* 159:1471, 1968.
11. MacBrinn, M.C., Okada, S., Ho, M.W., Hu, C.C. and O'Brien, J.S.: Generalized gangliosidosis: Impaired cleavage of galactose from a mucopolysaccharide and a glycoprotein. *Science,* 163:946, 1969.
12. Thomas, G.H.: β-D-Galactosidase in human urine: Deficiency in generalized gangliosidosis. *J Lab Clin Med,* 74:725, 1969.
13. Okada, S. and O'Brien, J.S.: Unpublished data, 1969.

Chapter VII

THE MUCOPOLYSACCHARIDOSES
Recognition and Diagnosis

C. Ronald Scott

SINCE the earliest part of the twentieth century, clinicians have recognized a group of similar appearing children who have had bone deformities associated with mental retardation. These children were reported in the medical literature from 1920 to the early 1950's as clinical curiosities. In 1952, Brante[1] isolated a substance from the liver of such an afflicted patient which was tentatively identified as a mucopolysaccharide, and later Dorfman and Lorinz[2] documented a marked excretion of mucopolysaccharide in the urine of similar patients. Subsequently, it has generally been accepted that the primary abnormality in these patients is a disorder of mucopolysaccharide metabolism. This concept has led to the categorization of patients who excrete in their urine or store in their tissues excess mucopolysaccharides under the term "mucopolysaccharidoses."[3]

It was recognized as early as the 1930's that patients with mucopolysaccharidoses accumulated lipid-like material within the central nervous system. This lipid storage, associated with obvious bony alterations, generated the term "lipochondrodystrophy" to describe the major clinical features of the disorder. Now there exist at least six major types of mucopolysaccharide disorders which can be distinguished on the basis of clinical features, inheritance pattern and biochemical criteria.[3] This delineation can primarily be credited to McKusick and was based on genetic interpretation of published pedigrees and patients personally examined by him (Table VII-I).

RECOGNITION OF THE MUCOPOLYSACCHARIDOSES

The recognition and classification of the mucopolysaccharidoses are dependent upon their physical appearance, mode of inheritance and type of mucopolysaccharide excreted in the urine.

93

TABLE VII-I

THE GENETIC MUCOPOLYSACCHARIDOSES

MPS Disorder (Eponyme)	Clinical	Genetic	Biochemical
I Hurler syndrome	Moderate-severe physical and mental alterations.	Autosomal recessive	Dermatan-SO_4 Heparan-SO_4
II Hunter syndrome	Moderate physical and mental alterations.	X-linked recessive	Dermatan-SO_4 Heparan-SO_4
III Sanfilippo syndrome	Mild physical changes. Severe mental deterioration.	Autosomal recessive	Heparan-SO_4
IV Morquio syndrome?	Severe bony changes. Moderate-severe physical changes. Variable intellectual development.	Autosomal recessive	a) Keratan-SO_4 b) Normal
V Scheie syndrome	Mild-moderate physical changes. Normal intelligence.	Autosomal recessive	Dermatan-SO_4 Heparan-SO_4
VI Maroteaux-Lamy syndrome	Severe bony changes. Moderate physical alterations. Normal intelligence.	Autosomal recessive	Dermatan-SO_4

Note: Modified slightly from the classification of McKusick.[3]

Hurler's Syndrome (MPS Type I)

The Hurler syndrome serves as the classic model of the mucopolysaccharidoses. Patients have major physical and mental alterations and accumulate and excrete large quantities of mucopolysaccharides. Affected children have coarse features characterized by a large head, wide-set eyes, a flat nasal bridge, large lips, coarse tongue and mild hypertrophy of the gums. There is usually a protuberant abdomen with enlargement of the liver and spleen. Corneal opacifications exist and are slowly progressive. Anatomic changes in the vertebral column produces a gibbous deformity of the back, and thickening of the synovial capsules produces limitation of flexion and extension of the major joints. There may be patches of thick roughened skin. Umbilical and inguinal hernias are common when the children are young.[4] Roentgen changes are prominent in all bony structures.

Growth failure is usually pronounced by three years of age. Mental development may appear normal during the first year, but usually plateaus between two and four years. Heavy, noisy respirations, chronic nasal discharge, nasal airway obstruction and pulmonary infections can present chronic problems requiring medical care.

The importance of the mucopolysaccharidoses to mental retardation raises interesting speculations. Although three of the mucopolysaccharidoses (Hurler, Hunter and Sanfilippo syndromes) are recognized as having central nervous system involvement, the remaining three groups (Morquio, Scheie and Maroteaux-Lamy syndromes) usually do not have associated central nervous system symptoms. Thus, the relationship of mental retardation to the accumulation of mucopolysaccharides within tissue or its excretion in the urine is not directly correlated with mental deterioration. Today there are no recognized therapies which will aid in the alleviation or prevention of the slowly progressive mental or physical deterioration associated with the Hurler, Hunter or Sanfilippo syndromes. Of prime importance is the early recognition of the mucopolysaccharidoses and their correct classification. With this approach one can offer the families of such patients a correct diagnosis and psychologically prepare them if mental retardation is a serious complication. Similarly, they can be reassured if mental retardation is not a component of the syndrome. Early recognition can be of value by anticipating physical problems prior to their development; this offers the physician the opportunity to give genetic counseling to families at risk for future affected children. Recent evidence would suggest that some of the mucopolysaccharidoses can probably be detected by antenatal techniques and, therefore, fetuses recognized as affected with such disorders may be therapeutically aborted under morally and legally acceptable conditions.

The major medical problem is the frequency of pneumonia during the first few years. Pneumonia is the primary cause of death up to the age of four years. Thereafter, cardiac failure from aortic or mitral insufficiency is common.

Hurler's syndrome is genetically transmitted as an autosomal recessive condition. It affects males and females in equal proportion. Although precise figures are not available on the incidence of the condition in the newborn population, it probably occurs less than one in 25,000 live births.

Affected children excrete two types of mucopolysaccharides in excess: dermatan and heparan sulfate. Each is increased five to ten times over the normal urinary concentration.

Hunter's Syndrome (MPS Type II)

Hunter's syndrome varies from the Hurler's syndrome in only two major features: it has a milder clinical course, and it is genetically transmitted on the X-chromosome.

Children affected with Hunter's syndrome are phenotypically similar to patients with Hurler's syndrome. Patients with Hunter's syndrome, however, usually have less severe mental retardation, fewer respiratory problems, clear corneas, greater final height, and live longer than patients with Hurler's syndrome. These children will often survive into the second decade before succumbing to neurological deterioration and pneumonia.

This syndrome is at least as common as the Hurler variety. Children with this syndrome excrete dermatan and heparan sulfate in similar quantities to patients with Hurler's syndrome.

Sanfilippo's Syndrome (MPS Type III)

Sanfilippo's syndrome differs markedly from the previous two disorders. The major clinical manifestation is mental deterioration. This severe mental involvement becomes manifest by two to three years of age as hyperactivity and a destructive behavioral disorder. There may be few clinical findings to suggest a mucopolysaccharide disorder. By the time an organic basis is suspected for the behavioral disorder, there may be a coarsening of facial features and a moderately chronic nasal discharge. The retardation becomes progressive after three or four years and there is increased loss of any social or self-help skills they may previously have gained.[4]

Roentgenographic bone changes are usually minimal and by themselves are usually not characteristic of the disorder. The major diagnostic aid comes from the identification of excess quantities of a highly sulfated mucopolysaccharide in the urine: heparan sulfate.

Most children with the Sanfilippo syndrome succumb between five and fifteen years of age from severe neurological deterioration.

Morquio's Syndrome (MPS Type IV)

Agreement among medical personnel as to what should be considered an example of Morquio's syndrome is not clear. There exists a variety of genetically determined skeletal dysplasias which bear a clinical and roentgenographic similarity to each other and which have been classified as Morquio's syndrome. Varying classifications of the "spondyloepiphyseal dysplasias" are constantly being presented in an attempt to clarify the genetic determinants and the phenotypic expression of different entities. There does exist at least one clinical form of Morquio's syndrome in which the patient excretes increased quantities of a keratosulfate-like material.[5] Because of this keratosulfate excreting form (which is currently accepted as an example of Morquio's syndrome), Morquio's syndrome has been classified within the mucopolysaccharidoses.

The important clinical feature of "Morquio's syndrome" is the combination of normal mentality associated with severe bony deformities. Some patients may have corneal clouding and an occasional patient may have less than normal intelligence.

This group of patients undoubtedly requires extensive investigation to delineate the genetic heterogeneity, the phenotypic variability and the mucopolysacchariduria that has been noted to occur in certain clinical entities called "Morquio's syndrome."

Scheie's Syndrome (MPS Type V)

A paucity of clinical information is available on this rare condition.[6] As children their first complaint is usually joint limitation which is slowly progressive. They have only mild physical changes suggestive of the Hurler syndrome. By the age of five to six years they demonstrate considerable joint limitation and a coarsening of the facial features. The head is slightly enlarged, eyebrows prominent, nasal bridge flattened and lips slightly thickened. They have corneal clouding which is slowly progressive. Enlargement of the liver is usually present. Their intelligence is normal. Their growth is retarded with an ultimate height of only five feet being achieved after puberty.

Roentgenograms of the bony structures reveal only mild to moderate changes, but similar to those seen in Hurler's syndrome.

Examination of the urine for mucopolysacchariduria confirms the excess excretion of dermatan and heparan sulfate. These compounds are increased three to five times above normal values.

There is no information available on longevity, but mucopolysaccharide deposition may produce symptoms in adulthood, especially of the corneas or cardiac valves. Development of the "carpal tunnel syndrome" during childhood has been a consistent clinical problem.

The Scheie syndrome is inherited as an autosomal recessive condition and little information is available to estimate the incidence of the disorder in the newborn population.

Maroteaux-Lamy Syndrome (MPS Type VI)

The syndrome of Maroteaux-Lamy is relatively rare and has been characterized by severe bony deformities, Hurler-like appearance, dwarfism, normal intelligence and the excretion of excess dermatan in the urine.[7] This disorder was recognized as an independent entity in 1963, but previous cases were reported as variants of Hurler's syndrome. Patients with this disorder are intellectually normal and their major problems are a consequence of joint limitation, bony abnormalities, short stature and cloudy corneas. Existing reports do not contain information on the life expectancy of these patients.

Patients with this syndrome are diagnosed by documenting the excess excretion of dermatan sulfate in the urine, unaccompanied by an increased excretion of heparan sulfate. The syndrome is genetically transmitted as an autosomal recessive condition.

CLASSIFICATION

The correct classification of a child with mucopolysaccharide disorder is extremely important. Correct medical management, vocational training and genetic counseling can only occur after the recognition of the disorder. The early recognition of a child with a disorder of mucopolysaccharide metabolism often leads erroneously to the concept that the child will be mentally retarded. As previously mentioned, in only three of the currently recognized varieties is mental retardation a significant factor in the disorder.

SCREENING TESTS FOR MUCOPOLYSACCHARIDE EXCRETION

The quantitation of mucopolysaccharides in urine should ideally be performed in an experienced laboratory, sophisticated in the isolation and quantitation of mucopolysaccharides. There exist, however, several screening tests which may be used as a qualitative estimation of increased mucopolysaccharide excretion. These tests are helpful in determining whether or not an increased excretion of mucopolysaccharides may exist in suspected cases of mucopolysaccharide disorders.

A test which has received wide popularity because of its simplicity is the "Berry spot test."[8] In this test $5\mu l$ to $25\mu l$ of clear urine is spotted directly on filter paper, stained with toluidine blue, and then washed with ethanol. The appearance of a purple color is suggestive of an increased mucopolysaccharide excretion. Similarly, freshly filtered or centrifuged urine which is visually clear can be placed in a test tube and an aqueous solution of cetyltrimethylammonium bromide added.[9] An obvious precipitate develops over a 30-minute period in the presence of excess mucopolysaccharides. Each of the above tests are simple to perform but have their limitations. Each test will consistently give a small percentage of false-positive tests which require further diagnostic studies. With the cetyltrimethylammonium bromide test it is important that filtered or centrifuged urine free of flocculation be used, and that the urine be at room temperature, for a precipitate will form in the presence of any urinary sediment or if the test is performed at lower than ambient room temperature. Urine from young infants may give a false-positive reaction with these tests because of an increased level of urinary mucopolysaccharides as compared to older children and adults.

A better semiquantitative test has been popularized by Dorfman and called the albumin turbidity test.[10] Fresh urine is dialyzed against tap water overnight and the dialyzed urine added to an acid albumin reagent. After setting at room temperature overnight, the solution is read spectrophotometrically for turbidity formation. In the presence of mucopolysaccharides, a definite turbidity develops which is proportional to mucopolysaccharide content.

In each of the described tests the presence of mucopolysaccharide is suggested by a positive reaction. This reaction should be confirmed by an experienced laboratory for accurate quantitation and identification of the type of mucopolysaccharide present in urine. As indicated in Table VII-I, the identification of the type of mucopolysaccharide is helpful in the classification of the genetic type of mucopolysaccharidosis.

Ancillary Procedures

Circulating mononuclear cells may be examined for metachromatic inclusion granules within the cytoplasm.[11] In mucopolysaccharidosis Type I, II, III and V such inclusions have been found in circulating lymphocytes or monocytes, mononuclear bone marrow cells or monocytes collected by the skin window technique of Rebuck.[12] A significant number of cells usually demonstrate discrete metachromatic cytoplasmic vacuoles when stained with toluidine blue or alcian blue at acid pH. It is believed that these granules represent the storage of acid mucopolysaccharides within lysosomal organelles. Similar types of storage material may be documented in fixed tissue macrophages obtained from skin, rectal mucosa or liver. The documentation of such inclusions helps to confirm the nature of the storage disease.

Studies using fibroblast cultures established from skin biopsies of patients with mucopolysaccharidoses have revealed several interesting clues into the nature of the chemical defect. Danes and Bearn[13] first showed that increased amounts of mucopolysaccharides could be visually demonstrated in fibroblast cultures of patients with Type I and II mucopolysaccharidoses, and it was subsequently confirmed for Types III and V. They stained fibroblast cultures established from patients with mucopolysaccharide storage with toluidine blue and observed metachromatic staining which appeared in the cytoplasm of the cells. Cells obtained from control patients, unaffected with a known storage disorder, usually do not demonstrate metachromatic staining with toluidine blue. The degree of staining, however, may vary between laboratories and the method of selecting control cultures. Taysi and co-workers demonstrated that 27 per cent of their control cells had positive metachromasia when children from a hospital ward were selected as control subjects for culture.[14] Furthermore, Danes and Bearn showed that heterozygotes for the genetic mucopolysaccharidoses would also demonstrate metachromatic staining of their fibroblasts when placed in culture, indistinguishable from homozygous patients. Evidence that the stainable material was a mucopolysaccharide which accumulated intracellularly was shown by Matalon and Dorfman by chemical analysis.[15]

Evidence that the basic derangement in the mucopolysaccharidoses was a defect in the ability of cells to break down synthesized mucopolysaccharides was supplied by Fratantoni, Hall and Neufeld.[16, 17] These investigators labeled cellular mucopolysaccharides with radioactive $^{35}SO_4$ and measured the retention of the ^{35}S within the cultured fibroblasts. Patients with

Types I, II and III mucopolysaccharidoses retained ^{35}S for a significantly longer period of time than cells from control patients. This retention of ^{35}S within cellular mucopolysaccharides was interpreted as being compatible with a defect in mucopolysaccharide catabolism.

Using the same methodology of ^{35}S labeling of intracellular mucopolysaccharides, the same investigators mixed cultures from Types I, II and III mucopolysaccharidoses with normal fibroblast lines and showed that the mutant cells no longer accumulated excess mucopolysaccharides.[17] This correction of the cellular metabolic defect by genetically different cells was attributed to some undefined "correction factor." Correction of the intracellular mucopolysaccharide accumulation in culture also occurred between the different types of mucopolysaccharidoses. This latter observation confirms the genetic dissimilarity between the mucopolysaccharidoses and offers the potential for a laboratory diagnostic test. A reference laboratory could maintain fibroblast cultures from patients with unambiguously classified mucopolysaccharide disorders and use these cells in "correction experiments" to classify new patients. Those cell types which did not mutually correct the cellular accumulation of mucopolysaccharidoses would be classified as genetically similar.

ANTENATAL DIAGNOSIS

In an attempt to identify as early as possible those children who may be affected with a disorder of mucopolysaccharide metabolism, increasing efforts have turned to their recognition before birth. In those families in which a previous child has been born with a mucopolysaccharide problem, future children are at risk for the same genetic disorder. Similarly, if a woman has a brother who suffers from Hunter's syndrome, she is at risk for being a heterozygote carrier of this condition and may transmit the disease to one-half of her sons. In such cases it would be advantageous to know early in pregnancy whether the child in the uterus is affected with the condition.

Three approaches have been used to answer this question. If the child is affected with a mucopolysaccharide disorder, amniotic cells grown in culture can be shown to demonstrate metachromasia when stained with toluidine blue. This technique has been shown to be positive in diagnosing a child with the disorder prior to birth.[18] However, the metachromatic staining is not specific for mucopolysaccharide disorders and does not differentiate between heterozygotes and homozygotes for the condition.

A second technique is to measure the rate of disappearance of radioactive sulfate incorporated into established amniotic cell cultures. In children with a disorder of mucopolysaccharide metabolism, the intracellular loss of incorporated radioactive sulfate is slower than normal. This technique has been used to demonstrate the disorder during early pregnancy.[19]

The third approach is perhaps the simplest. Amniotic fluid can be analyzed directly without culturing the amniotic cells. Quantitative mucopolysaccharide content of amniotic fluid is determined and compared to gestational age-matched controls. This method has indicated that if the developing fetus is affected with a known disorder of mucopolysaccharide metabolism, the apparent urinary excretion of mucopolysaccharides by the fetus will increase the concentration of mucopolysaccharides in the amniotic fluid.[20]

CLINICAL MANAGEMENT

The problem of clinical management is dependent upon the type of mucopolysaccharidosis. Most treatment is symptomatic and there is no rational therapeutic approach which has offered any promise in correcting the basic defect. In those cases where severe mental retardation is a serious problem (Sanfilippo, Hunter and Hurler), the major goal should be keeping the child comfortable and happy, and to relieve the parents of as much stress as possible. It is important that they have an accurate prognosis for their child and the availability of medical and emotional support. In the Hurler and Hunter syndrome the surgical repair of hernias and hydroceles may be necessary. Adenoidectomy may be indicated if airway obstruction becomes a major problem. Nervous system depressants may be given to control hyperirritability and hyperactivity. Hearing amplification may be of help in children with the Hurler and Hunter syndrome who suffer from hearing loss.

In those conditions which do not have mental retardation as a major component and in which the life expectancy may be normal, more vigorous therapeutic approaches are indicated. Physical therapy for joint contractions and a vigorous exercise program to maintain range of motion of all major joints may be helpful. Similarly, the early recognition of the "carpal tunnel syndrome" in the Scheie syndrome and its surgical alleviation is important. Constant emotional support for these children, carefully planned school programs to achieve maximum school performance, and vocational counseling and training are all an important aspect of their management. Their eventual independence and a self-supporting occupation will usually depend upon their intellectual capacity rather than their ability for physical performance.

SIMILAR DISORDERS WHICH MAY BE CONFUSED WITH MUCOPOLYSACCHARIDOSES

A group of storage diseases similar in nature to the classical mucopolysaccharidoses has been defined (Table VII-II). These are severe debilitating diseases of young children with limited life expectancy. The earliest to be recognized was referred to as "familial neurovisceral lipidosis."[21] It is now recognized that this particular disorder, although the clinical appearance and x-ray changes are similar to those seen in the Hurler syndrome, is clinically and genetically distinct. In this disease ganglioside GM_1 accumulates in neural tissue, and is now called "generalized gangliosidosis."[22] The basic defect in this disease is a deficiency of the lysosomal beta-galactosidase.[23]

A second ganglioside storage disease, referred to as juvenile GM_1 gangliosidosis, has also been identified.[24] In this disorder a deficiency of beta-galactosidase exists, but the deficiency is not as severe as that of generalized gangliosidosis.[25] In juvenile GM_1 gangliosidosis, somatic changes similar to those observed in Hurler's syndrome do not exist, and the only presenting symptom is slow neurological deterioration in a young child. A number of other disorders which appear to be quite rare, but which may present with storage of glycoprotein-like substances and a phenotypic appearance similar to Hurler's syndrome have been reported. These include such disorders as "I-cell disease,"[26] fucosidosis,[27] mannosidosis[28, 29] and "lipomucopolysaccharidosis."[30, 31]

TABLE VII-II
THE GENETIC LIPID-MUCOPOLYSACCHARIDOSES

Disorder	Clinical	Genetic	Biochemical
Generalized gangliosidosis	"Hurler-like" phenotype. Severe bony changes. Visceromegaly. Severe neurological degeneration.	Autosomal recessive	GM_1 and MPS storage in viscera. β-galactosidase deficiency. Normal MPS excretion.
Juvenile GM_1 gangliosidosis	Normal phenotype. Neurological degeneration. Normal bones.	Autosomal recessive	GM_1 storage in brain. Partial β-galactosidase deficiency. Normal MPS excretion.
Fucosidosis	"Hurler-like" phenotype. Bony alterations. Slow neurological degeneration.	Autosomal recessive	Glycolipid storage in viscera. Fucose in storage material. α-L-fucosidase deficiency. Normal MPS excretion.
Mannosidosis	"Hurler-like" phenotype. Bony alterations. Slow neurological degeneration.	?	Glycoprotein (?) storage in viscera. Mannose in storage material. α-Mannosidase deficiency. Normal MPS excretion.
I-cell disease	"Hurler-like" phenotype. Bony alterations. Neurological degeneration.	Autosomal recessive	Coarse granulation in cultured fibroblasts. Normal MPS excretion.
Lipomucopolysaccharidosis	Mild "Hurler-like" appearance. Mild bony alterations. Slow neurological degeneration.	Autosomal recessive	Coarse granulation in cultured fibroblasts. Normal MPS excretion.

In each of these diseases material seems to accumulate within lysosomal structures and the patients present with progressive mental and motor deterioration with onset in early childhood. These disorders should be considered when evaluating young children for mucopolysaccharide accumulation.

REFERENCES

1. Brente, G.: Gargoylism: A mucopolysaccharidosis. *Scand J Clin Lab Invest*, 4:43, 1952.

2. Dorfman, A. and Lorincz, A.: Occurrence of urinary acid mucopolysaccharides in the Hurler syndrome. *PNAS*, 43:443, 1957.

3. McKusick, V., Kaplan, D., Wise, D., Hanley, W., Suddarth, S., Sevick, M. and Maumenee, A.: The genetic mucopolysaccharidoses. *Medicine*, 44: 455, 1965.

4. LeRoy, J. and Crocker, A.: Clinical definition of the Hurler-Hunter phenotype. *Am J Dis Child*, 112:518, 1966

5. Robbins, M., Stevens, H. and Linker, A.: Morquio's disease: An abnormality of mucopolysaccharide metabolism. *J Pediatr*, 62:881, 1963.

6. Scheie, H., Hambrick, G., Jr. and Barness, L.: A newly recognized forme fruste of Hurler's disease (gargoylism). *Am J Ophthalmol*, 53:753, 1962.

7. Maroteaux, P. and Lamy, M.: L'oligophrenie polydystrophique. *Press Med*, 72:291, 1964.

8. Berry, H. and Spinanger, J.: A paper spot test useful in the study of Hurler's syndrome. *J Lab Clin Med*, 55:136, 1960.

9. Perry, T., Hanson, S. and MacDougall, L.: Urinary screening tests in the prevention of mental deficiency. *Can Med Assoc J*, 95:89, 1966.

10. Dorfman, A.: Heritable diseases of connective tissue: The Hurler syndrome. In *The Metabolic Basis of Inherited Disease* (Eds. Stanbury, J., Wyngaarden, J., Frederickson, D.). New York, New York, McGraw-Hill, 1966, p. 979.

11. Reilly, W.: The granules in the leucocytes in gargoylism. *Am J Dis Child*, 62, 489, 1941.

12. Carlisle, J. and Good, R.: The inflammatory cycle. *Am J Dis Child*, 99: 193, 1960.

13. Danes, B. and Bearn, A.: Hurler's syndrome: Demonstration of an inherited disorder of connective tissues in cell culture. *J Exp Med*, 123:1, 1966.

14. Taysi, K., Kistenmacher, M., Punnett, H. and Mellman, W.: Limitations of metachromasia as a diagnostic aid in pediatrics. *N Engl J Med*, 281:1108, 1969.

15. Matalon, R. and Dorfman, A.: Hurler's syndrome: Biosynthesis of acid mucopolysaccharides in tissue culture. *PNAS*, 56:1310, 1966.

16. Fratantoni, J., Hall, C. and Neufeld, E.: The defect in Hurler's and Hunter's syndromes: Faulty degradation of mucopolysaccharides. *PNAS,* 60:699, 1968.

17. Fratantoni, J., Hall, C. and Neufeld, E.: Hurler and Hunter syndromes: Mutal correction of defect in cultured fibroblast. *Science,* 162:570, 1968.

18. Nadler, H.: Antenatal detection of hereditary disorders. *Pediatrics,* 42: 912, 1968.

19. Fratantoni, J., Neufeld, E., Uhlendorf, B. and Jacobson, C.: Intra-uterine diagnosis of the Hurler and Hunter syndromes. *N Engl J Med,* 280:686, 1969.

20. Matalon, R., Dorfman, A., Nadler, H. and Jacobson, C.: A chemical method for the prenatal diagnosis of mucopolysaccharides. *Lancet,* I:83, 1970.

21. Landing, B., Silverman, F., Craig, J., Jacoby, M., Lahey, M. and Chad-wick, D.: Familial neurovisceral lipidosis. *Am J Dis Child,* 108:503, 1964.

22. O'Brien, J.: Generalized gangliosidosis. *J Pediatr,* 75:167, 1969.

23. Okada, S. and O'Brien, J.: Generalized gangliosidosis: Beta-galactasidase deficiency. *Science,* 160:1002, 1968.

24. Derry, D., Fawcett, J., Anderman, F. and Wolfe, L.: Late infantile systemic lipidosis. *Neurology,* 18:340, 1958.

25. O'Brien, J.: Five gangliosidoses. *Lancet,* II:805, 1969.

26. LeRoy, J., DeMars, R. and Opitz, J.: I-cell disease. Proc First Conf on the Clin Delin Birth Defects, Bergsma, D., McKusick, V. (Eds.), Vol 5. p. 174, 1969.

27. Durand, T., Borrone, C. and Della Cella, G.: Fucosidosis. *J Pediatr,* 75: 665, 1969.

28. Kjellman, B., Gamstorp, J., Brun, A. and Palmgren, G.: Mannosidosis: A clinical and histopathological study. *J Pediatr,* 75:366, 1969.

29. Ockerman, P.: Mannosidosis: Isolation of oligosaccharide material from brain. *J Pediatr,* 75:361, 1969.

30. Spranger, J. and Wiedemann, H.: Lipomucopolysaccharidoses—a second look. *Lancet,* II:270, 1969.

31. Spranger, J., Schuster, W., Tolksdorf, M., Graucob, E. and Ceasar, R.: Lipomucopolysaccharidoses. *Z Kinderheilk,* 103:285, 1968.

Chapter VIII

HISTIDINEMIC-LIKE BEHAVIOR IN CHILDREN RECOVERED FROM KWASHIORKOR

CARL J. WITKOP, JR.

FORTY-TWO children who had been hospitalized for severe protein malnutrition (kwashiorkor) and had recovered, plus 248 children who had not been hospitalized were studied to determine whether the recovered kwashiorkor child exhibited defects similar to those shown by children with histidinemia.

HISTORICAL REVIEW

Evidence that children with frank kwashiorkor and some with chronic protein deficiency have low levels of histidase and phenylalanine hydroxylase activities has accumulated in a number of studies. Cheung et al.[1] found an abnormally high ratio of phenylalanine to tyrosine in the urine of children with acute kwashiorkor. Cravioto et al.[2] demonstrated similar findings in the free amino acids of blood plasma. Dean and Whitehead[3] demonstrated that children with kwashiorkor had a positive ferric chloride urine test following phenylalanine loading. Whitehead[4] and Whitehead and Milburn[5] found that on giving children with kwashiorkor 5.0 gm oral loads of L-phenylalanine or L-histidine, the intermediate metabolites of phenylpyruvic and imidazolepyruvic acids, respectively, appeared in the urine of these children. This work further suggested that activities of histidine alpha deaminase, urocanase, phenylalanine hydroxylase, and p-hydroxyphenylpyruvic acid oxidase were deficient in these children. These enzymes appeared to recover normal activities as measured by a return to a normal phenylalanine-tyrosine ratio and a normal response to oral loading tests after the child

Note: Through the auspices of Dr. Moises Behar, Director, Instituto de Nutricion de Centro America y Panama, facilities at INCAP were utilized for the study conducted during the period of June 20 to August 15, 1967.

108

had been on a high biological value protein milk diet for twelve days. Rao, Deodhar and Hariharan[6] demonstrated in protein malnourished rats that a nutritionally reversible partial block existed in histidase and urocanase but that the activity of histidine-pyruvate transaminase was unaffected. Habicht and Witkop[7] demonstrated that older children, twelve to fourteen years of age, with chronic protein-calorie malnutrition, may also spill imidazolepyruvic or phenylpyruvic acids in their urine, sufficient to give a positive ferric chloride test following oral loads of histidine and phenylalanine respectively. Children with maramus (balanced protein-calorie intake but total food was insufficient) did not have an abnormal response to load tests. These and other studies suggested that children with kwashiorkor might exhibit histidinemic-phenylketonuric-like behavior.[8]

Histidinemia, first described by Ghadimi, Partington and Hunter[9] is a rare hereditary metabolic condition in which the enzyme histidase is missing or inactive.[10] Histidase catalyzes the deamination of histidine to form urocanic acid which is further metabolized to form iminoglutamic acid which enters the tetrahydrofolic acid cycle to form active methyl and formyl groups utilized in purine and pyrimidine synthesis. Approximately twenty-three patients have been described as histidinemics,[11, 12] however, some have also demonstrated elevated plasma alanine levels which suggests that genocopies of classical histidinemia exist.[12] Since not all of these patients demonstrated the same clinical findings, it has not been established whether all of the clinical defects described are the result of the metabolic error.

The most consistent defect found in all but eight of the histidinemic cases tested (exceptions: Ghadimi *et al.,*[9] Davies and Robinson,[13] Auerbach *et al.*[12]) is a disorder of articulation and language. Three different diseases possibly involving defects in histidine metabolism associated with defective speech, are the apparently lethal form associated with increased infantile growth and progressive degenerative brain disease of Waisman,[14] the formimino-transferase-deficiency syndrome reported by Arakawa and others;[15] and the dominantly inherited stammering reported by Galamon and Szulc-Kuberska[16] from Poland. A family similar to the latter condition resides in North Carolina, where it is known as the "Clucking-John" syndrome.

In La Du's patients personally examined, the speech defect appeared to have two distinct components.[17] One component could be described as a problem in articulation, and the other component, one of short auditory memory recall or a problem in auditory tracking.

Articulatory difficulty was encountered when children attempted to pronounce consonants requiring independent movement of tongue and mandible (i.e. English language, t, d, n, l). For example, "la, la, la" became "ya, ya, ya." Vowel distortions were sporadically evident, depending on the preceding or ensuing vowels and/or consonants. Such speech had been encountered in children with speech defects thought to be ascribable to defects in oral sensation, i.e. they appeared to lack the oral sensory clues for tongue position rather than a defect in the motor portion of the reflex arc. These latter children had difficulty recognizing different forms presented orally. Poor ability to identify forms presented orally was also encountered in adults with pernicious anemia—a defect in the tetrahydrofolic acid cycle. Histidinemic children, when tested for oral perception ability, also had very low scores compared to age and sex-mates.

The other component of the speech problem in histidinemic children was manifest as a problem of language organization. These were relatively mild when compared to most aphasic children. Errors in syntax and noun usage were common. Peripheral hearing was normal when tested by pure tone audiometry, but problems in sequential speech recall suggested central nervous system scrambling. Two to three-phrase sentences, even when repeated four times by the investigator, were scrambled nominally, syntactically and serially, with errors in pattern changing on each attempt. Appropriate responses to serial gestures indicated normal visual-cortical tracking. Teachers experienced with these children described them as "visual learners."

Mental retardation is the next most frequently reported trait among histidinemic children.[10] As nearly all children designated histidinemic have had positive ferric chloride urine tests (exceptions are cases of Davies and Robinson,[13] Hudson, Dickerson and Ireland[18]) similar to PKU patients, the high number showing mental retardation may reflect an ascertainment bias. One case had mental retardation without speech defect,[13] four cases demonstrated speech defects without mental retardation. Ghadimi and Zischka[11] suggest from the study of histidinemic siblings, one who had been on a high protein diet during infancy and has a speech defect and the other on a normal diet and does not have defective speech, that protein intake during infancy may influence whether this moiety is affected.

The exact chemical basis for the speech and mental retardation in histidinemia is not known,[10, 12] but various suggestions involving brain chemistry have been offered, mostly concerning inhibition of 5-hydroxytryptophan-dopa decarboxylase by histidine (and phenylalanine) pyruvates and lactates inhibiting the production of serotonin,[19, 20] which has been reported to be low in some patients with histidinemia,[21, 22] but not in others.[10]

Studies on motor-language development in severely malnourished children have been reviewed by Cravioto.[23] In general, these studies demonstrated that children with kwashiorkor had lower performance scores for all the behavior fields tested than children utilized as standards. In general, the better scores among kwashiorkor children were in motor development, and the greatest retardation was in language. As a rule, older patients exhibited more marked deficits[24] with language returning toward normal at the slowest rate as treatment of the malnutrition progressed.[22]

It has been suggested that serious malnutrition in the preschool child interferes with development of the central nervous system and lowers his adaptive capacity. In order to test intersensory organization, Cravioto, de Licardie and Vega[25] tested touch, vision and kinesthesis in a primary school population of a Guatemalan village with a history of acute and chronic protein malnutrition among the children. The study employed the method of Birch and Lefford[26] to test vision, kinesthesis and haptic touch utilizing eight geometric forms. As a visual stimulus, the form was presented directly in front of the child. For haptic stimulation, the form was presented out of sight of the subject behind an opaque screen and the child actively explored the form with his hand. The kinesthetic test was performed in a like manner with the investigator guiding the child's hand through a path describing the geometric form.

The results demonstrated that each pair of intersensory relationships increased with age in both the rural and urban children with the error curves almost identical in shape; the only difference being that urban children were significantly more advanced (see Fig. 3, Cravioto[23]). Both curves showed a rise in the error score among ten year olds to a point equivalent to seven to eight year olds. When height was used as a measure of nutritional status, intersensory performances of rural children in the upper height quartile were significantly better than rural children in the lower height quartile. This relationship was not demonstrated in the urban children. The lack of association in the urban group was interpreted as an indication that such a correlation exists only when height differences reflect a different nutritional background. Studies on parent-child height correlations among urban and rural subjects demonstrated a positive correlation in the urban sample, but no correlation in the rural sample. Thus, height was interpreted in the rural sample to strongly reflect accumulated nutritional experience.[23]

In view of the previous findings discussed above, this investigation was undertaken as a pilot study to test whether children recovered from kwashiorkor might exhibit defects similar to those shown by histidinemic children. Recovered kwashiorkor children were selected because it was felt that any defects of long-term significance to the learning and functioning capacities of the children would be evident in the recovered cases. It was hypothesized that if the kwashiorkor children demonstrated histidinemic-like characteristics, they should demonstrate poor haptic identification of forms presented orally, poor auditory memory, a relatively better visual tracking ability and normal audiograms.

POPULATION SELECTION

Recovered kwashiorkor patients were selected from among a list of patients provided by Dr. Fernando Viteri, Chief, Biomedical Division. From this list, forty-two discharged recovered kwashiorkor patients were relocated, geographically distributed within Guatemala City and the rural villages and farms of the Department of Guatemala and Santa Rosa. These departments were selected as they contain a higher proportion of Spanish speaking Ladino population and fewer Indians. Attempts were made to include only native Spanish-speaking Ladinos in order to avoid a possible language bias. The forty-two kwashiorkor children ranged in age from four years, eleven months to fifteen years, three months. Of these, twenty-four resided in Guatemala City and eighteen in rural communities. An attempt to select only male kwashiorkor subjects was made, however, one female, who because she had a masculine name, was brought in for examination.

Because the risk of kwashiorkor is associated with many cultural and socioeconomic factors, it is impossible in a study of this type to select a true control population in which malnutrition is the only variable that could conceivably affect the moieties tested. Therefore, comparison populations were selected so that the subjects came from the same social class and, when possible, from the same immediate location as the kwashiorkor subjects.

A comparison population for the urban children was obtained from a day nursery for lower class working mothers (Guarderia, Number 3) for ages four through seven and from a lower class public school (Escuela Federal de Pamplona, Zone 12) for children eight through fifteen years.

A comparison population for the rural children were obtained from the communities wherein the kwashiorkor subjects resided,

TABLE VIII-I

DISTRIBUTION OF SUBJECTS BY AGE, SEX AND RESIDENCE

Type of Subject	4	5	6	7	8	9	10	11	12	13	14	15	Total
Rural control males				7	7	7	7	7	6	9	7	9	66
Control females				4	5	4	6	3	5	4	10	6	47
Kwashiorkor males				3	2	4		2	1	2	1	2	18
Urban control males	3	7	7	7	7	7	7	7	7	7	8	7	81
Control females					6	6	6	6	6	12	6	6	54
Kwashiorkor males	1	6	4	1	4			1	2	3	1		23
Kwashiorkor females										1			1
													290

such that approximately seven children were seen for each kwashiorkor child. All subjects used for comparison were children who had not been hospitalized for any reason.

Although all kwashiorkor cases but one were male, both male and female subjects were included in the comparison population to see if sex differences were apparent in the test used. Table VIII-I gives the distribution of the subject tested by age, sex and residence.

TESTING PROCEDURE

A history was obtained for each kwashiorkor subject from hospital records. From each subject (from parents) a history was obtained of hospitalization, hearing loss or speech problem. Heights and weights were measured, and an oral examination was made which included palate and lingual function and oral abnormalities such as bifid uvula, notching of the posterior border of the hard palate, clefts and ankyloglossia. Each subject was tested as follows:

1. *Audiogram.* A pure tone air conduction audiogram was made utilizing a Zenith portable audiometer model ZA 110T for frequencies 125 through 8,000 cycles per second —calibrated to ISO 1964, reference thresholds.

2. Visual tracking was tested by an additive series of hand signals demonstrated by the investigator and repeated by the subject. Signal 1 was demonstrated by the investigator and the subject asked to reproduce it. Then signal 1 and 2 were demonstrated and the subject was asked to reproduce them. Then signal 1, 2 and 3, etc. until the subject made an error. He was then given one reinforcement by the investigator who repeated the series in which the error was made. The subject was given a score equal to the highest series completed without error after one reinforcement. A similar scoring procedure after one reinforcement was used in the number series and the phrase series.

3. Number series were presented orally by the investigator at the rate of 1 per second and the subject asked to repeat the series in the same additive manner used in the visual tracing. Numbers were selected from a random series of simple digit numbers as: 3,1,4,2,7,9,5. As described by

Lashley,[27] the process of serial order temporal integration is basic to the language process and for analytic purposes involves four facets of auditory memory.

a. Span, which describes not only the duration of auditory alteration, but the number of bits of auditory information.

b. Sequence, the order in which auditory events are recalled.

c. Patterning of rhythm, stress and inflection.

d. Patterning of phonetic detail.

A number series was used in addition to phrase memory recall as it was felt that a number series would emphasize span and sequency while the phrases would more likely elicit defects in patterning as well.

4. Auditory tracking and speech defects were tested by an additive series of five short phrases which additively produce a complete sentence. These had been pretested on children of various ages. Only one examiner tested, interpreted the tapes and scored all subjects. Pronunciation variations were interpreted as errors only if in the opinion of the speech therapist, they were different than the age specific and local pronunciation variations. Two sets of five phrases were used for each subject. One example was as follows:

a. El gato de Poli.

b. El lindo gato de Poli.

c. El lindo gato de Poli tiene una cola.

d. El lindo gato de Poli tiene una cola delgada.

e. El lindo gato de Poli tiene una cola delgada como de rata.

Children were reinforced once in any phrase they did not complete on the first try. A tape recording was made of the subject's answers and scored for errors such as phrase incompletions, word omissions, word transpositions, word substitutions and mispronunciations. Phrase incompletions, word omission, transposition and substitution errors were weighed depending upon the phrase in which the error occurred. For example, errors of these types were deemed

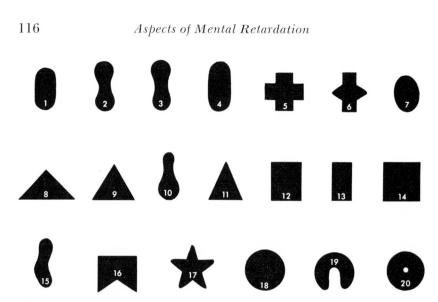

Figure VIII-1. Forms and numbers randomly assigned to subjects for testing oral sterognosis and visual matching.

more serious if they occurred in phrase 1, than in phrase 5. So error scores were weighed as follows: 5:1, 4:2, 3:3, 2:4, 1:5. As mispronunciations tended to be constant throughout each phrase, an unweighed score was given for this type of error. A final score for those errors relating to auditory memory and an error score for pronunciations were computed for each subject.

5. Oral stereognosis and visual matching were tested by using the NIH set of twenty oral plastic forms.[28] A board on which twenty different geometric shapes were mounted was placed in front of the subject. Prior to the beginning of each test, the forms and test procedure were explained. It was emphasized that time was not a factor and throughout the test the subject was reminded repeatedly to take his time. The investigator then presented a duplicate of each form visually, and the subject indicated the same form on the board by pointing. Errors in visual matching were noted and forms repeatedly presented until the subject could match all forms visually without error. The

investigator then presented each form by shielding it from the subject's vision and placing it in his mouth. The subject then felt of the form using his tongue, teeth and lips and indicated by pointing to a figure on the board the form he thought he had in his mouth. No time limit was set for the subject, but the number of seconds taken to make a decision was recorded. Answers were recorded and when errors were made, the form number indicated in error was also noted. A total error was computed for each subject. The forms and numbers randomly assigned to them are shown in Figure VIII-1.

TEST RESULTS

Inspection revealed no significant differences between male and female subjects for any test, so all subjects were combined with-could account for these findings.

Audiometrics

Using a 30 dB loss at any frequency tested as a criterion for hearing loss, no significant differences were found among the groups tested. Three children in the control sample and one in the kwashiorkor sample showed a hearing loss of 30 dB or greater. Two of these gave a history of accidents or injury which out regard to sex.

Visual Tracking

Visual tracking score means improved with age in all groups. In general, the groups in order of best performance score means were urban controls, rural controls, urban kwashiorkor and rural kwashiorkor (Fig. VIII-2). Because of the small size of the sample, the entire kwashiorkor population was compared to the entire comparison population for tests of significance. Age specific median scores for the comparison population were calculated and compared to the number of kwashiorkor children scoring above or below this median utilizing a modified sign test. Utilizing this test, the differences among the two populations yielded $p < .05$ (Table VIII-II). The curves of both control groups demonstrated slight inflections in slope at 12.5 years of age.

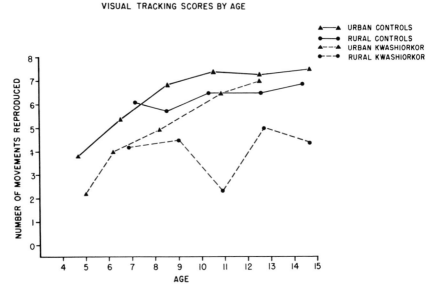

Figure VIII-2. Visual tracking performance scores by age for urban controls, rural controls, urban kwashiorkor and rural kwashiorkor.

Number Series

The mean ability to repeat an additive series of numbers increased (Fig. VIII-3) with age in all groups. The number series test did not clearly demonstrate the order of best performance urban controls, rural controls, urban kwashiorkor and rural kwashiorkor, but tended to group the subjects into control and kwashiorkor groups. However, the relative and absolute differences were slight and appear to be insignificant in the age groups up through seven years. One of the striking findings was that kwashiorkor children frequently responded with only the last digit in a long series when the capacity for a series of digits was exceeded. That is, a child may have repeated a three digit series correctly, but upon presentation of the four digit series, would forget the first digits and give back only the last one. This type of error was more common than the transposition or deletion error made by the controls when the digit capacity was exceeded. The modified sign test of significance between the total comparison and kwashiorkor population gave a probability value of $p < .01$ (Table VIII-II).

TABLE VIII-II

Age Group	All Controls Decimal Mean Age	N	All Kwashiorkors Decimal Mean Age	N	Visual Tracking r	p	Modified Sign Test Number Series r	p	Oral Forms r	p	Auditory Tracking r	p
4-5	4.7	10	5.0	7	1	.13	5	.77	1	.13	2	.45
6-7	6.8	25	6.4	8	1	.07	1	.07	1	.07	1	.07
8-9	8.4	49	8.4	10	3	.34	2	.11	1	.02	0	.01
10-11	10.4	49	10.6	6	2	.68	1	.22	1	.22	0	.03
12-13	12.7	56	12.5	8	3	.29	0	.01	2	.30	0	.01
14-15	14.5	59	14.7	3	0	.25	0	.25	0	.25	0	.25
Total		248		42	10	.05	9	.01	6	.004	3	.001

Note: r = number of kwashiorkor children scoring better than the median of the control children.

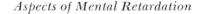

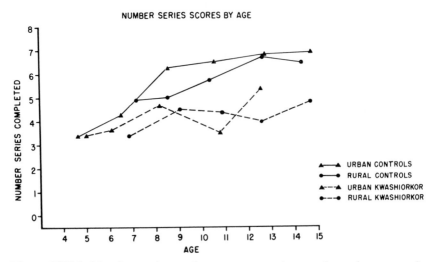

Figure VIII-3. Number series performance scores by age for urban controls, rural controls, urban kwashiorkor and rural kwashiorkor.

Auditory Tracking

Auditory tracking showed a continuous increase in ability with age for all groups tested. The kwashiorkor children made from two to three times the number of errors for age when compared to their rural or urban counterparts. The mean and +2 standard deviation curves are shown in Figure VIII-4 for all controls with the plots of individual kwashiorkor scores. When the total comparison population and the total kwashiorkor population were plotted by yearly age specific groups, the curves (Fig. VIII-5) were remarkably like those for manual haptic-kinesthetic error curves found by Cravioto[22] (see Fig. VIII-3); both demonstrating an inflection in the ten to eleven year age group which had higher mean errors than the eight to nine year olds. Both urban and rural kwashiorkor children scored lower than the mean of the controls and higher than +2 standard deviations of the controls in about the same proportions as were present in the total study population. The combined data were analyzed using a modified sign test and indicated that the total kwashiorkor distribution was different from the total control population at the p < .001 level (Table VIII-II).

Analysis of the type of response errors made in auditory tracking sharply differentiated the control population from the kwashiorkor population. Proportionally, twice as many kwashiorkor children as control children made each type of error.

Not only was the prevalence of the errors greater in the kwashiorkor children, but the severity of the errors per child making errors were greater when expressed as weighted error score means (Table VIII-III).

The per cent of children making each type of error in the ur-

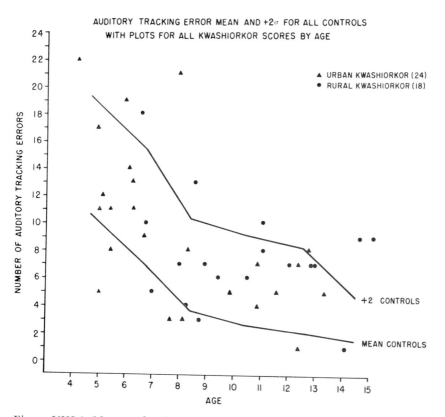

Figure VIII-4. Mean and +2 standard deviation curves for auditory tracking errors by yearly age intervals for controls and for kwashiorkor populations.

ban and rural groups were amazingly constant, differing only
in that 16 per cent of the rural controls could not complete one
or more phrases, while 25 per cent of the urban controls made
incompletion errors. The errors in order of decreasing frequency
were identical in the urban and rural controls and were transpositions, omissions, substitutions, phrase incompletions and pronunciations.

Among kwashiorkor children, the order was omissions,
transpositions, phrase incompletions, substitutions and pronunciations. The greatest difference in the prevalence of the errors
among kwashiorkor children and control groups was in phrase
incompletions.

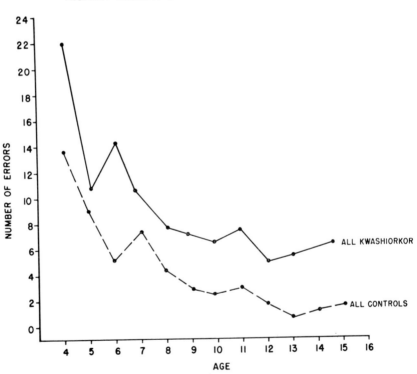

Figure VIII-5. Total comparison population and total kwashiorkor population scores by age and number of auditory tracking errors.

TABLE VIII-III

TYPES OF ERRORS FOUND IN AUDITORY TRACKING RESPONSES

Urban Controls—135 Children

Type of Errors	No. Children Making Errors	% Children Making Errors	Mean Error Score per Child Making Errors
Transpositions	59	44	2.8
Omissions	53	39	2.8
Substitutions	45	33	1.8
Incompletions	34	25	2.1
Pronunciations	6	4	—

Rural Controls—113 Children

Transpositions	50	44	3.5
Omissions	44	39	2.5
Substitutions	37	33	2.5
Incompletions	18	16	2.0
Pronunciations	5	4	—

All Kwashiorkor—42 Children

Transpositions	30	71	3.9
Omissions	34	81	3.4
Substitutions	26	62	2.7
Incompletions	27	64	2.7
Pronunciations	9	21	—

Other types of errors such as additions occurred so rarely that they were not analyzed separately.

Pronunciation Errors

Errors in pronunciation tended to remain constant throughout each test phrase in which they occurred. All children making pronunciation errors were less than eight years of age but one. The exception was a fourteen-year-old rural control. Children making auditory tracking errors such as omissions, transpositions and substitutions did not have an increased number of pronunciation errors in words immediately following these errors as were observed in the histidinemic children.

Oral Stereognosis

In general, the mean ability to identify forms presented orally increased as a function of age in all groups. The same

general shaped error curve was demonstrated by each group and
these curves were very similar to those for auditory tracking in
this study and haptic-kinesthetic curves by Cravioto,[23] even to
the detailed peaking at ten to eleven years of age. The means
for each group by age are shown in Figure VIII-6. As with other
tests, the relative position of each group was urban controls,
rural controls, urban kwashiorkor and rural kwashiorkor in order of increasing errors for comparable ages. All control means
and +2 standard deviations with plots for all kwashiorkor cases
are shown in Figure VIII-7 and indicates that about the same
proportion of urban and rural kwashiorkor cases are distributed
over the graph. The data for all kwashiorkor scores were compared to all controls using a nonparametric modified sign test
and indicated that the kwashiorkor distribution differed from
the controls at the p < .004 level of significance (Table VIII-II).

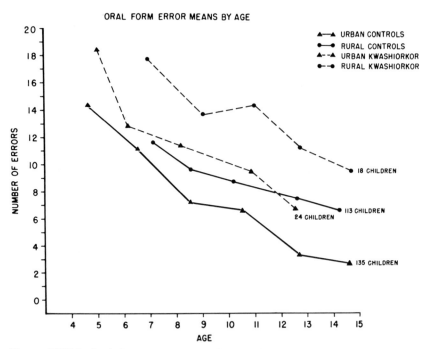

Figure VIII-6. Oral form error means by age for urban controls, rural controls, urban kwashiorkor and rural kwashiorkor.

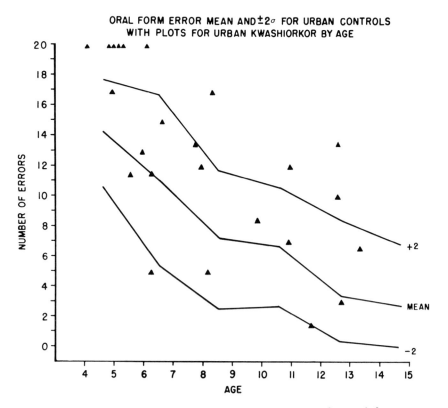

Figure VIII-7. Mean and +2 standard deviation curves for oral form error by age for urban controls and urban kwashiorkor population.

Visual Matching

Differences in the ability to match the forms visually was not significantly different in any of the groups except in four to five year olds in the kwashiorkor group. Three of the kwashiorkor children and one control had marked difficulty in matching forms presented visually and scored 20, 20, 19, 18 errors respectively on the oral stereognostic test. These were the only children who made more than four errors on the first visual match. All other subjects matched all forms correctly on two trials.

Other Comparisons

Regression of oral stereognostic error scores against auditory tracking error scores indicated that among the kwashiorkor children those making high error scores on one test were not necessarily those making high error scores on other tests. While as a group, the kwashiorkors had high error scores on both tests, the same individuals did not contribute equally to the high mean scores in both tests. Only three of the sixteen kwashiorkor patients scoring more than +2 standard deviations on the oral form test also scored more than +2 standard deviations on the auditory tracking test. When those scoring more than +2 standard deviations on either test are regressed against age at which they were hospitalized for kwashiorkor, there is a suggestion that those scoring more than +2 standard deviations on the oral form test were younger and those scoring more than +2 standard deviations on the auditory tracking test were older at the time of hospitalization. The mean age of hospitalization of the more than +2 standard deviation oral form test children was 2.5 (median 1 year 11 months) range 1.4 to 5.11 while for the +2 standard deviation auditory tracking subjects, the mean age was 4.1 (median 3 years, 6 months) range 1.3 to 9.6 (Table

TABLE VIII-IV

AGE DISTRIBUTION AND MEAN (M) OF KWASHIORKOR CHILDREN
SCORING MORE THAN +2 STANDARD DEVIATIONS OF CONTROL
CHILDREN FOR AUDITORY TRACKING (8) AND ORAL FORM
ERRORS (16) BY AGE OF HOSPITALIZATION

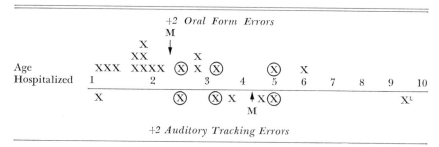

Note: Three subjects at 2 years, 5 months; 3 years, 2 months; and 5 years scored more than +2 standard deviation on both tests. 1. Subsequent investigation showed that this subject was treated for Kwashiorkor previously at 4 years, 2 months of age.

VIII-IV). Among all kwashiorkor subjects, these same trends appeared but did not reach the level of statistical significance. Those who were hospitalized prior to 25 months of age had adjusted mean scores of 8.1 auditory tracking errors and 13.0 oral form errors, while those older than 29 months at the time of hospitalization had 9.5 auditory tracking errors and 12.0 oral form errors.

The comparison of each control population and their kwashiorkor counterparts showed that the differences in the mean error scores were approximately constant at about 3 errors for the urban and 5 for the rural at each age interval. However, because of the curve form, the relative scores expressed in age increased greatly. That is, an eight-year-old urban kwashiorkor scored the same as a six-year-old urban control, a difference of two years, but a twelve-year-old kwashiorkor child scored the same as an eight-year-old control—a difference of four years, indicating that the kwashiorkor children were about 30 per cent retarded for age.

Time required for decision was calculated for each subject by adding the decision time on each form and dividing by 20. Among the kwashiorkor subjects who had oral form error scores greater than $+2$ standard deviations, the age adjusted mean time was 5.3 seconds compared to 7.9 seconds for those scoring less than $+2$ standard deviations. Among the fifty-six controls of eleven to twelve years, those having error scores higher than the 75 percentile had mean decision times of 3.8 seconds while the remainder had a mean of 6.2 seconds.

DISCUSSION OF RESULTS

As there are no adequate controls for kwashiorkor populations such as used in this study, two comparison populations were used which shared some characteristics with the children recovered from kwashiorkor. However, it became apparent that some of the children used as controls also had evidence of protein malnutrition; noteworthy that among the rural controls, two children were referred into the hospital with edema as was one relapsed kwashiorkor. The differences between the urban and rural controls most likely not only reflect socioeconomic differences but also nutritional differences. In this respect, it could be argued that the differences among the urban controls and the rural kwashiorkor are the extremes of nutritional status in this population. If this were the true picture, and assuming a nutritional influence on the moieties tested, then we feel that the urban kwashiorkor children should be closer to the rural kwashiorkor children than the graphs indicate for oral stereognosis and visual tracking. The auditory tracking curves, the number series scores, and the proportion of children making speech errors suggest that the urban kwashiorkor children are not just rural children transplanted to the city.

Despite attempts to select only Ladino children for the study, one Indian kwashiorkor and two Indian controls were included in the study. These did not contribute to low scores in any of the verbal or other tests as the one Indian kwashiorkor scored best on all tests of any kwashiorkor child as did one Indian control who had the best scores of the control group.

In all tests except the number series test, the general relationship of the groups in order of best performance was urban controls, rural controls, urban kwashiorkor and rural kwashiorkor. As the number of kwashiorkor cases by age category and residence is insufficient to give valid tests of significance, the data were combined and analyzed using a nonparametric modified sign test. Combining the data into all controls and all kwashiorkor changes two rural and two urban kwashiorkor children in relation to the residence specific two standard deviation line, but they still maintain their relative positions in relation to the median in the sign test and do not change the significance of the p value.

The slopes of the curves at different age periods are remarkably similar for various tests with a steep slope from about four to seven, a plateau at seven to ten, a steep slope from ten to twelve and another plateau from twelve to fifteen. These curves roughly resemble, and the ages approximately coincide with, the periods of proceritas and tugor of physical growth. Considering that this study involved very few subjects in any age category, the details of these curves may not be subject to interpretation. However, the peaking of the oral haptic curves at eleven years of age, is remarkably like the peak seen in manual haptic testing at ten years of age shown in Figure 3, of Cravioto;[23] and in manual haptic-kinesthetic tests of North American school children by Birch and Lefford.[29] This may reflect only differences in samples, but may also suggest that there is a readjustment in intersensory moieties from ten to eleven years of age. Manual haptic moieties may mature earlier than oral haptic and auditory moieties, a problem which could be tested in larger samples. The consistent finding in four studies (Birch and Lefford,[29] Cravioto,[23] McDonald and Aungst,[30] this study) that either ten year olds (manual haptic or eleven year olds (oral haptic) make higher mean error scores than children one to two years younger, suggests that there is something peculiar about the intersensory relationships of ten or eleven year olds. That it occurs in widely different populations under different social-economic conditions suggests that it may involve an intrinsic factor related to growth.

Mean error scores by age indicate that kwashiorkor children made $1\frac{1}{2}$ to 2 times the errors made by comparable controls similar to the haptic-kinesthetic errors made manually in the Cravioto[23] study. This might suggest that there is a panhaptic deficit in protein malnourished children affecting both oral and manual stereognostic ability. However, it is not known how mental ability as measured by IQ affects the results of the oral test and whether these findings represent a true haptic loss or reflect a general depression in mental ability. Moser, LaGourgue and Class[31] made an analysis of oral stereognostic ability among normal, blind and deaf subjects and indicated that mental ability as measured by IQ contributes about 10 per cent of the variance in oral test scores and vice versa. If this were generally true, then a real haptic loss difference probably exists between the groups tested.

The one striking comparison which indicates differences between all controls and all kwashiorkor is the analysis of the types of speech errors made in the two groups of children. The percentage of children making each type of error in the rural and urban controls is remarkably constant, and if this were to obtain for other "normal" populations, it would be a new and unique epidemiologic tool.

Table VIII-III indicates that the most frequently made error among the controls was transposition, while among the kwashiorkor children, it was an error of omission. Further, the greatest proportional difference between the control children and kwashiorkor children was incompletion errors. It might be argued that the control children made less serious errors in that a transposition is probably less serious than an omission and that a substitution is probably less serious than the inability to complete a phrase. In this respect, the control children showed more originality in that they transposed and substituted words rather than omitting them, and attempted to complete the phrase— things that the kwashiorkor children did less frequently.

The question arises whether these tests really demonstrate anything more than a general loss of ability among kwashiorkor children, and that kwashiorkor children might not have any specific moiety affected proportionally more than another. Both sides of the question could be argued from the data in this study.

While ten kwashiorkor children scored better than the median visual scores of their comparison age mates compared to only three kwashiorkor children who exceeded the median control scores for auditory tracking, the numbers in this study are insufficient to conclude that the visual moiety is relatively less affected.

There is some suggestion in this pilot study that severe protein malnutrition at different ages may result in depression of different moieties. Again, as in former studies, it does not clearly differentiate whether malnutrition per se or the social-psychic dislocation accompanying hospitalization results in the depression of the functions tested. However, the author is unaware of any study showing a haptic loss in children associated with hospitalization per se. Further, the finding of Cravioto,[23] of a similar manual haptic deficit in chronically malnourished children who had not been hospitalized suggests that hospitalization per se is not the reason for the observed behavior. These data indicate that while recovered kwashiorkor children have high mean error scores for both oral stereognostic and auditory tracking, the children who score more than +2 standard deviations on one test are not the same as the children who score more than the +2 standard deviation on the other test. Only three children of the sixteen scoring more than +2 standard deviations on the oral stereognostic test also scored more than +2 standard deviation on the auditory tracking test. As eight children scored more than +2 standard deviations on the auditory tracking test, this is about the number expected by chance association. This fact might be argued as evidence suggesting a general depression rather than a deficit resulting from a more or less specific biochemical defect, if the histidinemia model obtains. However, the fact that all but two of the children scoring more than +2 standard deviations on the stereognostic test were hospitalized between the ages of one year, four months and three years, two months; while all but two of the children scoring more than +2 standard deviations on auditory tracking were hospitalized between two years, five months, and five years; suggests that oral perception may be affected severely if the insult occurs from about one to three years, two months of age; while severe auditory tracking errors occur when the insult is from two years, five months to five years of age. Two of the children having both moieties severely affected were in the overlap age from two years, five months to three years, two months. Considering the variable conditions under which these children live and are brought to medical attention, those children hospitalized beyond five years of age who had severe defects could have had an earlier episode of severe malnutrition within the age ranges given above which could account for their defect if the relationship between age and the moiety affected is a true one. The only child who could not be accounted for among the twenty-one subjects by this hypothesis is the child at one year, three months who had an auditory tracking error only. This child scored six oral form errors at fourteen years, seven months of age about the mean score for rural controls of this age (Fig. VIII-7). Considering the relative crudeness of the tests and the large variables in a study of this sort, these exceptions might be expected. Regression of age of hospitalization against these scores for all kwashiorkor children did not result in statistically significant different means when divided into those hospitalized before two years of age and those after two years, but the mean scores are in the direction expected under the above hypothesis.

SUMMARY

The objective of this study was to determine if children recovered from kwashiorkor manifest signs and symptoms similar to children with histidinemia. It was postulated that if they did, the kwashiorkor child would have normal audiograms, a depressed auditory tracking and oral stereognostic ability and a relatively better visual tracking ability. Four Ladino Spanish-speaking groups were tested—urban controls, rural controls, recovered urban kwashiorkor and recovered rural kwashiorkor children. The results of the study indicate that recovered kwashiorkor children have normal audiograms, depressed auditory tracking and oral stereognostic ability, but also have a depressed visual tracking ability. It is true that the proportional number of errors made on visual tracking is not as great as in auditory tracking and stereognosis, but the differences are not great enough to be able to say that the visual moiety is relatively less affected.

Oral stereognostic error curves in the kwashiorkor children are similar to haptic-kinesthetic manual error curves found by Cravioto[23] for malnourished rural Guatemalan children. Auditory tracking errors in the kwashiorkor children differ quantitatively and qualitatively from the errors made by the controls; the kwashiorkor children making a higher proportion of the more serious type errors such as phrase incompletions and omissions. Except for audiograms, each moiety tested improved with age in all groups. The general relationship of best performance in each test was urban controls, rural controls, urban kwashiorkor, rural kwashiorkor except in the type of speech errors made in response to the auditory tracking test. These latter were identical for the urban and rural populations and sharply separated the control from kwashiorkor populations. The general shape of the error curves and the ages at which slopes inflect correspond roughly to the periods of proceritas and tugor of physical growth. The finding in this and three previous studies of inflections in error curves, such that ten or eleven-year-old children make more errors than eight or nine year olds, suggests that intrinsic rather than social factors make these ages ones in which intersensory moieties are readjusted. The relative differences in all tests except audiometrics among the kwashiorkor groups and their comparison counterparts indicated that recovered kwashiorkor children were from 30 to 40 per cent retarded for age. A suggestion of hyperkinesthetic type of behavior was found in that kwashiorkor children made faster decisions than their control counterparts as did those controls in the upper 25 percentile of the error scores for stereognosis, this despite repeated instructions before and during the test to take all the time they needed.

The fact that kwashiorkor children who scored over +2 standard deviations on the auditory tracking test were not the children who scored over +2 standard deviations on the stereognosis test except as chance association would expect, makes it difficult to ascribe these findings to a histidinemic-like lesion, and would seem to indicate some general depressions among kwashiorkor children. However, considering the relatively small sample size, the fact that kwashiorkor children had auditory tracking errors qualitatively and quantitatively different than the control, and that most children making a high error score in stereognosis had severe protein malnutrition from one year to three years, two months of age while most with high error scores for auditory tracking were hospitalized between two years, five months and five years of age, may be some evidence that a histidinemic-like basis for these defects could exist.

SIGNIFICANCE OF THIS WORK

Studies of Bond and Tinker[32] and Lashley[27] have indicated that a large proportion of persons with idiopathic dyslexia have short auditory phrase memories. Thus, children recovered from acute infantile protein-calorie malnutrition and perhaps chronic malnutrition may have considerable difficulty in learning to read. Further, short auditory memory has been found by Bradley[33] to occur in PKU children and the severity of the defect correlates with the age at which the dietary treatment is started.[34] While the results of loading tests on chronically malnourished children are not reported here, those findings coupled with this present study bears on the significance of this entire area. Among thirteen to fourteen-year-old nonpregnant girls who were 30 per cent under height for age and had not had frank kwashiorkor, 40 per cent gave positive ferric chloride urine tests after loading with histidine at 360 mg/kg or phenylalanine 100 mg/kg. These studies done under field conditions did not permit evaluation of their plasma levels, but it appears that plasma levels must reach 15 mg/100 ml before the pyruvates appear in the urine in sufficient quantities to be detected by the methods used.[35] Thus, these subjects appear to handle test loads of the amino acids somewhere between a heterozygote and homozygote for the corresponding hereditary defects. Should subjects with this degree of enzymatic defect subsequently become pregnant, then the fetuses would be exposed to an intra-uterine environment not unlike that of fetuses of homozygous mothers in the genetic diseases. Nearly all such children of PKU mothers are severely retarded.[36]

Studies reporting or suggesting defects in the histidine pathway indicate that alterations in the metabolism of this amino acid are associated with alterations in speech,[10, 14-16] among other symptoms.

Acute infantile protein malnutrition or the social-psychic factors associated with it puts the child at a distinct disadvantage early in life and this continues after the dietary defect is corrected. If dyslexia is shown to be significant among these children, then it would imply that some children in programs such as Head Start may already be at an intrinsic disadvantage by the time they reach the age of entry into the program. If there is a significant difference in the severity of the visual-auditory tracking defects, it would suggest that visual means of teaching may yield better results than auditory means in protein malnourished populations. Infantile protein malnutrition may account for some cases of idiopathic dyslexia in the United States. These findings coupled with the previous reported and unreported biochemical findings, suggest that treatment for kwashiorkor which is now prolonged (six to eighteen months of hospitalization in our sample) may benefit by starting children on low phenylalanine-histidine diets. It suggests that village feeding programs such as AID milk program, in which cows' milk which has two to three times the amount of phenylalanine contained in human milk,[12] given once a week may result in the maximum damage one could conceive. If such feeding programs are undertaken, they should be intensive, continuous and prolonged. It implies that PKU detection programs, especially heterozygote detection, would have a large source of error in protein malnourished populations and would require dietary reinforcement to detect true heterozygotes.

While this author is unfamiliar with the literature concerning educational deficits in the blind, this hypothesis would predict that children with retrolental fibroplasia would be one group of blind subjects who would have marked difficulty in learning to read braille due to a marked haptic deficit. Such subjects are for the major part, premature children who have been exposed to high oxygen tensions in incubators resulting in retinal damage. Premature children have immature enzyme systems, especially those along the histidine-phenylalanine pathway. Hence, much like the histidinemic, PKU, and protein-calorie, malnourished children are at high risk for overloading of these amino acids and haptic damage.

REFERENCES

1. Cheung, M.W., Fowler, D.I., Norton, P.M., Snyderman, S.E. and Holt, L.E., Jr.: Observations on amino acid metabolism in kwashiorkor (a preliminary report). *J Trop Pediatr,* 1:141, 1955.
2. Cravioto, J., Gomez, F., Ramos-Galvan, R., Frenh, S., Montano, E.L. and Garcia, N.: Metabolismo proteico en la desnutricion avanzada: concentration de aminoacidos libres en el plasma sanguineo. *Bol Ofic Sanitaria Panama,* 48:383, 1960.
3. Dean, F.A. and Whitehead, R.G.: The metabolism of aromatic amino acids in kwashiorkor. *Lancet,* 1:188, 1963.
4. Whitehead, R.G.: Amino acid metabolism in kwashiorkor I. Metabolism of histidine and imadozole derivatives. *Clin Sci,* 26:271, 1964.
5. Whitehead, R.G. and Milburn, T.R.: Amino acid metabolism in kwashiorkor II. Metabolism of phenylalanine and tyrosine. *Clin Sci,* 26:148, 1967.
6. Rao, D.R., Deodhar, A.D. and Hariharan, K.: Histidine metabolism in experimental protein malnutrition in rats. *Biochem J,* 97:311, 1965.
7. Habicht, J. and Witkop, C.J., Jr.: As quoted by Witkop, C.J., Jr.: Genetics and nutrition. *Fed Proc,* 26:148, 1967.

8. Witkop, C.J., Jr.: Genetics and nutrition. *Fed Proc*, 26:148, 1967.
9. Ghadimi, H., Partington, M.W. and Hunter, M.D.: A familial disturbance of histidine metabolism. *N Engl J Med*, 265:221, 1961.
10. La Du, B.N.: Histidinemia. In: Stanbury, J.B., Wyngaarden, J.B. and Fredrickson, D.S. (Eds.). *The Metabolic Basis of Inherited Disease*, 2nd ed., New York, McGraw-Hill, 1966, p. 366.
11. Ghadimi, H. and Zischka, R.: Histidinemia. In: Nyhan, W.L. (Ed.): *Amino Acid Metabolism and Genetic Variation*. New York, McGraw-Hill, 1967.
12. Auerbach, V.H., DiGeorge, A.M. and Carpenter, G.G.: Histidinemia. In: Nyhan, W.L. (Ed.): *Amino Acid Metabolism and Genetic Variation*. New York, McGraw-Hill, 1967.
13. Davies, H.E. and Robinson, M.J.: A case of histidinemia. *Arch Dis Child*, 38:80, 1963.
14. Waisman, H.A.: Variations in clinical and laboratory findings in histidinemia. *Am J Dis Child*, 113:93, 1967.
15. Arakawa, R., *et al.*: Forminotransferase-deficiency syndrome: A new inborn error of folic acid metabolism. *Ann Pediatr*, 205:1, 1965.
16. Galamon, T. and Szulc-Kuberska, J.: Hereditary abnormality of histidine metabolism in stammering. In: *Third Meeting of the Federation of European Biochemical Societies*. Warsaw, Poland. Apr. 4-7, 1966, New York, Academic Press, p. 317.
17. Witkop, C.J., Jr. and Henry, F.V.: Sjögren-Larsson syndrome and histidinemia: hereditary biochemical diseases with defects of speech and oral functions. *J Speech Hear Disord*, 28:109, 1963.
18. Hudson, F.P., Dickinson, R.A. and Ireland, J.T.: Experience in the detection and treatment of phenylketonuria. *Pediatr*, 31:47, 1963.
19. Quay, W.B.: Effect of dietary phenylalanine and tryptophan on pineal and hypothalamic serotonin levels. *Proc Soc Exp Biol Med*, 114:718, 1963.
20. Woolley, D.W. and van der Hoeven, T.: Serotonin deficiency in infancy as a cause of mental defect in experimental phenylketonuria. *Int J Neuropsychol*, 1:529, 1965.
21. Auerbach, V.H., DiGeorge, A.M., Baldridge, R.C., Tourtellotte, C.D. and Brigham, M.P.: Histidinemia. A deficiency in histidase resulting in urinary excretion of histidine and of imidazole-pyruvic acid. *J Pediatr*, 60:487, 1962.
22. Holton, J.B., as quoted by La Du, B.N.: Histidinemia. In: Stanbury, J.B., Wyngaarden, J.B. and Fredrickson, D.S. (Eds.): *The Metabolic Basis of Inherited Disease*, 2nd ed., New York, McGraw-Hill, 1966, p. 366.
23. Cravioto, J.: Nutritional depreciation and psychobiological development in children. In: *Deprivation in Psychobiological Development*. Pan American Health Organization, Scientific Publication No. 134, 1966. p. 38-54.

24. Cravioto, J. and Robles, B.: Evolution of adaptive and motor behavior during rehabilitation from kwashiorkor. *Am J Orthopsychiatry*, 35: 449, 1965.

25. Cravioto, J., de Licardie, E.R. and Vega, L.: Amino-acid-protein malnutrition and mental development. In: Nyhan, W.L. (Ed.) : *Amino Acid Metabolism and Genetic Variation*. New York, McGraw-Hill, 1967.

26. Birch, H.G. and Lefford, A.: Two strategies for studying perception in brain damaged children. In: Birch, H.G. (Ed.) : *Brain Damage: The Biological and Social Aspects*. Baltimore, Williams and Wilkins, 1964.

27. Lashley, K.S.: *The Neurophysiology of Lashley, Selected Papers*. New York, McGraw-Hill, 1960.

28. Bosma, J.F. (Ed.) : *Symposium on Oral Sensation and Perception*. Springfield, Ill., Charles C Thomas, 1967.

29. Birch, H.G. and Lefford, A.: Intersensory development in children. Monographs *Soc Res Child Dev, Serial No. 89*, 28:5, 1963, p. 17.

30. McDonald, E.T. and Aungst, L.F.: Studies in oral sensorimotor function. In: Bosma, J.F. (Ed.) : *Symposium on Oral Sensation and Perception*. Springfield, Ill., Charles C Thomas, 1967, p. 202-220.

31. Moser, H., LaGourgue, J.R. and Class, L.W.: Studies of oral stereognosis in normal, blind and deaf subjects. In: Bosma, J.F. (Ed.) : *Symposium on Oral Sensation and Perception*. Springfield, Ill., Charles C Thomas, 1967, p. 244-286.

32. Bond, G.L. and Tinker, M.: *Reading Difficulties: Their Diagnosis and Correction*. 2nd ed., New York, Appleton-Century-Crofts, 1967.

33. Bradley, D.: Personal communication, speech pathologist, University of North Carolina, Chapel Hill, North Carolina, 1968.

34. Stewart, J.M. and Ashley, C.G.: Phenylketonuria report of the Oregon detection and evaluation program. *The Journal-Lancet* (Minneapolis) , 87:162, 1967.

35. Armstrong, M.D. and Low, N.I.: Phenylketonuria VIII, relation between age, serum phenylalanine level and phenylpyruvic acid excretion. *Proc Soc Exp Biol Med*, 99:219, 1958.

36. Mabry, C.C., Denniston, J.C., Nelson, T.L. and Son, C.D.: Maternal phenylketonuria: A cause of mental retardation in children without metabolic defect. *N Engl J Med*, 269:1404, 1963.

Chapter IX

POSSIBLE BIOCHEMICAL APPLICATIONS IN THE TRAINING OF THE MENTALLY RETARDED

Edward Glassman and John E. Wilson

IGNORANCE OF BRAIN FUNCTION

MENTALLY retarded people can be helped by the application of special methods of training and care. It is clear, however, that even with the development of improved or new training methods, additional approaches will be necessary to achieve the desired goals. The major obstacle to the development of new approaches is a lack of information concerning the mechanisms underlying mental retardation. It is difficult to describe and deal with the abnormal when the characteristics of the normal condition are not known. This lack of information is due mainly to a deficiency of appropriate basic research on the nature of brain function. Thus, it is not known which regions of the brain malfunction in a mentally retarded person. Even if this knowledge were available, it would be difficult to decide whether to attempt to increase the performance of that part or to stimulate another area to perform new functions. This would depend partly on whether mental retardation is due to abnormal brain metabolism or to abnormal neuronal circuitry. It is not unlikely that both factors are operating, one influencing the other, and there may be much that might be done to improve brain function of the mentally retarded to make training more effective.

One possibility is the development of chemical treatments

Note: This research was supported in part by research grants from the Geigy Chemical Corporation, the United States Public Health Service (GM-08202; NB-07457), the National Science Foundation (GB-18551) and by a Research Career Development Award (GM-K3-14) to E. Glassman from the Division of General Medical Sciences, National Institutes of Health.

138

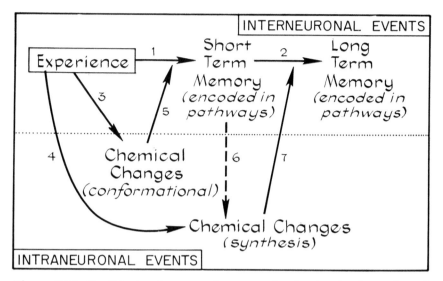

Figure IX-1. Possible involvement of macromolecules in the formation of short- and long-term memory. In this scheme, certain experiences trigger chemical changes that produce intraneuronal modifications. These allow the formation of intraneuronal pathways in which experiential information is stored.

that would stimulate mental performance, so the specialized training methods now in use are even more effective. Such chemicals could possibly be applied to localized brain regions to overcome deficient processes in that region or to compensate for deficiencies in other areas. Alternatively, the chemicals might be applied systemically with the subsequent stimulation of many parts of the brain. This type of therapy might induce improved response to appropriate training methods in a mentally retarded person.

The lack of insight into the basic chemical and physiological processes necessary for normal brain function hinders the development of such effective chemical therapy for the mentally retarded. Much more basic research is necessary if we are to obtain this information. Recent biochemical research related to learning and memory consolidation, while not specifically directed toward this end, is perhaps a useful example of the type of work that has potential application.

THE STORAGE OF MEMORY

Much research suggests that the storage or consolidation of memory involves successive stages (Fig. IX-1). Right after training, memory seems to be retrievable from a short-lived form, short-term memory. This decays within hours, but by that time memory is retrievable from a more permanent form, long-term memory. A number of approaches indicate the existence of at least two phases. First, in a variety of mammals, lesions in the area around the hippocampus are reported to cause rapid forgetting after a task has been learned.[1, 2] Memory for events learned prior to the production of the lesion seems unimpaired. Removal of the ventral lobe of the octopus brain has a similar effect.[3] Thus, short-term memory, but not long-term memory, can be formed in these lesioned animals. Second, many experiments show that the *formation* of long-term memory is prevented by agents that have no effect on short-term memory, or on long-term memory once it is formed.[4] There might be significant therapeutic help for the mentally retarded if the processes involved in the formation of long-term memory could be enhanced by chemical treatment.

Unfortunately, this approach is made difficult because the exact role of chemicals in these reactions is not known. While it is not likely that chemicals encode experiential information within their own structure, they probably are involved in producing changes within nerve cells that lead to the formation of neuronal pathways which do encode information. Because the formation of short-term memory is not sensitive to the inhibitors of RNA or protein synthesis,[5–10] this process may not be directly dependent on the synthesis of these macromolecules. This does not rule out the participation of macromolecules in the formation and maintenance of short-term memory since conformational changes of some type could take place at the synapse of the cell.

The formation of long-term memory, however, is interfered with if inhibitors of protein or RNA synthesis are given before or immediately after training,[7, 11, 12] and it is possible that this process depends on the synthesis of these macromolecules. Long-term memory, once it is formed is not sensitive to these inhibitors, and thus its maintenance is probably not specifically dependent on the continuous synthesis of RNA and protein at high levels. There are data that suggest that other agents known to affect memory fixation processes such as ECS and KCl-induced spreading depression may also affect protein synthesis,[13-15] and it is therefore possible that many, if not all, agents that affect memory fixation do so by affecting the synthesis of RNA or protein. These data have given rise to the notion that chemicals necessary for memory fixation are synthesized during the early stages of the formation of long-term memory. It is tempting to speculate that inducing localized changes in the brain RNA or protein with chemicals may have the effect of increasing memory fixation in mammals, a result that may have great significance for improving mental processes in the mentally retarded. This process may be occurring when various chemicals produce increased memory fixation in mice.[16] This is another area where basic research might prove fruitful.

The model shown in Figure IX-1 suggests that neuronal electrical activity by itself will not produce these chemical changes,[17, 18] but some form of excitement (arousal) may also be necessary, as indicated by McGaugh[19] and Barondes and Cohen.[11] Indeed, it is possible that certain types of novel or intense sensory stimulation can produce this excitement and the subsequent chemical events without the formation of short-term memory, and would account for many of the chemical changes caused by novel sensory stimulation.[20] Chemicals that have this effect on excitement levels might be of use when training the mentally retarded.

BIOCHEMICAL APPROACHES

Clearly, extensive coordinated research projects involving many basic neurobiological disciplines are necessary to produce data that can be applied to the problem of enhancing memory processes in the mentally retarded. Such a project exists within the Neurobiology Program of the University of North Carolina. A behavioral task that is rapidly learned by a mouse was used in order to measure the incorporation of precursors into RNA, proteins, lipids and other substances while the mouse was learning. In this way the synthesis of macromolecules associated with memory fixation might be detected. Only RNA has been studied. The mouse was chosen because it has been used extensively in behavioral, biochemical and genetical studies, but recent studies with the rat have also produced comparable data.[21] To minimize genetic variation, only six to eight-week-old males of the C57Bl/6J strain supplied by the Jackson Laboratories were used, but female mice show the same chemical changes when conditions are right. The methods and the data have been published in detail elsewhere.[21-26]

The training apparatus consists of a box divided into two sections with a common electric grid floor.[23, 27] One mouse is placed in each section. A light and a buzzer are attached to the outside of the box so that each mouse receives equal stimulation. The sections are identical except that one side has an escape shelf. The light and buzzer are presented for three seconds after which an electric foot shock is applied. Initially, both mice jump in response to the shock. The shock is terminated as soon as the animal that has the shelf uses it as a haven. After fifteen seconds the mouse is then removed from the shelf, placed on the grid floor and another trial commences. The training lasts for fifteen minutes, and between twenty-five and thirty-five trials are carried out in this interval. The mouse that has the shelf will usually start to avoid the shock in response to light and buzzer by the fifth trial, and is performing to a criterion of nine out of ten by ten minutes. The untrained mouse also receives equivalent handling at random during the training. Thus, with respect to lights, buzzers, shocks, handling and injection, the untrained mouse is *yoked* to the *trained* mouse.

The mice are injected intracranially or interperitoneally with radioactive uridine, a precursor of RNA, thirty minutes before training. After the training period, the mice are sacrificed and the brains of the trained and the yoked mouse are homogenized and the amount of radioactivity in RNA isolated from nuclei, ribosomes or polyribosomes is determined.[23, 25] The radioactivity in UMP isolated from the supernatant fraction is a useful indicator of the relative amount of uridine that entered brain cells, and it is used as a correction factor. Coded, blind experiments were carried out. Only after the biochemical analysis was completed and all data were computed was it revealed which mice were trained.

RESULTS

Almost every trained mouse incorporated more radioactivity into brain RNA or polysomes than did its untrained control.[23, 25] For technical reasons, these differences cannot be unequivocally ascribed to increased synthesis of RNA in the trained animal, and we refer only to a change in the amount of incorporation of radioactive uridine. Trained and untrained animals had no significant differences in the incorporation of radioactive uridine into RNA or polysomes of liver or kidney, while these same animals showed pronounced differences in the brain.[23, 25] It is therefore concluded that while tissues other than the liver and kidney might be responding to the experiences, the effect is probably specific to the brain.

Chemical analyses of brains after gross dissection into six parts have indicated that the changes in RNA occur primarily in the diencephalon and associated areas.[28] Autoradiography has confirmed this.[26] Although our analysis has not proceeded to the point where we can catalogue all of the areas that show a difference between trained and untrained animals, there are nuclei throughout the limbic system (olfactory and entorhinal cortices, hippocampus, amygdala, thalamus, hypothalamus and mamillary body) in which there is incorporation in trained mice with much less incorporation into their untrained yoked controls. In contrast to these structures, the outer layers of the neocortex showed the reverse situation, i.e. there is less radioactivity incorporated in the cells of this region of trained mice than in their untrained yoked controls. This is in agreement with the previous report based on gross dissection[23] that there is a significantly lower incorporation in this part of the brain of a trained mouse than in that of its yoked control. Most areas and cells of the brain, however, seem to incorporate similar amounts of radioactivity in trained and untrained animals. The knowledge of the functional relationships between the cells and areas of the brain where the chemical changes take place might have important implications for chemical treatments involving mentally retarded people. Much more basic research is required. Autoradiography, and perhaps histochemistry, seem well suited for elucidating these cellular relationships.[29]

SIGNIFICANCE OF BIOCHEMICAL STUDIES ON MEMORY PROCESSES

During the past decade much research has been published indicating that macromolecules, particularly RNA, undergo changes when experiential information is coded in the nervous system.* The behavioral trigger for such chemical changes has not been elucidated. It may be that the learning, per se, or the special stresses and emotional and motivational effects of learning are responsible for triggering such chemical responses. It is also possible, however, that the changes in macromolecules are due to nonspecific stimuli or to the activity associated with the training experience. Visual,[42–44] auditory,[45] rotary,[46–51] olfactory,[52] and stress stimulation[53, 54] have been reported to cause changes in RNA or polysomes in the nervous system. It is not unexpected that such stimuli would be effective during training. Such nonspecific stimuli have been eliminated in our research, but the exact mechanism has not been delineated.[55] This does not necessarily mean that the encoding of the experience in the nervous system is the trigger for the chemical reactions. It may well be that the special stresses, levels of excitement, emotional responses and other phenomena that may be related to the learning process are operating here. This is another area where more basic research is needed. Knowledge of the behavioral trigger might have therapeutic value during training of the mentally retarded.

The nature of the RNA is crucial to many hypotheses.[20] Our work revealed that the increased radioactivity in brain RNA during training was not confirmed to a single species of RNA, and the data resembled those found after RNA synthesis had been stimulated in liver by hydrocortisone or in uterus by estrogen.[23] This suggested that a general increase had occurred in the synthesis of rapidly-labeled RNA owing to a metabolic stimulation of brain cells. There was no evidence for a unique RNA with a function that does not involve protein synthesis; indeed

_____
* See references 21-26, 28-36, 38-41.

the RNA is similar to RNA extracted from other tissues. Further work is needed to determine whether this brain RNA is involved in the synthesis of new proteins or in the replenishment of an increase in the proteins already present.

The function of these macromolecules in the brain is another area where basic knowledge of brain function may be extremely important with respect to enhancing mental processes in the mentally retarded. Their role could be to replenish chemicals used in nerve activity, similar to the restorative role macromolecules play in all cells, and thus are responsible for the maintenance of function and the health of cells. Another possibility is that the changes in macromolecules are related more specifically to new pathway formation by changing connectivity between neurons through the alteration of the probability that a postsynaptic neuron will fire when impulses arrive from presynaptic nerves. This could be accomplished through processes that change the effectiveness of the neurotransmitter, by increasing its concentration, by decreasing the activity of enzymes that inactivate it, or by increasing the number or effectiveness of the receptor sites on the postsynaptic neuron. Regulating one or more of these processes by chemical treatment might have very beneficial effects on the mental performance of the mentally retarded.

Until it is known whether the changes in macromolecules have anything to do with the learning process, per se, or with an incidental process, it will be extremely difficult to correlate our results with the consolidation of memory (Fig. IX-1), although it is extremely tempting to do so. The RNA might code for proteins that may be involved in this process (Fig. IX-1, step 7), possibly by rendering permanent the synaptic associations that developed during short-term learning (Fig. IX-1, step 2). The protein may be related to the peptide(s) postulated to be involved in the maintenance and retrieval of memory by Flexner and Flexner[12] and Bohus and deWied.[56] If so, such molecules might have very beneficial effects on mentally retarded people when combined with appropriate methods of training and care.

The intermediate chemical and physiological steps that lead to increased incorporation into RNA and polysomes are also important. In mammals, this usually involves an hormonal intermediate. We have been studying uridine incorporation into brain polysomes during training in animals with various glands removed. The goal is to establish whether the biochemical response that occurs during fifteen minutes of avoidance training is dependent on the release of hormone from a functioning gland during this time. Long-term debilitating effects of gland removal were avoided. The data indicate that the adrenal, the pituitary, the testes and the ovary are not necessary for a mouse to learn the avoidance task, or for the increased incorporation of uridine into RNA that accompanied it.[21, 24] The possible effects of other glands are being investigated. In addition, changes in histones, norepinephrine, cyclic AMP and adenyl cyclase are also being studied. These substances are believed to be related to increased incorporation into RNA in other mammalian tissues, and they may be important to this brain response as well. Knowledge of the involvement of all the biochemical and physiological reactions in memory processes may lead to testable hypotheses concerning chemical approaches to the enhancement of mental performance in mentally retarded persons.

It should be clear that while the problems of increasing the mental capacity of the mentally retarded has special characteristics that must be dealt with in specific ways, the problem of augmenting mental processes is a general one, and has broad applicability to many types of people, whether they are normal, geniuses, senile or disadvantaged. All could benefit from chemical treatments that improve brain function, and such a development is a much desired goal if it is not misused. It is hoped that there will be an increase in basic research in those areas of behavior and biochemistry that are necessary if we are to gain the knowledge needed before safe chemical enhancement of mental processes is a reality.

REFERENCES

1. Douglas, R.J.: *Psychol Bull,* 67:416, 1967.
2. Gross, C.G., Black, P. and Chorover, S.: *Psychon Sci,* 12:165, 1968.
3. Young, J.Z.: *Proc Roy Soc (London),* 163:285, 1965.
4. John, E.R.: *Mechanisms of Memory.* New York, Academic Press, 1967.
5. Barondes, S.H. and Cohen, H.D.: Delayed and sustained effect of acetoxy-cycloheximide on memory in mice. *PNAS,* 58:157, 1967.
6. Shashoua, V.E.: RNA changes in goldfish brain during learning. *Nature,* 217:238, 1968.

7. Agranoff, B.W., Davis, R.E., Casola, L. and Lim, R.: Actinomycin-D blocks formation of memory shock-avoidance in goldfish. *Science,* 158:1600, 1968.
8. Barondes, S.H. and Jarvik, M.E.: The influence of actinomycin-D on brain RNA synthesis and on memory. *J Neurochem,* 11:187, 1964.
9. Flexner, L.B., Flexner, J.B. and Roberts, R.B.: Memory in mice analyzed with antibiotics. *Science,* 155:1377, 1967.
10. Agranoff, B.W., Davis, R.E. and Brink, J.J.: Memory fixation in the goldfish. *PNAS,* 54:788, 1965.
11. Barondes, S.H. and Cohen, H.D.: Arousal and the conversion of "short-term" to "long-term" memory. *PNAS,* 61:923, 1968
12. Flexner, L.B. and Flexner, J.B.: Intracerebral saline: Effect on memory of trained mice treated with puromycin. *Science,* 159:330, 1968.
13. Vesco, C. and Giuditta, A.: *J Neurochem,* 15:81, 1968.
14. Macinnes, J.W., McConkey, E.H. and Schlesinger, K.: Changes in brain polyribosomes following an electro-convulsive seizure. *J Neurochem,* 17:457, 1970.
15. Bennett, G.S. and Edelman, G.M.: Amino acid incorporation into brain proteins during spreading cortical depression. *Science,* 163:393, 1969.
16. McGaugh, J.L. and Petrinovich, L.F.: *Int Rev Neurobiol,* 8:139, 1965.
17. Edstrom, J.E. and Grampp, W.: Nervous activity and metabolism of ribonucleic acids in the crustacean stretch receptor neuron. *J Neurochem,* 12:735, 1965.
18. Bondeson, C., Edstrom, A. and Beviz, A.: Effects of different inhibitors of protein synthesis on electrical activity in the spinal cord of fish. *J Neurochem,* 14:1032, 1967.
19. McGaugh, J.L.: A multi-trace view of memory storage processes. In Bovet, D.F., Bovet-Nitti, F. and Oliverio, A. (Eds.): *Attuali Orientamenti della Ricerda Sull Appredimento e la Memoria.* Volume CIX. Rome, Accademia Nazionale de Lincei, 1968.
20. Glassman, E.: The biochemistry of learning: An evaluation of the role of RNA and protein. *Ann Rev Biochem,* 38:605, 1969.
21. Coleman, M.S., Pfingst, B., Wilson, J.E. and Glassman, E.: Brain function and macromolecules. VIII. Uridine incorporation into polysomes of hypophysectomized rats and ovariectomized mice during avoidance conditioning. Report, 1970, in preparation.
22. Coleman, M.S., Wilson, J.E. and Glassman, E.: Grain function and macromolecules. VII. Uridine incorporation into polysome of mouse brain during extinction. Report, 1970, in preparation.
23. Zemp, J.W., Wilson, J.E., Schlesinger, K., Boggan, W.O. and Glassman, E.: Brain function and macromolecules. I. Incorporation of uridine into RNA of mouse brain during short-term training experience. Proceedings of the National Academy of Sciences. *PNAS,* 55:1423, 1966.
24. Adair, L.B., Wilson, J.E. and Glassman, E.: Brain function and macro-

molecules. IV. Uridine incorporation into polysomes of mouse brain during different behavioral experiences. *PNAS,* 61:917, 1968.

25. Adair, L.B., Wilson, J.E., Zemp, J.W. and Glassman, E.: Brain function and macromolecules. III. Uridine incorporation into polysomes of mouse brain during short-term avoidance conditioning. *PNAS,* 61:606, 1968.

26. Kahan, B., Krigman, M.R., Wilson, J.E. and Glassman, E.: Brain function and macromolecules. VI. Autoradiographic analysis of the effects of a brief training experience on the incorporation of uridine into mouse brain. *PNAS,* 65:300, 1970

27. Schlesinger, K. and Wimer, R.: Genotype and conditioned avoidance learning in the mouse. *J Comp Physiol Psychol,* 63:139, 1967.

28. Zemp, J.W., Wilson, J.E. and Glassman, E.: Brain function and macromolecules. II. Site of increased labeling of RNA in brains of mice during a short-term training experience. Proceedings of the National Academy of Sciences. *PNAS,* 58:1120, 1967

29. Beach, G., Emmens, M., Kimble, D.P. and Lickey, M.: Autoradiographic demonstration of biochemical changes in the limbic system during avoidance training. *PNAS,* 62:692, 1969.

30. Bateson, P.P.G., Horn, G. and Rose, S.P.R.: Effects of an imprinting procedure on regional incorporation of tritiated lysine into protein of chick brain. *Nature,* 223:534, 1969.

31. Bogoch, S.: *The Biochemistry of Memory.* London, Oxford University Press, 1968.

32. Bowman, R.E. and Strobel, D.A.: Brain metabolism in the rat during learning. *J Comp Physiol Psychol,* 67:448, 1969.

33. Delweg, G., Gerner, R. and Wacker, A.: Quantitative and qualitative changes in ribonucleic acid of rat brain dependent on age and training experiments. *J Neurochem,* 15:1109, 1968.

34. Hyden, H. and Egyhazi, E.: Nuclear RNA changes of nerve cells during a learning experiment in rats. Proceedings of the National Academy of Sciences. *PNAS,* 48:1366, 1962.

35. Hyden, H. and Egyhazi, E.: Glial RNA changes during a learning experiment in rats. *PNAS,* 49:618, 1963.

36. Hyden, H. and Egyhazi, E.: Changes in RNA content and base composition in cortical neurons of rats in a learning experiment involving transfer of handedness. *PNAS,* 52:1030, 1964

37. Hyden, H. and Lange, P.W.: A differentiation in RNA response in neurons early and late during learning. Proceedings of the National Academy of Sciences. *PNAS,* 53:964, 1965.

38. Machlus, B. and Gaito, J.: Detection of RNA species unique to a behavioral task. *Psychon Sci,* 10:253-254, 1963.

39. Machlus, B. and Gaito, J.: Unique RNA species developed during a shock avoidance task. *Psychon Sci,* 12:111, 1968.

40. Rose, S.P.R., Bateson, P.P.G., Horn, A.L.D. and Horn, G.: Effects of an imprinting procedure on the regional incorporation of tritiated uracil into chick brain RNA. *Nature*, 225:650, 1970.

41. Shashoua, V.E.: RNA metabolism in goldfish brain during acquisition of new behavioral patterns. *PNAS*, 65:160, 1970.

42. Appel, S.H., Davis, W. and Scott, S.: Brain polysomes: Response to environmental stimulation. *Science*, 157:836, 1967.

43. Talwar, G.P., Chopra, S.P., Goel, B.K. and D'Monte, B.: Correlation of the functional activity of the brain with metabolic parameters. III. Protein metabolism of the occipital cortex in relation to light stimulus. *J Neurochem*, 13:109, 1966.

44. White, R.H. and Sundeen, C.D.: The effect of light and light deprivation upon the ultrastructure of the larval mosquito eye. I. Polyribosomes and endoplasmic reticulum. *J Exp Zool*, 164:461, 1967.

45. Hamberger, C.A. and Hyden, H.: Cytochemical changes in the cochlear ganglion caused by acoustic stimulation and trauma. *Acta Octolaryngol [Stockholm] (Supplement)*, 61:1, 1945

46. Hamberger, C.A. and Hyden, H.: Production of nucleoproteins in the vestibular ganglion. *Acta Otolaryngol [Stockholm] (Supplement)*, 75:53, 1949.

47. Hamberger, C.A. and Hyden, H.: Transneuronal chemical changes in Deiters' (sic) nucleus. *Acta Otolaryngol [Stockholm] (Supplement)*, 75:82, 1949.

48. Watson, W.E.: An autoradiographic study of the incorporation of nucleic-acid procursors by neurones and glia during nerve stimulation. *J Physiol*, 180:754, 1965.

49. Attardi, G.: Quantitative behavior of cytoplasmic RNA in rat Purkinje cells following prolonged physiological stimulation. *Exp Cell Res (Supplement)*, 4:25, 1957.

50. Jarlstedt, J.: Functional localization in the cerebellar cortex studied by quantitative determinations of Purkinje cell RNA. I. RNA changes in rat cerebellar Purkinje cells after proprio- and exteroreceptive and vestibular stimulation. *Acta Physiol Scand*, 67:243, 1966.

51. Jarlstedt, J.: Functional localization in the cerebellar cortex studied by quantitative determinations of Purkinje cell RNA. II. RNA changes in rabbit cerebellar Purkinje cells after caloric stimulation and vestibular neurotomy. *Acta Physiol Scand (Supplement)*, 271:1, 1966.

52. Rappoport, D.A. and Daginawala, H.F.: Changes in nuclear RNA of brain induced by olfaction in catfish. *J Neurochem*, 15:991, 1968.

53. Altman J. and Das, G.D.: Behavioral manipulations and protein metabolism of the brain: Effects of motor exercise on the utilization of leucine-[3]H. *Physiol Behav*, 1:105, 1966.

54. Bryan, R.N., Bliss, E.L. and Beck, E.C.: Incorporation of uridine-^{3}H into mouse brain RNA during stress. *Fed Proc*, 26:709, 1967.

55. Glassman, E. and Wilson, J.E.: The effect of short experience on macro-molecules in the brain. *Proceedings of the Parkside Symposium,* in press, 1970.

56. Bohus, B. and deWeid, D.: Inhibitory and facilitatory effect of two re-lated peptides on extinction of avoidance behavior. *Science,* 153:318, 1966.

Chapter X

HAND ABNORMALITIES IN MALFORMATION SYNDROMES ASSOCIATED WITH MENTAL RETARDATION

MURRAY FEINGOLD

A LARGE number of mental retardation syndromes are associated with some type of hand malformation.

HAND DEVELOPMENT

Embryologically, the arm bud is present by the 26th day, the hand plate by the 38th day, the finger rays by the 43rd day and complete separation of the fingers by the 47th day. The central nervous system is developing simultaneously and an insult to the embryo at this stage may cause abnormalities of both the central nervous system and the hands.

There are a great variety of hand abnormalities and some of the more significant ones include: abnormalities of size and shape; for example, a broad hand; long and narrow fingers (arachnodactyly); short fingers (brachydactyly); hyperextensible fingers; flexion deformities; extra fingers (polydactyly); clinodactyly (abnormal positioning of the fingers); thumb anomalies including a broad thumb, short thumb or a distally placed thumb; and shortened metacarpals. The major nail abnormalities include dysplastic (malformed) or dystrophic (maldeveloped) nails, convex nails and abnormal markings of the nails. Abnormal palmar creases are quite significant; the most common one is the so-called four-finger or simian line. Dermatoglyphic abnormalities, although frequently found in mental retardation syndromes, will not be discussed in this chapter.

Some of the syndromes in which the hand malformation is a major component are Apert's syndrome (many of these children are not retarded), Cornelia DeLange syndrome, Lawrence-Moon-

Note: Detailed descriptions of the syndromes listed in this chapter can be found in references 3 and 4.

Biedl syndrome, mucopolysaccharidoses, oto-palato-digital syndrome (mental retardation, if present, is mild), pseudohypoparathyroidism and the Rubinstein-Taybi syndrome.

THE RUBINSTEIN-TAYBI SYNDROME

A representative example of this group is the Rubinstein-Taybi syndrome. Patients with this syndrome have a characteristic facial appearance which includes frontal bossing, beaking of the nose, hypoplastic facial bones, micrognathia, anti-mongoloid slant of the eyes, ptosis and a high arched palate (Fig. X-1). Broad thumbs (the toes are also broad), which may be angulated, are the most striking feature on examination of the hand (Fig. X-2). Other hand abnormalities in this syndrome include broadness of the terminal phalanges of the other fingers, clinodactyly, short fifth finger, polydactyly and a simian line. The diagnosis is made clinically and the physician should suspect this syndrome

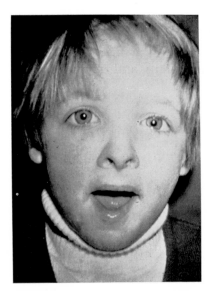

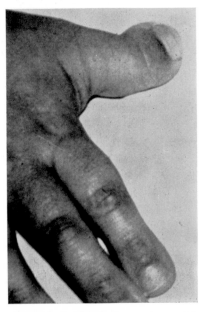

Figure X-1. Patient with Rubinstein-Taybi syndrome showing microcephaly, anti-mongoloid slant of the eyes and a beaked nose.

Figure X-2. Hand of a patient with Rubinstein-Taybi syndrome showing a broad thumb with angulation of the distal phalanx.

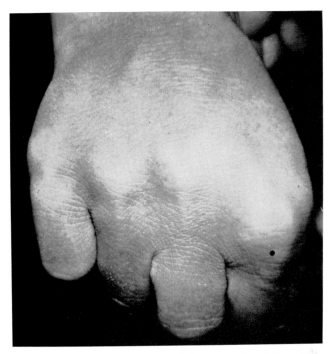

Figure X-3. Hand of a patient with pseudohypoparathyroidism. Note the concave shape of the knuckle line which is secondary to shortening of the third and fourth metacarpals.

when he finds broad thumbs and toes associated with mental retardation and the classical facial appearance.[1]

PSEUDOHYPOPARATHYROIDISM

Pseudohypoparathyroidism is another good example of the patient's hands directing the physician to the proper diagnosis. In this syndrome, usually the fourth metacarpal and sometimes the other metacarpals may be short.[2] When patients with this syndrome make a fist, the knuckle line assumes a concave instead of the normal convex shape due to the shortening of the fourth and third metacarpals (Fig. X-3). This type of hand abnormality, when associated with mental retardation, obesity, rounded facies, short stature and eye abnormalities should help lead the examiner to the proper diagnosis.

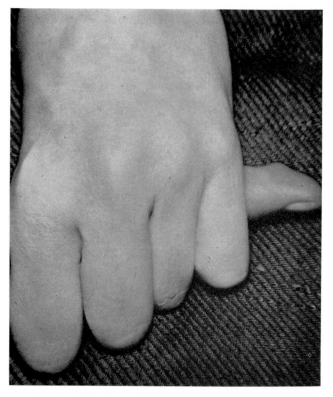

Figure X-4. Patient with Marfan's syndrome and "thumb sign."

ARACHNODACTYLY

The hand can also be helpful in differentiating between two similar, but different syndromes. For example, arachnodactyly is present in both Marfan's syndrome and homocystinuria. However, patients with Marfan's syndrome have hyperextensibility of the fingers while in homocystinuria there is rigidity. Therefore, the thumb sign (extension of the thumb beyond the ulnar border of the hand when a fist is made and the thumb is tucked under the fingers) is present in patients with Marfan's syndrome (Fig. X-4), but not in patients with homocystinuria who have a difficult time in making a fist because of rigidity of the fingers.[1]

MUCOPOLYSACCHARIDOSES

There are many syndromes associated with a short, broad hand and a good example of this would be the hand of the patient with one of the mucopolysaccharidoses such as the Hunter or Hurler syndromes (Fig. X-5). Of course, there are many other features present in this group of syndromes besides the broad hand, but when a patient presents with mental retardation, coarse facial features and broad hands, this syndrome complex should be considered. The Berry spot test is a diagnostic aid in most, but not in all of the patients with the mucopolysaccharidoses.

CHROMOSOMAL ABNORMALITIES

Patients with chromosomal abnormalities associated with mental retardation also have hand malformations.[3] Perhaps best

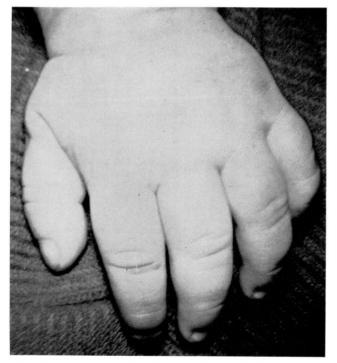

Figure X-5. Broad and short hand of a patient with Hurler's syndrome.

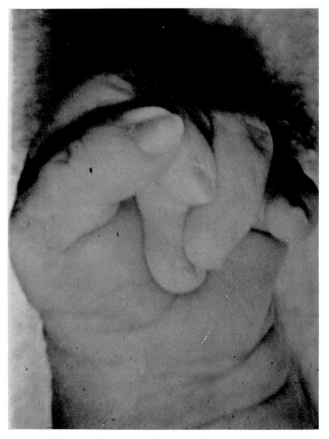

Figure X-6. Hand of a patient with Trisomy 18. Note the overlapping of the second finger over the third.

known is the hand of the patient with Down's syndrome. The hand is short and stubby with clinodactyly of the fifth finger, a missing or short middle phalanx of the fifth finger and a simian line. The physician who rarely sees patients with Trisomy 13 or Trisomy 18 may be helped in differentiating between the two by examining the hand. In Trisomy 13 the fifth finger usually overlaps the fourth, but in patients with Trisomy 18, the second finger usually overlaps the third and occasionally the fifth finger overlaps the fourth (Fig. X-6). Other hand abnormalities present in these two syndromes are hyperconvex nails, polydactyly and flexion deformities of the fingers and wrists. Although mental retardation is uncommon in Turner's syndrome, it is frequently found in Noonan's syndrome. Dorsal edema of the hands (and feet) and dysplastic nails in infancy are important clues to the diagnosis of both syndromes.

SHORT BROAD HANDS

Numerous mental retardation syndromes are associated with short hands and brachydactyly.[4] As mentioned before, patients with most of the mucopolysaccharidoses will have a short hand which is also broad. Because of the shortened metacarpals, patients with pseudohypoparathyroidism also have a short hand. The patient with the Prader-Willi syndrome frequently has short hands plus clinodactyly, short fifth finger, syndactyly and a simian line. Some other syndromes with short hands are cleidocranial dysostosis, Conradi's syndrome, and the Cornelia DeLange syndrome.

NAIL ABNORMALITIES

Dysplastic or dystrophic nails are usually not an outstanding feature in mental retardation syndromes.[4] For example, dysplastic nails may be present in Trisomy 18 but this is certainly not a major feature of the syndrome. There are some syndromes with dysplastic or dystrophic nails in which mental retardation may or may not be present. They include: focal dermal hypoplasia (Goltz's syndrome), nail-patella syndrome, Ellis-van Creveld syndrome and incontinentia pigmenti syndrome. In Trisomy 18, Noonan's syndrome and leprechaunism, mental retardation is usually a constant feature.

Cornelia DeLange syndrome is a classical example of severe mental retardation, a classical facial appearance and various hand abnormalities. These abnormalities include clinodactyly, a short fifth finger, syndactyly, thumb deformities, short metacarpals, "lobster claw" hand, hypoplastic terminal phalanges, and a simian line. Phocomelia is also associated with this syndrome (Fig. X-7).[3]

These are just a few of the many mental retardation syndromes associated with hand abnormalities which serve to illustrate the importance of a careful examination of the hand.

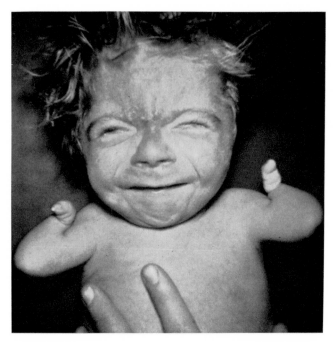

Figure X-7. Classical facial features of the Cornelia DeLange syndrome. Note the phocomelia.

The diagnostic clues gained from such an examination will often lead the physician to the proper diagnosis.

REFERENCES

1. Johnson, C.F.: Abnormal thumbs and physical diagnosis. *Clin Pediatr,* 9: 131:1970.
2. Gellis, S.S. and Feingold, M.: *Atlas of Mental Retardation Syndromes.* U.S. Department of H.E.W., U.S. Government Printing Office, 1968.
3. Smith, D.: *Recognizable Patterns of Human Malformations.* Philadelphia, W.B. Saunders, 1971.
4. Feingold, M.: List of hand abnormalities and syndrome diagnosis. In Gellis, S.S. (Ed.): *Yearbook of Pediatrics.* Chicago, Yearbook Medical Publishers, 1966.

Chapter XI

"SIMPLE" MENTAL RETARDATION

Robert F. Murray, Jr.

USUAL MODES OF INHERITANCE

EVEN after all the best diagnostic methods have been focused on a population of patients who present with mental retardation, at least 75 per cent of them will remain without a specific etiologic diagnosis. Dealing with this group of patients is, to say the least, exceedingly frustrating. In contrast to the very illuminating presentations of specific etiologies of mental retardation in earlier chapters, this chapter will be an attempt at some clarification of the mechanisms of inheritance of mental retardation that can be called "simple," that is, mental retardation uncomplicated by obvious physical abnormalities or detectable cellular or metabolic abnormalities. This discussion will serve, primarily, to demonstrate the tremendous amount of study that is still needed in this field.

The terms "uncomplicated" or "undefined" or "essential" might be more accurate than "simple" since the root causes of the retardation in this undiagnosed group are hardly simple and are probably, at least, as numerous as those already discussed. But for the sake of this discussion accept as the definition of "simple mental retardation" those patients whose only clear phenotype characteristic is the presence of mental retardation in some degree.

This chapter is divided into three parts. Initially it will deal with some of the evidence for the polygenic causes basic for the inheritance of mental retardation. Then there will be a brief review of some studies of "familial retardation" and finally there will be a short presentation of the environmental hypothesis for mental retardation with particular reference to the role of poverty and malnutrition in its production.

POLYGENIC ETIOLOGY OF SIMPLE
MENTAL RETARDATION

A review of the literature since 1963 when the revised and up-dated edition of Penrose's book *The Biology of Mental Defect*[1] was published reveals that very little new information has been contributed in the somewhat gray and nebulous area of hered-itary mental retardation. This is probably a result of the fact that there is still no reliable way to isolate the dual effects of heredity and environment in producing the phenotype men-tal retardation which is being studied and also because of the difficulty in trying to define the phenotype of mental retarda-tion. An exception to this is the study of Huntley.[2] Using the concept of heritability developed by Falconer he has presented estimates of the heritability of general intelligence based on his own data and that obtained from other studies suggesting that verbally determined IQ has a heritability of 60 to 70 per cent. The heritability is that proportion of the variability in IQ ob-served in a population which is under genetic control. Finger-prints which are known to be primarily genetically controlled have a 98 per cent heritability. It is important to note that herita-bility estimates are valid only for the population in which they are determined.

It is commonly assumed that mental retardation is a conse-quence of deficient "general intelligence."[3] This is a concept that is often supposedly measured by one, but should preferably be estimated by several IQ tests. Mental retardation and IQ cannot be equated but are closely associated since there is significant correlation between IQ and classification of individuals into graded categories of mental deficiency by other means.[4] A prop-er estimate of mental retardation involved a clinical evaluation of development, adaptive behavior and intellectual function. Where the clinical estimate of mental retardation is inconclusive, the IQ is usually used to make the phenotype classification.

There is no universally accepted definition of mental retarda-tion. The American Association on Mental Deficiency defines mental retardation as follows:

Mental retardation refers to subaverage general intellectual functioning which originates during the developmental period and is associated with impairment in adaptive behavior.[5]

Other definitions have been proposed, such as the following:
1. The mentally retarded are those who measure approximately 50 to 75 IQ and are in the lowest 2 per cent of the school population in learning ability.[6]
2. Socially incompetent; mentally subnormal; retarded intellectually from birth or early age; retarded at maturity; constitutionally mentally deficient; essentially incurable.[6]
3. Individuals who, for temporary or chronic reasons function intellectually below the average of their peer groups; whose social adequacy is not in question, but if in question there is likelihood that the individual can learn to function independently and adequately.[6]

All these definitions have serious inherent deficiencies which make them unsatisfactory.

For practical purposes mental retardation is often defined by an IQ below 70. In following this definition it is assumed that IQ is normally distributed in the population but in reality, the distribution is skewed to the left. At the extreme negative tail of the distribution is an excess of very low IQ values that comprise that distribution of IQs in the population of mentally retarded individuals with clearly defined organic, metabolic, single gene, or chromosomal causes for their mental retardation and who are, as a result, eliminated from consideration in this discussion.

Despite the shortcomings of IQ tests[6, 7] and the arbitrary nature and inadequacy of using an IQ of 70 to define mental retardation many investigators find it convenient and continue to use it. It is probable that there are subgroups of mental retardation with quite different patterns of disability[4] and as these are more clearly defined this simplistic and inadequate definition of mental retardation currently used will be discarded.

Carter[8] lists four criteria which have been proposed as tests for the polygenic or multigenic hypothesis for the inheritance of a particular common trait.

1. Risks in relatives compared with those of general population would be absolutely greater but proportionately less as the incidence of the abnormality increases.
2. The risk of relatives will vary from family to family. The risk will increase if two affected persons are already in the family.
3. More severe degrees of abnormality carry a higher risk to relatives.
4. An increase in parental consanguinity is expected, since it is a form of assortive mating.

Studies of mental retardation have shown that it fits these criteria. When the frequency of mental retardation among the parents and sibs of individuals with mental retardation is somewhere between 7 and 9 per cent, the frequency among the general population is only 1 per cent.[9] Reed and Reed[10] in a similar study, found a frequency of 12 to 13 per cent.

When the recurrence of mental retardation in specific families is studied,[10] it appears that the union of a normal individual who has one retarded sibling with a normal individual without retarded sibs has a 1.9 per cent risk of producing a retarded child. If the first parent has two or more retarded sibs there is a 3.6 per cent chance of having a retarded child. In other words, the risk of a retarded offspring increases with the number of affected individuals in the family.[10]

Although the severely retarded have *fewer* retarded relatives, that is, a lower frequency of retarded relatives than *higher* grade retardates, they have, *more frequently,* relatives who are *also severely* retarded. That is, severely retarded individuals have severely retarded relatives.

With reference to the fourth category, that of consanguinity, an analysis of the data from Reed and Reed[10] indicates that of 230 families where mental retardation arose from possible genetic causes that could not be related to specific syndromes, 7.4 per cent involved consanguineous matings. This is much greater than the usual 0.05 per cent frequency in the general United States population.

The behavior of mental retardation in families and populations, then, is consistent with that which one would expect in a polygenic or multifactorial trait.

The currently accepted view of the operation of polygenic traits is that the phenotype seen is a composite of the small additive effects of several pairs of genes and the environment. Regression analyses estimating the mental similarity of sibs, half-sibs and cousins have been carried out. The observed mean IQ of those relatives of patients with an IQ of *50 or above* was only 2 points from that which would be expected on the additive gene hypothesis. This hypothesis does not seem to hold for the relatives of patients with an IQ below 50, suggesting that polygenic factors may not be as influential below an IQ of 50.

The number of genes involved is not known, but models postulating five[11] and ten[12] pairs of genes have been proposed and both give rise to theoretical distributions of IQ from 50 to 150 that fit well with curves derived from the population.

Since "general intelligence" and presumably mental retardation is under such complex control there is in this category no *"usual" mode of inheritance* as the title of this presentation implied, rather, there are statistical patterns of occurrence of mental retardation and these are a function of the relatedness of the individuals in question. Hereditary mental retardation with polygenic determinants which occurs more than once in a family, including third-degree relatives, is called *familial*.

SIMPLE MENTAL RETARDATION IN FAMILIES

Familial traits are not always genetic nor are genetically determined traits always familial. But at least mental retardation which occurs in a familial fashion may possibly have significant or major genetic determinants.

The studies of Reed and Reed[10] have shed considerable light on the pattern of recurrence of mental retardation in families. Their data do not define a pattern of inheritance but they do enable workers who are dealing with the families of retardates to give recurrence risks to parents who may already have had a retarded offspring or retarded relatives.

These authors compiled the pedigrees of the descendants of the grandparents of 289 probands with mental retardation beginning with records compiled fifty years before. By collecting school records, IQ scores and occupational data, they determined the mental status of all individuals in the study. One hundred and one (101) of the 289 index cases of probands had mental retardation which clearly fell into the simple or undefined category and was probably genetically determined, but by their criteria 123 were of undetermined origin. These, although they comprise a heterogeneous group of cases, would be counted in this presentation as one of the "simple" or "undefined" or "essential" group of mentally retarded, since it is certainly possible that a large number of such isolated cases were examples of single instances of mental retardation due to polygenic or rare autosomal recessive traits occurring by chance only once in certain families.

From their very extensive data they have developed empiric risk figures for normal couples who have not had any children and for normal and retarded persons with at least one retarded child. Table XI-I shows the risk figures for the former group. Note that when there are no retarded children in the family of Normal X Normal the risk is one-third of that when one parent has one retarded sib and one-sixth of that when one parent has two retarded sibs.

The exceedingly high risk that is found when a normal individual with a retarded sib marries a retardate shows the seriousness of unions with retarded individuals.

Table XI-II shows the marked increase in the risk when a couple has already had one retarded child. When normals with one retarded child have no family history of a retarded sib, their recurrence risk is almost 6 per cent and it is almost 13 per cent

TABLE XI-I

EMPIRIC RISK FIGURES FOR NORMAL PERSONS WHO HAVE NOT
HAD ANY CHILDREN

Type of Union	*Chance That the First Child Will Be Retarded (As a Percentage)*
1. a. Normal (with retarded sibling) × retardate	23.8
b. Normal (with retarded sibling) × normal	
(1) First parent had only one retarded sibling	1.8
(2) First parent had two or more retarded siblings	3.6
2. Normal (with all siblings normal) × normal	0.53

Reproduced with permission of authors and publisher (Reference 10) .

TABLE XI-II

EMPIRIC RISK FIGURES FOR NORMAL OR RETARDED PERSONS
WHO HAVE HAD AT LEAST ONE RETARDED CHILD

Type of Union	Percent Retarded After the First Retarded Child
1. Retardate × retardate	32 out of 76 (42.1%)
2. Retardate × normal or unknown	63 out of 317 (19.9%)
3. Normal × normal	
a. One normal parent had one or more retarded siblings	18 out of 139 (12.9%)
b. All siblings of one normal parent known to be normal	6 out of 104 (5.7%)

Reproduced with permission of authors and publisher (Reference 10).

if one parent has a retarded sib. Unions between one retarded and one normal individual after one retarded child have a 20 per cent risk of recurrence and two retarded parents have a 40 per cent chance of having another retarded offspring.

A vital factor, then, in evaluating the group of patients with "simple" or "essential" mental retardation, involves taking a careful pedigree. It is especially important to get first-hand evidence of normality if at all possible. This latter point has been highlighted by the experience of Wortis.[13] He found that 15 out of 102 sibs of retardates that had been reported in the family history as normal by the mothers were actually retarded when examined. It was later discovered that the mothers did actually recognize the child's mental deficit, but for unknown reasons failed to report it. Under ideal circumstances the sibs of retardates and also of parents should be examined and tested by a professional since in almost all cases the presence of mental retardation in parental sibs is associated with a significant increase in the recurrence risk.

SIMPLE MENTAL RETARDATION AND THE ENVIRONMENT

Among several factors which significantly influence IQ test scores is the socio-cultural-economic situation of the child.[4] Test scores are often depressed in children from deprived socio-cultural environments. The tests are also biased against lower socio-economic class children for they measure performance which is strongly influenced by learning opportunities and experience. The tests measure intelligent behavior not intelligence per se.[14]

Not only cultural but also physical deprivation strongly influences the intellectual development of children. It has been shown that marked protein deprivation can result in speech defects.[15] Studies in rats have demonstrated that undernutrition in the newborn period will produce physical, chemical and functional changes in the brain.[15] Studies of children exposed to severe early malnutrition is associated with perceptual defects. Retardation was seen in other studies of malnourished children but they were inadequately controlled.[15] When there is severe malnutrition in early life, development is retarded but the two have not been conclusively proven to have a cause and effect relationship.

In the group of mentally retarded individuals, the poor, nonwhite and especially the blacks are overrepresented.[6, 16] Most investigators feel that this is a consequence of environmental factors like those mentioned above. The children of these people are more frequently subjected to serious socio-cultural deprivation and malnutrition as well as to other environmental stresses and strains like disease and family instability.

This large group of individuals with high level mental retardation have the same phenotype as individuals with a true primary genetic etiology but it has been estimated that as many as 80 per cent of those with mental retardation at the 50 to 70 IQ level may be victims of environmental deprivation.[6] What is important is that it is possible to treat these individuals by supplying the environmental deficit or removing the environmental stress.

One should not forget that in all genetic conditions, especially those of polygenic causation there is a greater or lesser degree of genetic-environmental interaction. It may be that a certain level of genetic predisposition is required for susceptibility to environmental deprivation. In any event since many factors influence the result of an IQ test a lowered test score should not be equated with lower intelligence.[7] All that appears to be mental retardation is not, and all the factors that influence behavior and test performance should be carefully evaluated. Some education psychologists, for example, feel that the person with an IQ of 60 to 70 probably has an unfavorable social and family environment or may have undesirable emotional traits.

At any rate, it is safer to assign one of the untreatable etiologies, i.e. heredity or brain damage, to a mentally retarded individual only when there is some evidence so that hope is not falsely abandoned for an individual who has socio-culturally determined mental retardation that might respond to some form of intensive psycho-social therapy.

It should be fairly clear that "simple" mental retardation is far from simple. Only the phenotype of this entity is simple. There are a number of possible factors or combinations of factors, the result of which will be mental retardation. Some non-geneticists seem to forget that the genotype of mental retardation is only inferred from an observation of the phenotype. This is true even when one or both parents are mentally retarded. One should also keep in mind the fact that we have little or no idea of the relationship between the phenotype and the underlying genotype not only in mental subnormality but in mental supernormality. One can intelligently discuss the operation of genetic factors in the production of mental retardation in individuals from particular families, but, because of what is known about the operation of genes in man, it is not justified to extrapolate from individual genetic behavior to that in large groups.[9]

PREVENTION OF SIMPLE MENTAL RETARDATION

In recent years some workers[4, 9] have been somewhat reluctantly suggesting again that severely retarded persons be encouraged to have compulsory sterilization. Even if there is adequate scientific evidence for this recommendation there is still a sticky moral-philosophical problem. Their case has some merit since fertile retardates making up 1 to 2 per cent of the total population produce 36 per cent of the retarded individuals of the succeeding generation. It is probably still premature to advocate such sterilization since the severely retarded persons have reduced fertility anyway. It will be necessary to study and understand thoroughly and learn to control for the effects of nutritional and social deprivation on mental development before any serious recommendations can be made along these lines. But, in the meantime, these people can be counseled to have much smaller families and to avoid marrying or mating with individuals with the same problem.

Certainly much of our future research effort could profitably be directed toward unraveling or sorting out the tangled web of causation that hinders our ability to deal constructively with this group of unfortunate people.

REFERENCES

1. Penrose, L.S.: *The Biology of Mental Defect* (2nd ed.). New York, Grune and Stratton, Inc., 1963.

2. Huntley, R.M.C.: Heritability of intelligence. J.E. Meade and A.S. Parkes (Eds.) : *Genetic and Environmental Factors in Human Ability.* London, Oliver and Boyde, Ltd., 1965.

3. Holt, S.B.: Inheritance of dermal ridge patterns. L.S. Penrose (Ed.) : *Recent Advances in Human Genetics.* London, Churchill, 1961.

4. Fraser Roberts, J.A.: Multifactorial inheritance and disease. *Progr Med Genet* 3:188, 1964.

5. Heber, R.: A manual of terminology and classification in mental retardation. *Am J Ment Defic (Supplement),* 3, 1961.

6. Hurley, R.L.: *Poverty and Mental Retardation: A Causal Relationship.* New York, Vintage Books, Random House, 1969.

7. Poser, C.M.: *Mental Retardation: Diagnosis and Treatment.* New York, Hoeber Medical Division, Harper and Row, Inc., 1969.

8. Carter, C.O.: Polygenic inheritance and common diseases. *Lancet,* 1:1252, 1969.

9. Penrose, L.S.: A clinical and genetic study of 1,280 cases of mental defect. *Sp Rep Ser Med Res Comm,* No. 229, London, H.M.S.O., 1938.

10. Reed, E.W. and Reed, S.C.: *Mental Retardation: A Family Study.* Philadelphia, W.B. Saunders Co., 1965.

11. Conrad, H.S. and Jones, H.E.: A second study of family resemblances in intelligence: Environmental and genetic implications of parent-child and sibling correlations in the total sample. *Yearbook Natl Soc Stud Educ,* 39:Part II, 97, 1940.

12. Pickford, R.W.: The genetics of intelligence. *J Psychol,* 28:129, 1949.

13. Wortis, J.: Prevention of mental retardation. *Am J Orthopsychiatry,* 35: 886, 1965.

14. Tredgold, R.F. and Soddy, K.: *Tredgold's Mental Retardation.* Baltimore, Williams and Wilkins Co., 1970.

15. Witkop, C.: Histidinemic-like behavior in children recovered from kwashiorkor. Washington, D.C., Howard University, Conference on the Genetic, Metabolic and Developmental Aspects of Mental Retardation, 1969.

16. Winick, M.: Malnutrition and brain development. *J Pediatrics,* 74:667, 1969.

17. Jensen, A.R.: A theory of primary and secondary familial mental retardation. *Int Rev Res Ment Retard,* 4:33, 1970.

Part II

DEVELOPMENTAL ASPECTS OF
MENTAL RETARDATION

Chapter XII

PERINATAL FACTORS IN THE PRODUCTION OF CEREBRAL DEFICIT

HARRIE R. CHAMBERLIN

A LTHOUGH birth trauma, especially asphyxia, is generally considered to be the primary factor which may produce severe or subtle damage to the central nervous system in the perinatal period, kernicterus, neonatal hypoglycemia, certain viral and bacterial infections acquired at that time and a variety of other perinatal events may also lead to future mental or motor disability. In addition, the immediate postnatal period is a time when a whole host of congenital defects first become evident, some acquired on a hereditary basis, some the result of acquired chromosomal defects, and some the result of agents which have distorted the environment of the developing fetus. In 1953 Dr. Theodore Ingalls[1] of Harvard wrote:

> The nearly insurmountable obstacle in the clinical study of prenatal sickness arises from the fact that the patient voices no complaint, remembers nothing about his illness, hides himself from view, and puts off his visit to the doctor until the last possible moment.

This statement is perhaps not quite so true today, in an age when we are learning to follow the status of selected fetuses by measuring maternal estriol outputs and when the new technique of transabdominal amniocentesis is beginning to make available a whole new approach to fetal diagnosis early in pregnancy. But in spite of these new approaches, Ingalls' statement is valid in most situations, particularly when nothing abnormal has been anticipated. If a pregnant woman develops rubella during the first trimester, it is immediately recognized by her obstetrician that her infant is running a very significant risk of being born with a variety of congenital defects. Yet the other two maternal infections which are universally recognized as capable of producing congenital defects, particularly of the nervous system, namely cytomegalic inclusion disease and toxoplasmosis, almost always go unrecognized in the mother. These maternal infections are thus diagnosed retrospectively. The thalidomide tragedy represents a dramatic example of what Ingalls referred to—some 8,000 infants, primarily in Germany, had been irretrievably damaged by the time the cause of this damage had been thoroughly recognized to end the distribution of the drug.[2]

If we focus, however, on conditions operative primarily in the perinatal period we narrow down largely to trauma, asphyxia, kernicterus, neonatal hypoglycemia and the whole problem of prematurity. The more common signs and symptoms of neonatal asphyxia suggest depression and include lethargy, hypotonia, areflexia, poor sucking, a weak cry and an incomplete Moro reflex. We must recognize, of course, that these signs may merely be the result of a mild excess of maternal anesthesia or even of prolonged labor without clear evidence of asphyxia. On the other hand, the infant whose nervous system has been damaged during the birth process may be hyperirritable, show spasticity with increased reflexes, develop opisthotonus and possibly develop seizures. Again hyperirritability alone does not necessarily indicate that damage has occurred. It is recognized that symptoms of this sort may instead be due to some form of congenital central nervous system defect, to neonatal hypoglycemia, or when they develop in conjunction with a rapid rise in the serum indirect bilirubin level, to kernicterus.

Among the causes of physical trauma at birth (often also associated with asphyxia) are prematurity (with precipitous delivery), breech and other abnormal presentations, hasty extraction (as when the infant is already showing some signs of distress), the use of instruments other than outlet forceps, maternal dystocia and an excessively large fetus. When intracranial trauma of significant degree has occurred in the neonate, this is usually associated with some degree of hemorrhage. Among the hemorrhagic lesions which may occur during the birth process are the following: subdural hemorrhage, which is still relatively common; massive intracerebral hemorrhage, which is usually fatal; subarachnoid hemorrhage, which occurs primarily in prematures; intraventricular hemorrhage, which also occurs primarily in prematures[3] and is usually fatal; subependymal hemorrhage, which is also usually fatal; and multiple, small cerebral hemorrhages, which are seen mainly in full-term infants.[4] Often these lesions will occur in combination. Although the hemorrhage itself, particularly when associated with thrombosis, may lead to severe brain damage or possibly to obstructive hydrocephalus, if the infant survives and there is residual impairment of central nervous system functioning, the impairment is likely due primarily to transient associated asphyxia, as from ischemia arising from the pressure of the hemorrhagic lesion. Ischemic damage to the cerebral mantle in subdural hematoma is a good example of this. Moreover, intraventricular hemorrhage is now considered to be more common than subdural hemorrhage and its genesis is clearly in part related to asphyxia.[5] It is also probably fair to say that for the majority of surviving infants who have acquired brain damage during the birth process, particularly when the damage is merely mild to moderate, anoxia of central nervous system tissue has probably played a greater etiologic role than actual physical trauma.[5]

The conditions which are especially prone to produce asphyxia in the perinatal period include maternal toxemia and other physical disabilities of the mother, premature separation of the placenta, prolapse of the umbilical cord, excessively lengthy general anesthesia, excessively prolonged delivery, and delayed resuscitation, as is frequently seen in prematurity or when there is obstruction of the airway. Significant slowing of the fetal heart rate and meconium staining of the amniotic fluid are signals during the birth process that asphyxia is occurring.

When perinatal asphyxia is severe and prolonged, profound retardation with spastic quadriplegia and microcephaly are likely to result. This asphyxia does not need to occur in the immediate perinatal period. Infrequently it results from a complication which follows the birth process; more rarely it precedes it. A most unusual patient, a female infant followed in the Division for Disorders of Development and Learning in Chapel Hill, is an example of the latter situation. In this case profound developmental retardation resulted from a bee sting. The mother was exceedingly allergic to insect bites and was stung by a common hornet in the eighth month of pregnancy, which had been unremarkable up to that point. She went rapidly into shock, was rushed to a physician's office where she was given epinephrine, and then to a hospital emergency room, where she was deeply cyanotic with almost no blood pressure, but gradually came around with the use of pressor drugs and intravenous fluids. She did not lose her fetus and went on to deliver the baby a month later, under the guidance of an obstetrician in a university hospital, with no evidence whatsoever of perinatal problems. The infant breathed promptly and normally at the time of delivery, but it became evident during the next few days that something was seriously wrong and she gradually developed a picture of spastic quadriplegia, microcephaly and failure to achieve any of the usual developmental milestones. She eventually died of pneumonia at 31 months and the autopsy revealed ulegyria and other findings typical of a past history of neonatal asphyxia.

If one looks retrospectively at children with major degrees of brain damage, particularly if there is significant motor deficit, one is apt to find that prematurity and other obstetrical complications appear to have played an important role in the etiology of many of the cases. The results of a retrospective study of obstetrical factors in 79 cases of cerebral palsy,[6] carried out several years ago in North Carolina, were quite typical of many similar studies. It was found that 39 per cent of the patients had been prematurely born and that 68 per cent of these had had prenatal or perinatal complications. Of the remaining 61 per cent, who weighed over 2500 gm at birth, 51 per cent had had prenatal or perinatal complications. In fact only 29 per cent of all the infants had been neither premature nor had prenatal or perinatal difficulties. Fifty-three per cent of this series were judged to be mentally retarded and it is likely that a far higher proportion of them would have demonstrated subtle mental deficits if more detailed studies had been carried out. Yet in the neonatal period only 13 per cent of the whole series were suspected of having brain damage.

It should be emphasized that the above study involved cerebral palsied persons and that obstetrical factors are generally recognized to play a greater role in the spectrum of etiologies of cerebral palsy than in the etiologies of other categories of developmental defects. The fact that almost four out of ten of these infants were premature speaks to the very important role of that condition. However, when an infant develops poorly following premature delivery or perinatal obstetrical problems, it is most important not to assume automatically that these problems were the cause of the developmental deficit. Often the deficit proves to have been congenital in origin, the underlying etiology, whatever it may have been, having predisposed to prematurity, or to difficult initiation of respiration at birth, or both. One might draw an analogy to the difficulty that the model-T Ford owner might have had years ago in trying to get his car started on a cold morning when one or two of the four sparkplugs were inoperative. The need for resuscitation of an infant at birth is obviously at times due to the presence on a congenital basis of an inadequate nervous system.

Another important observation which was made in the North Carolina study and which is characteristic of similar studies, relates to the fact that only 13 per cent of the infants in this series were suspected in the neonatal period of having any form of brain damage. This underscores the point, which will be amplified later, that it may be most difficult, especially if a detailed neurological evaluation is not done, to demonstrate mild or even moderate degrees of brain damage in the neonatal period. It is actually more the rule than the exception to assume that an infant is going to develop normally when in fact he is not.

The many studies of the incidence of developmental deficits following prematurity show strikingly variable results.[7-12] Part of the discrepancy relates to the above-mentioned situation: although prematurity per se may often be directly responsible for brain damage, often the prematurity and the brain damage detected later appear to be the results of some underlying cause. In addition, the definition of the premature as being any infant born with a birth weight under 2500 gm does not take into account variations in gestational age and in maturity, even when weights are identical. Lastly, follow-up studies on prematures rely on widely differing criteria in the assessment of brain dysfunction.

The findings obtained by Drillien in Edinburgh in a follow-up of forty-nine very small prematures are quite typical.[9] It is generally recognized that the smaller the premature the more likely the possibility of a developmental deficit. In this case infants were chosen whose birth weights were under 1360 gm (3 lb). The study revealed that only 25 per cent of the forty-nine children were managing adequately in a normal school setting. An additional 39 per cent were in special education classes. Of forty-two children tested, 90 per cent had an IQ under 100; 78 per cent of them had developed behavior problems of one sort or another. Among the thirty of the forty-nine children who had siblings, 73 per cent were mentally slower than all of their siblings.

Because prematurity clearly does play a significant role in the production of cerebral deficits, a review of some of its apparent causes is appropriate. They include, on the part of the mother, poor nutrition, poor hygiene, chronic infections, fatigue, an unusually young age, toxemia, hydramnios, high altitude, placental abnormalities and fetal abnormalities. Although infants born of a multiple pregnancy weighing under 2500 gm are generally more mature for their weight than single infants, the multiple pregnancy alone may often predispose to true prematurity. Beyond this list, and many other generally less common etiologies, the cause of premature labor and delivery is unknown in the majority of cases.

It is well known that figures on prematurity rates when compared with socioeconomic status show a relationship between the two.[11, 13] This fact is a major guide for attempts at prevention. Although individual studies give markedly differing premature rates even when the variable of socioeconomic status is relatively controlled, it is unequivocally clear that the mother whose socioeconomic background is low, and who frequently receives either no prenatal care or a minimum of it, has a greater risk of producing a premature infant than does the mother who is carefully followed by an obstetrician.

The cornerstone for the prevention of central nervous system damage at the time of birth is thus a matter of good obstetrical care, in both the prenatal and perinatal periods. Other factors include proper management of hyperbilirubinemia and of neo-natal hypoglycemia,[14] and the recognition, as will be discussed later, of a possibility that neonatal asphyxia and the respiratory distress syndrome may be more closely interrelated than was once thought.

The relatively complete prevention of kernicterus, which once accounted for some 5 per cent of all cases of cerebral palsy, has been a giant step. New approaches, in addition to the well-estab-lished exchange transfusion, are now being made in this dis-ease, including prior desensitization of the mother[15] and the use of light of specific wave lengths which impede the develop-ment of jaundice by promoting the degradation of indirect bili-rubin.[16] It has long been known that certain drugs such as sul-fonamides and vitamin K compete with indirect bilirubin for binding sites on serum albumin and these drugs should hence be avoided or used in only small amounts when indirect bilirubin levels are abnormally high. Increasingly it is being recognized that kernicterus can often be demonstrated pathologically in small prematures who fail to survive, even when indirect serum bilirubins have not surpassed 10 to 13 mg%.[17] The possible roles in such circumstances of anoxia with acidosis, variations in al-bumin binding capacities or other mechanisms remain unclear.

If we extend our efforts at prevention to include prevention of congenital, as well as of perinatally acquired, central nervous system defects, such approaches as family planning and genetic counseling become important. A check for a rise in maternal serum antibody titers to rubella, when indicated, will demon-strate whether or not a mother has actually had rubella during pregnancy if the clinical picture is uncertain. The compilation of high risk rosters based on genetic histories, histories of previ-ous pregnancies and other pertinent data can be helpful in spotting possible difficulty early, this often leading to ameliora-tion, if not prevention, of a specific developmental problem.[18, 19]

An entirely new approach to the prevention of congenital ab-normalities has recently become possible with the advent of techniques for prenatal diagnosis. These involve the study of amniotic fluid cells, which are fetal in origin, obtained on am-niocentesis generally during the fourteenth to sixteenth week of pregnancy, early enough to allow therapeutic abortion.[20, 21] This approach has been used most frequently for the prenatal diagnosis of chromosomal aberrations, particularly of Down's syndrome. With control of high quality, both the fetal sex and karyotype can be determined on cultured and noncultured cells. The prenatal determination of sex alone can greatly enhance genetic counseling with respect to the sex-linked diseases, if specific intrauterine diagnosis cannot be attained. Moreover, specific prenatal diagnosis of a rapidly increasing number of inborn errors of metabolism, when individually sought because of the family history, is now becoming possible, largely through measurement of specific enzyme levels in amniotic fluid cells grown in tissue culture. These methods, which give new precision to genetic counseling, while of tremendous value, do raise many moral and legal considerations with which both individuals and the states must grapple during the coming years. Although this exciting new field does not involve the perinatal period, like the latter it is an area in which the obstetrician and the pediatrician must closely share.

Returning to factors operative in the perinatal period which may lead to cerebral deficits, it is important to review the possible implications of the remarkable work by Dr. William F. Windle of New York University on neonatal asphyxia in the rhesus monkey.[22, 23] His studies, for which he received the Lasker Award,[24] are now well known to many and are concerned with the detailed clinical and neuropathological follow-up of monkeys subjected to carefully controlled asphyxia at the time of birth. He demonstrated that asphyxia of the neonatal monkey for less than seven minutes generally appeared to produce no damage. When asphyxia extended from seven to eleven minutes, the basic neuropathology was limited to certain brain stem centers which are associated with general body sensation and with hearing, but not with vision, primarily the inferior colliculus and certain thalamic nuclei; motor systems were generally spared. Asphyxia of from 12 to 17 minutes produced more profound neuropathology. Despite associated early clinical abnormalities, even some of these monkeys eventually became grossly normal neurologically, although their brains were subsequently shown to be riddled with lesions in the afferent input systems and the more severe cases also showed additional nuclear lesions in the cerebellum, basal ganglia, cerebral cortex and even in the spinal cord in the most severe instances. Although seven minutes of asphyxiation is a long period, it should be recognized that, when an infant with an excessively slow heart rate is delivered, we often do not know how long perinatal asphyxia has lasted prior to the time of birth, even if resuscitation is relatively easy. The fact that many of the monkeys who were asphyxiated for over seven minutes soon appeared neurologically normal may occasionally parallel the apparent normality of many infants when they are finally sent to the nursery after difficulty in resuscitation; it seems possible that this observation may lead to a false sense of security on the part of the physician.

One of the most impressive observations arising from Dr. Windle's studies is that linking the presence of the respiratory distress syndrome in his neonatal monkeys to initial asphyxia. The syndrome developed in thirty-four of sixty-eight, or 50 per cent of the monkeys which had undergone controlled asphyxia at birth; it developed in only four of ninety nonasphyxiated monkeys. Pathological studies on the lungs of the neonate monkeys who experienced the respiratory distress syndrome revealed typical hyaline membranes. It appeared in these studies that the respiratory distress syndrome was an effect of asphyxia neonatorum. Moreover, and most important, when the respiratory distress syndrome did appear, far more lesions were later found in the cerebral cortex. It must be emphasized, however, that despite these statistically significant findings in rhesus monkeys, a causal relationship between perinatal asphyxia and the respiratory distress syndrome in humans is not generally recognized.[25] Several studies,[12, 26] moreover, have shown no increase in the incidence of the developmental deficits which may follow prematurity when the prematurity was also associated with the respiratory distress syndrome.

Also important, among Dr. Windle's findings, is the observation that when the monkeys developed neurological signs, these signs often gradually disappeared within the next year or two, with the occasional exception of mildly impaired manual dexterity and reduced spontaneous activity. Yet Windle's group was surprised to discover that, despite this gradual disappearance of gross neurological findings, on pathological study they found a steady increase in depletion of nerve cell populations in regions that had not been affected by the initial asphyxic insult, a finding that was particularly striking in the third and fourth layers of the cerebral cortex. With reference to this, Windle points out that approximately 1.5 per cent of infants being followed in the Collaborative Perinatal Study of the National Institute of Neurological Diseases and Stroke showed definite neurological abnormality at one year and yet many infants who had deficits persisting during the first year had lost them by four years. He therefore raises the exceedingly important suggestion that, even in the face of diminution or disappearance of neurological signs in these infants, the same neuronal degeneration may continue to occur which he has seen in his monkeys. This hypothesis suggests that the 1.5 per cent of infants with neurological abnormality at one year may still show an abnormal degree of subtle perceptual, perceptual-motor, or integrative dysfunction when carefully tested in early school age, even if their standard neurological examinations are normal. Support for this view appears to be present in certain follow-up studies on perinatal asphyxia which include sophisticated psychological testing,[27, 28] whereas a correlation between perinatal asphyxia and later deficit is often absent when the follow-up evaluation is less intensive.

A half century ago there was a tendency for the lay public and also for many physicians to implicate the birth process automatically as the cause of a large proportion of all cases of cerebral palsy and of otherwise unexplained moderate to severe mental retardation. It is now evident that there are many scores of known causes of mental deficit. With the reasonably good obstetrical care available to most of our population, perinatal factors have more recently been thought responsible for only a tiny portion of all cases of mental retardation, estimated as perhaps 3 per cent in one residential population.[29] It may be, however, that as we intensify our study of the very common broad spectrum of conditions often called "minimal brain dysfunction," "central processing dysfunction," or from the educators' point of view, "specific learning disorders," our ideas on this matter may change. Many of these problems appear to be related to maturational lags and others can be ascribed to subtle congenital defects. Yet the hazards of the birth process may also prove to play a highly significant etiologic role.

This kind of thinking leads to even more unorthodox thoughts. What is our real mental potential? Is the actual level of functioning by each of us well below his original potential? Does this possibly depressed level of functioning result in part from an accumulation of subtle and not-so-subtle insults: genetic, fetal, perinatal and postnatal? It is easy to brand such ideas as absurdly speculative, but many professional persons are beginning to think along these lines and our newer knowledge seems to be pointing increasingly in this direction. Certainly, although there are only shreds of suggestive evidence thus far, ideas of this sort are most provocative.

REFERENCES

1. Ingalls, T.H.: Preventive prenatal pediatrics. *Adv Pediatr,* 6:33, 1953.
2. Joseph, N.C.: Thalidomide and congenital abnormalities. *Dev Med Child Neurol,* 4:338, 1962.
3. Srsen, S.: Intraventricular hemorrhage in the newborn and "low birthweight." *Dev Med Child Neurol,* 9:474, 1967.
4. Dekaban, A.: *Neurology of Infancy.* Chap. 3, Baltimore, Williams and Wilkins, 1959.
5. Tizard, J.P.M.: Indications for oxygen therapy in the newborn. *Pediatrics,* 34:771, 1964.
6. Nebel, W.A. *et al.:* Obstetrical factors in cerebral palsy: A North Carolina Study. *N C Med J,* 23:329, 1962.
7. Harper, P.A., Fischer, L.K. and Rider, R.V.: Neurological and intellectual status of prematures at 3 and 5 years of age. *J Pediatr,* 55:679, 1959.
8. Knobloch, H. and Pasamanick, B.: Prematurity and development. *J Obstet Gynaecol Br Commonw,* 64:729, 1959.
9. Drillien, C.M.: The incidence of mental and physical handicaps in school-age children of very low birth weight. *Pediatrics,* 27:452, 1961.
10. Dann, M., Levine, S.Z. and New, E.V.: A long-term follow-up study of small premature infants. *Pediatrics,* 33:945, 1964.
11. Robinson, N.M. and Robinson, H.B.: A follow-up study of children of low birth weight and control children of school age. *Pediatrics,* 35:425, 1965.

12. Bacola, E. *et al.:* Perinatal and environmental factors in late neurogenic sequelae. *Am J Dis Child,* 112:359 and 369, 1966.
13. Rider, R., Taback, M. and Knobloch, H.: Associations between premature birth and socioeconomic status. *Am J Public Health,* 45:1022, 1955.
14. Greenberg, R.E. and Christiansen, R.O.: The critically ill child: hypoglycemia. *Pediatrics,* 46:915, 1970.
15. Diamond, L.K.: Protection against Rh sensitization and prevention of erythroblastosis fetalis. *Pediatrics,* 41:1, 1968.
16. Behrman, R.E. and Hsia, D.Y.Y.: Summary of a symposium on phototherapy for hyperbilirubinemia. *J Pediatrics,* 75:718, 1969.
17. Gartner, L.M. *et al.:* Kernicterus: High incidence in premature infants with low serum bilirubin concentrations. *Pediatrics,* 45:906, 1970.
18. Oppe, T.E.: Risk register for babies. *Dev Med Child Neurol,* 9:13, 1967.
19. Alberman, E.D. and Goldstein, H.: The "at risk" register: A statistical evaluation. *Br J Prev Soc Med,* 24:129, 1970.
20. Nadler, H.L. and Gerbie, A.B.: Role of amniocentesis in the intrauterine detection of genetic disorders. *N Engl J Med,* 282:596, 1970.
21. Milunsky, A. *et al.:* Prenatal genetic diagnosis. *N Engl J Med,* 283:1370, 1441, and 1498, 1970.
22. Windle, W.F.: An experimental approach to prevention and reduction of the brain damage of birth asphyxia. *Dev Med Child Neurol,* 8:129, 1966.
23. Faro, M.D. and Windle, W.F.: Progressive degenerative changes in brains of monkeys surviving neonatal asphyxia in *Brain Damage in the Fetus and Newborn from Hypoxia or Asphyxia.* Proceedings of a Ross Laboratories Pediatric Research Conference, Las Croabas, Puerto Rico, 1967, p. 24.
24. Windle, W.F.: Brain damage at birth; functional and structural modifications with time. *JAMA,* 206:1967, 1968.
25. Nelson, N.M.: On the etiology of hyaline membrane disease. *Pediatr Clin N Am,* 17:943, 1970.
26. Ambrus, C.M. *et al.:* Evaluation of survivors of respiratory distress syndrome at 4 years of age. *Am J Dis Child,* 120:296, 1970.
27. Schachter, F.F. and Apgar, V.: Perinatal asphyxia and psychological signs of brain damage in childhood. *Pediatrics,* 24:1016, 1959.
28. Graham, F.K. *et al.:* Development three years after perinatal anoxia and other potentially damaging newborn experiences. *Psychol Monographs,* 76:no. 3, 1962.
29. Yannet, H.: Mental deficiency. *Adv Pediatr,* 8:217, 1956.

Chapter XIII

CASTE, CLASS AND INTELLIGENCE

Leon Eisenberg

INTELLIGENCE is that characteristic of the human organism that taxonomists have selected as the designation of its uniqueness by assigning the species name: sapiens. In this era of strife within and between nations, of gross inequities in the allocation of resources within and between nations, of runaway increase in human populations and massive uncontrolled pollution of our biosphere, to call our species "wise" would seem the ultimate irony, perhaps even the revenge of the gods for Linnaeus' hubris. Yet we clearly exceed all other animals in our ability to solve these problems we are willing to put to ourselves. The deficit lies in the one-sided development of that problem-solving capacity; namely an enormous growth in its technological capabilities without a corresponding gain in its social qualities.

The failure of our educational institutions to have devoted equal time to the cultivation of the social roots of intelligence is a consequence of a gross misconception of its nature. Human intelligence is, in fact, a social product; that is, a product of the interaction between men. The misconception of intelligence as an autonomous individual trait has not lacked for leading thinkers to have challenged it; indeed, the challenge goes back at least as far as the French Encyclopedists. But the individualistic view was indelibly impressed upon educational institutions during the period of rapid growth of state supported schools in response to the manpower needs of industrialization. The dominant political model of the nineteenth century depicted national progress as resulting from the venturesome activity of the individual entrepreneur under a government policy of economic laissez faire. This model was given a pseudobiological justification when Spencer, taking from Darwin only the catch phrase "survival of the fittest," managed to misrepresent the very delicate balance of cooperative and competitive factors in ecology as a replica of his own privileged view of society.[1] That philosophy of industrial capitalism-cum-Spencerism continues to influence contemporary child rearing and schooling.

A SET OF PREMISES

Let me at the outset set forth a very different set of premises that I believe are warranted by the available theory and evidence in behavioral science. First, intelligence develops and does not spring forth full blown at the moment of conception. Second, its development is a social process, strictly dependent upon the quality and organization of the human environment in which it evolves. Third, human intelligence is social intelligence; the problems on which it cuts its teeth, the methods it is able to elaborate and the solutions it creates are set by the social context in which they are posed and solved. Fourth, these theses, though academic in phraseology, carry revolutionary implications for social policy. The burden of argument will be their justification.

To say that intelligence develops faces us at once with what is meant by development.[2] The term may be used in a Platonic sense; the changes over the time are seen as the realization of what was immanent from the first; that is, the attainment of an ideal given by the gods or by the genes, as you will. In this sense, there is in fact nothing new between adult and infant, merely the unfolding in the former of that whose essence was already fully present in the latter, much as the opening of a rose from its bud. Such a view is incompatible with the concepts of modern biology.

We can agree that nothing can appear in the adult organism, the capacity for which was not present in its genetic complement by definition. That assembly of genes, while necessary, is not a sufficient condition of development. That is, given an embryo with certain genetic constituents, the transitions that occur over time are dependent on the interactions between those nuclear components and the surrounding cytoplasm of the cell, between the cell and its neighbors, between the organized cell mass of the embryo and its uterine environment, between the uterus and the body fluids of the mother and between the mother and her physical and social environment. At particular stages in the developmental sequence, certain opportunities as well as certain vulnerabilities are present; before that stage they cannot be induced; after it, they cannot be recouped.

The most convenient illustrations of this principle come from experimental embryology. As the optic cups are extruded from the forebrain, they induce, in the overlying ectoderm, the formation of a crystalline lens. If the optic cups are removed before this stage, the lens fails to form; delayed replacement of optic cups from another embryo will not be successful in inducing lens formation if the time lag is excessive.[3] To take another example, the forerunner of the pancreas becomes determined as pancreas only if surrounded by mesenchyme. That is, even though the cells of the pancreatic rudiment have all their genes intact, they will not evolve into mature pancreas without a substance supplied by nonpancreatic tissue. Contrariwise, once the influence has been exerted, pancreatic development continues in the absence of further contact with mesenchyme.[4] At the level of systems, the development of fully mobile joints is dependent upon the random activity of muscles that produce the phenomenon we recognize as fetal movements. The intrauterine injection of curare (which produces paralysis of muscles) into pregnant sheep results in the birth of lambs with ankylosed— that is, frozen joints.[3] Examples need not be multiplied. The point is that development is sequential and interactional or, as Aristotle termed it, epigenetic.

A second premise underlying my argument has even more ancient Greek roots. It is to be found in the Hippocratic dictum that the brain is the organ of the mind. I do not suggest that mind is fully to be explained by brain, but that intactness of brain is a precondition for proper function of mind. Thus, our concern with the development of intelligence must include a concern for the development of brain. Setting aside for the moment phylogenetic considerations, let us consider ontogeny.

THE CASTE STRUCTURE OF SOCIETY

There are many biological factors capable of influencing central nervous system development in the fetus and young organism: time limits us to a few that are particularly salient to contemporary conditions. Complications of pregnancy and parturition (such as toxemia, bleeding and prematurity) are associated with brain defects in children who display clinical disorders that extend from cerebral palsy and epilepsy through mental deficiency and learning disabilities.[5] These "biological" disorders in the mother are class related; the toll increases as the socioeconomic scale is descended. Animal studies provide unequivocal evidence that protein deficient diets during pregnancy and lactation impair fetal and infant development and lead to permanent sequelae in adult life. The offspring of mothers so treated never attain the stature of control foster-reared litter mates, exhibit irreversible metabolic defects, and display impaired learning.[6] Clinical and epidemiological data attest to similar phenomena in infants of malnourished mothers and in infants exposed to the twin evils of malnutrition and infection in the first two years of life; witness the ghastly tragedy that took place in Biafra. Unlike the catch-up that occurs when malnourishment is succeeded by repletion later in childhood, early affliction leads to permanent stunting of stature and performance.[7] Access to food and vulnerability to infection, I need not add, are functions of class and ethnic status. I put *caste and class* because to be poor is not the same as to be black, and to be black and poor is quite different from being white and poor, so one must make these distinctions. Thus the caste structure of society has major consequences for the biological integrity of the children who grow up in it. This is a profoundly important political, as well as a scientific question. The toll is the highest in the underdeveloped nations of the world, but is certainly not insignificant in the United States; the same morally intolerable and technologically inexcusable crippling of children occurs in the underdeveloped areas of so-called "developed" a country as our own. There is no more telling example of the gap between economy and moral development.[8]

Our abbreviated enumeration of the necessities of brain development, however, has only begun. The central nervous system requires far more than protection from injury and adequate nutrition; its structures are critically dependent upon a proper balance between excitation and inhibition for their very maintenance let alone their maturation. The clearest illustration is to be found in the visual system; retina, optic nerve, geniculate body and striate cortex.[9–11] At birth, the retina is already intricately organized. It serves as a visual analyzer; there are cell groups that respond only to horizontal light fronts, others to verticals, still others to obliques, some to fronts moving left to right, others, right to left. Moreover, each eye commands fields of striate cells that it alone can trigger off as well as fields that are bilaterally responsive. Here we have a prime example of apparently autonomous development, for this organization predates visual experience. Yet, and this is its particular salience for my argument, these systems do not persist in the absence of adequate external reinforcement. If one eye of a newborn kitten is deprived of patterned visual input for several months, there is marked shrinkage in the striate fields it is able to excite and the surrender of much of its shared command; these changes persist indefinitely even after all obstruction to vision is removed. These functional changes are accompanied by shrinkage in the cell aggregate of the geniculate body served by that eye. A similar period of restriction later in life has no such effect.

If such processes as sensation and intersensory coordination display exquisite sensitivity to environmental contingencies, we can anticipate that higher order psychological functions will be even more responsive. In all vertebrates that have been studied, rearing in a restricted physical environment—which always involves social isolation as well—results in markedly deviant behavior. Songbirds, which in the wild sing in so species-typical a fashion that their songs identify them as precisely as their morphology, will, if reared in isolated soundproof chambers, emit no more than abortive caricatures of their normal lyric.[12] Dogs so reared fail to solve simple barrier problems, whirl in futile circles and cannot compete against control litter mates reared in domestic environments.[13] In monkeys so deprived, the mechanics of copulation itself, a process one might have supposed to be innate, so fundamental to species survival as it is, becomes an almost impossible enterprise; if successfully impregnated, such females function abysmally in mothering their young.[14]

Evolution trades the security of reflex automatisms in exchange for the selective advantage of initially riskier but ultimately more adaptive learned behavior; this process reaches its apex in man. The human infant is born the most immature of animals with a brain only one fourth its final size. In consequence, the infant is dependent upon adult caretaking for the most prolonged period, but a period during which he is enabled to acquire the behavioral repertoire necessary for successful adult function. Parenthetically, that period is the longer, the more technologically elaborate society into which he is born; culture here has imitated nature.[8] The sensitivity to environmental subtleties, so clearly evident in lower forms, is therefore all the greater in man.

The evidence is clinical rather than experimental but it is compelling in its extent and its consistency. It is reported that King Frederick of Prussia, in his zeal to determine whether the original language of mankind was Hebrew or Greek, ordered that babies be reared in a nursery without any words spoken to them; his linguistic experiment terminated unexpectedly when the babies languished and died. No one would today "deliberately" raise human infants in deprived environments but our consciences are not yet sufficiently nice to keep us from permitting those very conditions to come about by social neglect. Unhappily, therefore, data on the effects of deprivation abound in this age of the great society.

PREVENTION OF STAGNATION IN INFANCY

We have a moral imperative to prevent stagnation in infancy. Infants who are reared in institutions staffed by few and inconsistent caretakers display marked retardation on all indices of physical and psychological maturation.[15] If nutrition and cleanliness are maintained at a higher level but without specific enrichment of adult-infant social interactions, the lag in adaptive behavior continues and results in developmental quotients in the defective range. If these conditions are allowed to persist throughout childhood, the youngsters exhibit the psychological stigmata of mental deficiency and become adults who function as poorly as those with intrinsic brain pathology. It is not known with certainty for how long severe psychosocial deprivation can be tolerated by the organism before the functional retardation becomes irreversible. Rapid and apparently complete recovery can occur following adoption into family life by the end of the first year.[16] Similarly gratifying results were obtained in the Skeels study by nursery school enrichment and home placement in the fourth year of life.[17] Other reports have been less sanguine.[18] The earlier the rescue and the more complete the restitutive measures, the better is the outcome. We have a moral imperative to prevent stagnation in infancy but we have no less a responsibility to continue efforts at resurrection for the older victim; lest we condemn tens of thousands of children, we dare not draw unwarranted inferences about irrecoverability on the basis of ethological concepts of critical periods valid for some species but not yet established for man.

Extremity of neglect with its inexorable consequences is of course the limiting case. It obtains for only a minority of children, though it should not be tolerated for a single child, given the means and the knowledge we have at hand. Epidemiologically, the major problem is far larger numbers of children who experience psychosocial deprivation in lesser degree than the orphanage prototype, but to an extent sufficient to impair developmental acquisition of the full range of cognitive abilities. These are the children of the poor, particularly those of low status ethnic groups. In the United States, those at greatest hazard are the black, the American Indian, the Mexican and the Puerto Rican, but serious risk is present for Appalachian and other whites in isolated pockets of poverty. Without exception, comparative studies of academic achievement find the children of the poor scoring far less well than their middle class age mates, with the children of the black poor doubly disadvantaged.[19] The gap in school performance becomes progressively greater with ascending age and reaches a crescendo in high percentages of dropping out of school, subsequent unemployability and what society labels as social deviance. It has been fashionable since at least the time of Herbert Spencer to ascribe these social class discrepancies to differences in biological fitness induced by assortative mating of the less capable.

Jensen, writing from California, and the physicist Shockley, also speaking from California, a favorite place these days for this viewpoint, concluded that, in fact, there are primarily genetically determined differences in intelligence between the races and that we ought to face this "fact."[20] This theory has the peculiar virtue of at once allowing those of us who have made it to glory in our superiority and at the same time of justifying economies in social welfare and educational measures on the ground that we deal with inherent and irremediable defects. What has happened, by the use made of the educational and material resources of this society, is that on the basis of depriving the blacks of the same opportunities the whites have, one then gets the blacks to the point where they test less well than the whites and then one uses the fact that they test less well to justify what one has done in the first place. One has a beautiful circular situation in which the evidence is always interpreted according to the belief of the person doing the interpreting. This belief persists, perhaps for these self-serving rationalizations, despite the progressive amassing of evidence that the most parsimonious explanation of these differences lies in social experience and that programs of early enrichment minimize, if they do not completely eliminate, the disadvantages associated with low caste.[21]

Unless there are changes in teacher attitudes, we can anticipate no benefit in the school system at all. The Rosenthal study indicates that the expectation of the teacher is a major variable in controlling the behavior of the children. American school teachers, black as well as white (that is one of the sad parts about it), expect very little from black children and get very little from black children. Our studies of psychological attitudes, among black teachers as well as white teachers in the ghetto, indicate a prevalence of extremely authoritarian, extremely restrictive, extremely limited attitudes. Perhaps the greatest curse of racism in its entirety is that the black population has been infected with the same kinds of negative ideas that are prevalent in the white culture.

There are, at best, low correlations between academic scores and professional peer ratings later in life. If you used the WISC IQ to predict which kid could survive living in a poor inner city neighborhood, you might well have a negative order of correlation. My child who had a "good" score on that test, and did well in school, and managed to get along in a quiet suburban part of the city in which I live (shaded, with nice policemen and protected from violence) just would not have made it had he grown up with the same traits in the ghetto; capacity to learn under conditions of extreme stress is not measured by any of the standard tests.

The "intelligence" displayed by the members of hunting and gathering societies is different from, but not necessarily inferior to, our own. This can be illustrated by a story that Nissen, the psychologist, tells of his experience on a visit to Africa, in the thirties, to study the social behavior of the chimpanzee. He had been ill advised and he arrived in the village which was to be his base during the rainy season. While he waited for the rainy season to end, being an ingenious psychologist, he decided to do some testing of the people who lived in the village and so gave them a series of performance tests which required matching geometric patterns. What he found was that the natives in this village did much worse than the American norms. When the rain stopped Nissen began to look for chimpanzees. The first day his guides took him right to where the chimpanzees were. The second day they took him to a different place and also on the third day, but each day to the chimpanzee colony.

He got increasingly curious because he did not see a thing until he was suddenly in the area where the chimpanzees were. "How do you know?" he asked. They looked at him and said the equivalent of "Man, where have you been?" "Now look at that branch that's turned a little to the side, and you see that little dropping, and you see that leaf." They had been alert to a number of aspects of the environment which had adaptive value for them to learn but that he could not see, and, in fact, never learned to see and did not have to because he had somebody who could take him where he had to be. These "natives" perform poorly when given tests of abstract geometric ability but succeed admirably in tracking animals in the wilds, a test most of us would fail (though no Australian or African Binet has yet bothered to standardize it as a basis for arguing the genetic inferiority of Caucasians).

The social invention which distinguishes man qualitatively from all other animals, his capacity for language, is a common discovery of all known human societies. Each healthy member of any given society is capable of learning any other language, at least if exposed to it early enough in life. Since only man has language, the capacity for language learning is genetic; what language is learned and how well it is learned is a function of individual social experience. The very possession of language—that is, symbols manipulated by rules of syntax—represents a high order of ability at abstraction. To be handicapped in social function by language impoverished in its vocabulary and its adherence to the grammatical rules of the standard-setting group in society is to suffer severe handicap indeed.

The problem really is that children from many black homes come to school with different language. Different is interpreted, usually, as meaning inferior. There is no evidence at all, although it is an investigatable question, that this language, in fact, fails in any way to convey any of the subtle nuances of information that are required in the context in which it is used; in fact, it is quite good in conveying information between two black "co-conspirators" with a white person present who misses all of the meaning in the conversation. In fact, it is extremely socially effective. The conversations that occur when blacks are together take on a very different tenor when a white enters, unless he is an unusually trusted individual. It is a language that is markedly varied, extremely subtle, has all the elements in it that exist in the standard language. The fact that the grammatical forms are different does not mean that the ability of that syntax to convey meaning is in any way inferior.

Then, should one teach ghetto children in ghetto language and sort of figure that is the end of it? I would suggest not, because since the blacks are some 10 per cent of this American population, and since the wealth and power are controlled by the whites who insist that you understand the white language to succeed, the task is to make black children bilingual. I would suggest that the task is to make white children bilingual, too. Black language is, in fact, enriching white. It reflects new nuances that develop with different social contacts.

The major barrier to healthy development in minority groups is racism. Its primary victims are the ethnic minorities who suffer physical insult and psychological assault. But those who are prejudiced and those who tolerate prejudice undergo a warping of their own psychological development, based as it is on a spurious sense of superiority. It rends nations in two and eats into the very fabric of the entire culture. The American crisis of race does not need recounting here; unhappily, racism is not a unique American phenomenon. Its most virulent public proclamations may be found in South Africa and Rhodesia but rare indeed is the nation that is free of it. Witness the antisemitism in Poland, the savageries against the Ibos in Nigeria, the restrictive immigration laws in England. Here again, we who as professionals see the evil consequences of prejudice for oppressor as well as oppressed have a moral imperative to speak out, however unwelcome the message may be and whatever the personal consequences.

The biosocial and psychosocial factors are intertwined with racism. The intolerable burdens are multiplied by the housing ghettos, the employment barriers, the lower pay scales for those who are employed and the barrage of psychological insult directed against those who are visibly different. Given the greater biological hazards and the cultural differences that make it very difficult to attain economic success, in a society where the amount of money you have determines how "good" you are, the further assault of a dominant culture that systematically degrades the characteristics that establish one's identity make the task of growing up whole a particularly difficult one for a black child. If one is to obtain a sense of potency, namely a conviction that one is a real man or a real woman, one has to believe that his own efforts will be able to determine his own destiny. How can you attain a feeling of personal confidence of your skin color, if you are black; of automation, if you are unskilled; of illness, when you are denied medical care; of false imprisonment, if you cannot get a lawyer; all issues beyond personal control, destroy your job, your savings, your dreams, no matter how hard working and how diligent you are?

I would suggest to you that there is one antidote that may

serve as a soul-saving measure, even while the major struggle for human dignity is being fought, and that antidote, though it is one not without toxicity, is pride in race. We have begun to observe the growing strength in the United States of the movement that asserts that black is beautiful and that African culture is better than Western. United by common beliefs, black communities have begun to assert the rights of local control in policing, business interests, schooling and urban planning. There is in my mind no question that all of this is a distinct psychological gain for the black *and for the white community* as well. Whether it will succeed politically is still an open question.

When we turn to the public school crisis, we find the movement for local autonomy confronted by the vested interest in job and tenure of the educational establishment from the most underpaid teacher to the most prestigious school board member. Mechanisms to enable local control and job security both to survive remain to be invented. In essence, the black community confronts us with these incontrovertible facts. Integration has not moved forward in a meaningful fashion in the twelve years since the Supreme Court decision. Black children will fall by the academic wayside. Could black run schools do worse? I do not believe so. Successes have been attained by street academies established by militant volunteers.

There is, as I see it, good reason to support "black power" from the strictly self-advantage of the whites. Black power accepts the segregated housing patterns in school districts as unavoidable phenomena of the near future. Nothing is going to change that within the next decade, even if this country had a commitment to do so, which it does not. At least some of the spokesmen for black control anticipate the time when reunion and reintegration will be possible once the blacks have obtained political power as attested by the history of each of the immigrant groups of these shores. Will this prove to be true? It is the more likely to be true the greater the commitment of professionals to its success. For those of us who are psychiatrists and psychologists, it will provide a unique opportunity to study the interaction between self-concept and personal development, if we make ourselves available to these new schools as contributors to their growth and investigators of the progress to their pupils. From the black power leaders, we will want to learn even as we teach. It is imperative that we abandon our pretentions of arrogance as standard bearers, that we become active participants and not pose as "neutral" scientific observers.

I do not suggest that these goals are easily attained or that no other significant problems remain. Indeed, history teaches us that each solution brings new challenges in its wake. There is no final state of grace. It is in the very process of striving for social betterment that man makes himself more human. A century ago, Frederick Douglas, a courageous black American who escaped from slavery to become a leader in the movement for the abolition of bondage, wrote: "Without struggle, there is no progress." I call upon you to join in that struggle in the name of children everywhere.

REFERENCES

1. Spencer, H.: *Social Statistics*. London, Williams and Norgate, 1902.
2. Eisenberg, L.: Clinical considerations in the psychiatric evaluation of intelligence. In Zubin, J. and Jervis, G.A. (Eds.): *Psychopathology of Mental Development*. New York, Grune and Stratton, 1967.
3. Coulombre, A.J.: Steps in embryonic development: Some implications for developmental pharmacology in drugs and poisons in relation to the developing nervous system. Public Health Service Publication No. 1791. Washington, U.S. Department of Health, Education and Welfare, 1967.
4. Grobstein, C.: Cytodifferentiation and its controls. *Science*, 143:643-650, 1964.
5. Pasamanick, B. and Knobloch, H.: Retrospective studies in the epidemiology of reproductive casualty. *Merrill-Palmer Quart Behav Dev*, 12: 7-26, 1966.
6. Chow, B.F., Blackwell, R.Q. and Sherwin, R.W.: Nutrition and development. *Borden Review*, 1968.
7. Cravioto, J. *et al.*: Nutrition, growth and neurointegrative development. *Pediatrics*, 38:319-372, 1966.
8. Eisenberg, L.: A developmental approach to adolescence. *Children*, 12: 131-135, 1965.
9. Wiesel, T.N. and Hubel, D.H.: Effects of visual deprivation on morphology and physiology of cells in the cat's lateral geniculate body. *J Neurophysiol*, 26:978-993, 1963.
10. Hubel, D.H. and Wiesel, T.N.: Relative fields of cells in striate cortex of very young, visually inexperienced kittens. *J Neurophysiol*, 26:994-1000, 1963.
11. Wiesel, T.N. and Hubel, D.H.: Single cell responses in striate cortex of

kittens deprived of vision in one eye. *J Neurophysiol,* 26:1003-1017, 1963.

12. Thorpe, W.H.: The ontogeny of behavior. In Moore, J.A. (Ed.) : *Ideas in Modern Biology.* New York, Natural History Press, 1965.

13. Melzak, R.: Effects of early experience on behavior. In Hoch, P.H. and Zubin, J. (Eds.) : *Psychopathology of Perception.* New York, Grune and Stratton, 1965.

14. Harlow, H.F. and Harlow, M.K.: The effectional systems. In Schrier, A.M., Harlow, H.F. and Stollnitz, F. (Eds.) : *Behavior of Non-Human Primates, Vol. II.* New York, Academic Press, 1965.

15. Dennis, W. and Najarian, P.: Infant Development Under Environmental Handicaps. *Psychol Mongr,* 71 (7) , 1957.

16. Sayegh, Y. and Dennis, W.: The effects of supplementary experience upon the behavioral development of infants in institutions. *Child Dev,* 36:81-90, 1965.

17. Skeels, H.H.: Adult Status of Children with Contrasting Early Life Experiences. *Monogr Soc Res Child Dev,* Serial #105.31 (#3) , 1966.

18. Goldfarb, W.: Emotional and intellectual consequences of deprivation in infancy. In Hoch, P.H. and Zubin, J. (Eds.) : *Psychopathology of Childhood.* New York, Grune and Stratton, 1965.

19. Eisenberg, L.: Reading retardation: 1. Psychiatric and sociologic aspects. *Pediatrics,* 37:352-365, 1966.

20. Jensen, A.R.: How much can we boost IQ and scholastic achievement? *Harvard Ed Rev,* Vol. 39, No. 1, Winter, 1969.

21. Eisenberg, L.: Social class and individual development. In Gibson, R.W. (Ed.) : *Crosscurrents in Psychiatry and Psychoanalysis.* Philadelphia, J.B. Lippincott Co., 1967.

Chapter XIV

THE DISADVANTAGED CHILD: HIS CULTURAL MILIEU AND EDUCATION

CLIFTON R. JONES

FOR more than fifteen years the education of disadvantaged youth has received more attention then perhaps any single problem in American education. During this period the Department of Education of practically every large city has established or experimented with some special program designed to raise the level of achievement of children from slum neighborhoods and to motivate the children to raise their aspirations to levels more consistent with the American ideal. Typical of these programs are the Higher Horizons Program of New York City, the Banneker Project of St. Louis, Project Mission in Baltimore and the Cardozo Project of Washington, D.C.

The education of disadvantaged youth has engaged the attention of both public agencies and private foundations, public school systems, and colleges and universities. Not the least of those committed to alleviating the problem is the Federal Government. During the past five years the Federal Government, through the United States Office of Education, has spent more than 4.5 billion dollars on the education of disadvantaged youth, under provisions of the various titles of the National Defense Education Act of 1964 and its numerous amendments since that time. This does not include appropriations for Head Start, administered by O.E.O., Title III Programs, under which disadvantaged youth obviously would benefit, or the Teachers Corps. Although this might appear to be an enormous sum, it falls far short of the amount needed to make any significant reduction in the problem.

How can we account for this concern over the education of the disadvantaged? The problem is certainly not a new one. As a matter of fact the problem has always been with us. However, it never reached the proportions that it has reached since World War II. The enormity of the problem was occasioned by a number of factors, including the general increase in school enrollment due to the increased birthrates during the War years and continuing thereafter. This increased enrollment resulted in a generally overcrowded condition in practically all schools, especially in urban schools. Teachers who were once tolerant of the few students in their classes who were not doing well, who appeared to be listless, who were frequently absent or who were serious disciplinary problems now seemed to be overwhelmed by the proportion to which these problems had grown. Moreover, it was apparent that these problems were concentrated in certain areas or neighborhoods—the slums and ghettos of the cities and the "pockets of poverty" in the rural areas.

In the urban centers, especially in the North, Mid-West and Far-West, the problem was further intensified by the immigration of hordes of rural parents—primarily Negro—and their children.[1] In many instances the children were already two or more grades behind for their age; as products of inferior rural schools they were unable either to keep up or catch up. Hence, the sheer weight of numbers of disadvantaged youth demanded that the education of this segment of the population be given serious attention.

In 1965 it was estimated that the disadvantaged youth in large urban centers such as New York, Philadelphia, Chicago, Baltimore, Washington and Detroit are 20 per cent of the total school enrollment, and in some instances it reached as much as 30 per cent.[2] Since 1965 there are reasons to believe that the proportion of disadvantaged has increased significantly, to as much as 40 per cent. No school system can afford to have 40 per cent of its enrollment fail or become dropouts. Neither can we as a nation, as a matter of national self-interest, afford to permit this to happen. If we assume a normal distribution of intelligence among the disadvantaged as in other segments of the population, however intelligence may be defined, each year we would be losing 20 per cent of persons of superior ability—the scientists, scholars, technicians, engineers, professionals and artists.

WHO ARE THE DISADVANTAGED?

Formulating a definition of disadvantaged youth is a difficult task. In the first place, disadvantage is a relative rather than an absolute condition, as Havighurst[2] suggests. Secondly, the definition depends upon the context in which the term is used. For those who regard disadvantage as a product of inadequate income, the term economic disadvantage is most frequently used. For those who view disadvantage primarily as a result of the deprivation of those cultural experiences to which every boy or girl "ought" to be exposed, the term cultural disadvantage or cultural deprivation is used. In reality the two are interdependent. Hence, any realistic definition must include both.

For our purposes, disadvantaged youth are those children of all ages: a) whose parents or guardians by virtue of inadequate income are unable to provide for their children the basic necessities of life above the minimum required for health and decency; b) who cannot afford to provide for their children adequate reading materials such as a daily newspaper, a weekly news magazine and children's books, to broaden their knowledge and stimulate their imagination; c) who cannot afford the price of admission to cultural events such as concerts and art exhibits; d) who, because of a lack of knowledge of and experience with these aspects of culture, do not encourage an appreciation for them in their children; and e) whose own low levels of educational achievement are inadequate to supplement the processes of formal education in which the child participates in the school. From the very beginning of the school experience, the disadvantaged child is handicapped in competition with children from homes where these disabilities do not exist.

The size of this segment of the population, by whatever standards poverty is measured, is shockingly large, numerically and proportionately. More specific data point up the enormity of the problem. Since poverty and cultural disadvantage are interdependent, we may use poverty as an index to the size of the problem. Without discussing the merits or demerits of the choice let us assume the poverty level as 3000 dollars annual income. Of the 46.3 million families in the United States in 1961, 21 per cent had an income of less than 3000 dollars. Of the total number of families, 27.6 million (60 per cent) had children, and 26.2 million (57 per cent) had children who were under eighteen years old.

Of the 26.2 million families with their own children, 4.2 million (16 per cent) were living in poverty. In addition there were about 500,000 families with related but not own children, of whom 36 per cent were living in poverty. In other words, a total of 4.7 million families with children were living in poverty in 1961.

It has been estimated that the children of the poor number nearly 16,000,000.[3] On the basis of this estimate "about one-fourth of all children under eighteen years of age are growing up in families whose incomes are clearly inadequate to meet their basic needs."[4]

With respect to race, in 1961 47 per cent of Negro families were living in poverty as compared with 14 per cent white. In other words, the rate of poverty among Negroes is almost three and a half times as high as the rate among whites.

Analysis of the data by race, region, rural or urban residence is even more revealing.

1. Of the 23,263,000 white families with own children in 1960, 3,145,-000 (14%) were classified as poor. Some 2,364,000 poor families (11% of all white families with own children) had a male head. Of these latter, 953,000 (6% of the total) were urban and 1,411,000 (21% of the total) were rural; 370,000 were urban South and 583,000 were urban non-South; 741,000 were rural South and 670,000 were rural non-South.

2. A total of 1,394,000 white families with own children in 1960 were headed by a female of which 790,000 (57%) were classified as poor. Of the 1,085,000 urban white families headed by a female, 580,000 (53%) were poor; and of the 309,000 rural white families with a female head, 210,000 (68%) were poor. Of the 278,000 urban South white families with a female head, 163,000 (59%) were poor; and of the 807,000 urban non-South white families with a female head, 417,000 (52%) are poor. Of the 134,000 South white rural families with a female head, 100,000 (75%) are poor; and of the 175,000 white non-South rural families with a female head, 110,000 (63%) are poor.

The contrast between Negro and white families with own children is striking. Yet, the story is a familiar one.

3. Of the 2,398,000 Negro families with own children in 1960, 1,124,-000 (47%) were classified as poor.

4. There were 1,901,000 Negro families with own children with a male head of which 723,000 (38%) were classified as poor. This contrasts with 11 per cent of white families with a male head classified as poor.

5. Of the total Negro families with own children with a male head, 1,388,000 were urban, of whom 374,000 (27%) were poor and 513,-000 were rural, of whom 349,000 (68%) were poor.

6. Of the 589,000 urban South Negro families with a male head, 240,000 (41%) were poor; 799,000 were urban non-South, of whom 134,000 (17%) were poor. Of the 433,000 rural South families with a male head, 319,000 (74%) were poor; and of the 80,000 rural non-South families with a male head, 30,000 (38%) were poor.

7. A total of 497,000 Negro families with own children had a female head. Of these, 401,000 (81%) were poor. This contrasts with 57 per cent of white families with a female head classified as poor.

8. Of the total Negro families with own children, 413,000 were rural, of whom 75,000 (89%) were poor.

9. There were 182,000 of these families in the urban South, of whom 156,000 (86%) were poor, and 231,000 in the urban non-South, of whom 170,000 (74%) were poor.

10. Of the 84,000 rural Negro families with a female head, 73,000 were in the South, of whom 66,000 (90%) were poor; and 11,000 were outside the South of whom 9,000 (82%) were poor.

Although the data included here are for 1961, there is no reason to assume that there has been any significant downward trend in the figures. To the contrary, 1971 data are likely to show a significant increase in each category in 1971, in view of a slowdown in the economy during the past two years and widespread unemployment.

It is these families, white and Negro, which produce the vast majority of the disadvantaged youth of our country. The statistical data reveal that while Negroes constitute slightly more than 10 per cent of the total population, they contribute more than a third of the estimated 18,000,000 disadvantaged youth. However, it should also be noted that, numerically, the number of white disadvantaged youth is considerably greater than the number of Negro disadvantaged youth.

THE CULTURAL MILIEU OF DISADVANTAGED YOUTH

Poverty is the condition into which the disadvantaged child is born and in which he develops. It is evident in the home, in the institutions with which he is likely to have most of his contacts, in the patterns of behavior to which he is exposed, many of which he acquires, and it influences the interaction which occurs between himself and those who are not poor. It is not intended to suggest here that poverty per se determines the nature of the organization within a given family, or that children of the poor cannot rise above their condition, or that they cannot aspire to positions of wealth, power, influence or high academic achievement. There are too many individual cases that refute this position. However, poverty is a disabling factor, a handicap far too great for any considerable number of the poor to overcome.

Although there are wide variations in family structure and function among the poor, it is to be observed that within this segment of the population there is a considerable degree of family disorganization. The "ideal" family in American society consists of two parents and their child/children, and they occupy a single dwelling unit. As a general rule, the father is the head of the family and the major "bread winner." Within the family, presumably, there is a more or less well-defined division of labor and differential status among family members. Although there are many variations from this ideal which are commonly accepted, particularly with the increased gainful employment of wives and mothers outside the home, any modification of family structure and function is always compared with this ideal type. It is the conception of this ideal type which is passed on from generation to generation and becomes a basis for comparison of the condition that exists in the family, individually or institutionally. Hence, separation, divorce and desertion are deviations from the ideal and are regarded as overt evidence of family disorganization.

Among the poor, rates of separation and desertion are high, and many children of the poor are brought up in homes with only one parent, usually the mother. There is not always a plausible explanation of where the other parent, usually the father, is. The disproportionate number of female heads of families among the poor imposes a burden on them of being breadwinner, homemaker and the center of authority. By virtue of poverty they are not likely to assume these functions successfully. In addition, a considerable number of female heads of families are unwed mothers. In these latter instances the child begins life not only with the handicap of poverty but with social stigma as well.

It goes without saying that the poor are unable to afford adequate housing. The dwelling units which they inhabit are marked by physical deterioration. The tenements which they occupy are below the minimum standards of health and safety; the neighborhood is characterized by filth and community neglect. Too often single dwelling units are occupied by two or more persons per room, and there is a minimum of privacy both within the family and between families.

Of greater importance than the physical characteristics of the home and the neighborhood in which the disadvantaged child lives are the patterns of behavior which he observes and acquires. Language is one of the first of these patterns of behavior which he acquires and it has a meaning which cannot be overemphasized.

The child's first contact with language is in the home. He acquires it from his parents, siblings and others who have contact with him there. The parents of the disadvantaged child are uneducated themselves and have a limited vocabulary. They have a limited knowledge of the formal rules of grammar and how to apply them. Conversations, more often than not, are carried on in monosyllables. The infrequent use of adjectives or adverbs is marked. And the narrow range of topics of conversation proscribe the world which the child can learn about vicariously. Whatever the limitations, this is the content of the language as he learns it, and as he speaks it in the family, in the neighborhood and in the school.

In addition to his learning about things through the language his parents use with him, language also reflects their attitudes which, in turn, are acquired by the child. Both points are dramatically illustrated by Havighurst[2] in his description of two mothers explaining the same event to their children. The mothers want to teach their children to sit properly on a bus seat, while the bus starts and stops suddenly:

Case A

Mother: Hold on tight to your seat.
Child: Why?
Mother: Hold on tight.
Child: Why?
Mother: You'll fall.
Child: Why?
Mother: I told you to hold on tight, didn't I?

Case B

Mother: Hold on tightly, darling.
Child: Why?
Mother: If you don't you will be thrown forward and then you'll fall.
Child: Why?
Mother: Because if the bus stops suddenly you'll jerk forward and bump against the seat in front.
Child: Why?
Mother: Now hold on tightly, darling, and don't make such a fuss.

The first thing that strikes the observer of these two cases is that the mother in Case A does not try to explain to the child. If this situation occurs again and again, the child may lose the habit of asking *why?* The next thing is that the vocabulary in Case A is more restricted than in Case B. Thus the child does not get practice in extending his vocabulary. Perhaps the next thing that will be noticed is that there is a difference in the relation *between* child and mother in the two situations. In Case A the mother asserts her authority through categorical statements. She does not really try to explain why the child should hold on tight, but *orders* the child to do so. The mother's authority is invoked almost at once, with the result that the natural curiosity of the child is pushed back, and the child is learning not to think for himself. In Case B the mother attempts to satisfy the child's curiosity with explanations. Although she finally resorts to authority, she had first given the child a chance to learn about the world in a relationship which permits him to challenge authority with questions.

"The child who experiences language and social relations of Case A during his early years is likely to develop a different kind of mind than the child who experiences language and social relations of Case B. The child in Case A is socially disadvantaged when compared with the child in Case B."[2]

Language consists of more than the formal rules of grammar and their correct usage. In the organization of our curricula it consists also of literature, beginning in the lower grades with Mother Goose stories, fables, Greek and Roman myths and advancing to ancient and modern literature in all its forms up to the present time. This requires reading. As a matter of fact, one of its functions is to teach reading. Reading is not a skill that the child acquires in school only, nor to be used there exclusively. It is facilitated when the child is read to, when he observes that his parents read frequently and when reading matter is available for him to read. In the family of the disadvantaged child the parents are not likely to read to him; they are poor readers themselves; and there is little reading matter in the home, possibly not even a daily newspaper. Indeed, reading may be discouraged for it may be regarded as a waste of time. Since the child's reading is largely limited to what he does in school, he is likely to be a poor reader.

The disadvantaged child grows up in a world where there is a fear of the law, but hardly a respect for it. He hears adults curse the police, boast of what they will do if the police threaten them. Yet he sees arrests made frequently. He sees the police abuse their authority and bully his friends, his parents or other adults. He soon learns that he has no protection *from* the law. If he should run afoul of the law his guilt is assumed; hence the rate of convictions following arrest is considerably higher for the disadvantaged than for any other class in society.[5] One of the reasons for the high rate of convictions is because these people are too poor to afford competent legal counsel. In any case, this is not a healthy situation from which the child can acquire the approved image of respect for the law and law enforcement officials.

The disadvantaged child grows up in a world in which physical violence occurs with considerable frequency. He experiences it in the home and in the neighborhood. Differences of opinion are settled by physical force or threats of physical force. The major proportion of crimes in the ghetto are crimes against persons.[6] Physical force, then, becomes a pattern of behavior which the disadvantaged child learns to use both defensively and offensively.

Recreation rates high in the value system of American society. We spend billions of dollars annually on amateur and professional sports, music, the theatre, the dance, public and private entertainment. Only a small proportion of the total is spent on recreation for the disadvantaged.

In the neighborhoods where the disadvantaged live, play space is severely limited. The child is forced to play in the streets, which incidentally is prohibited by law unless streets are roped off for this purpose. Playgrounds are often too far away to be accessible to the smaller children. Playground equipment is inadequate for all but a small proportion of the total who would want to use it. Playgrounds are understaffed; hence, a great deal of play goes unsupervised. When disadvantaged children venture forth from their limited world in legitimate search for recreation and play in the world of the middle class they are made to feel unwanted.

This brief description by no means includes all of the cultural milieu in which the disadvantaged child develops. However, it does suggest the source of the patterns of behavior which disadvantaged youth acquire. These patterns of behavior have survival value for him within his own neighborhood, but they bring him into conflict with the larger world outside the ghetto where the accepted and approved cultural patterns are different. Yet he is expected to adjust to them. Even though he is introduced to this world early in life, he is taught, consciously and unconsciously, by members of his own world and by members of the other world, that he is different, and different means inferior.

These attitudes are expressed in different ways, depending upon the situation in which he is involved. Since our concern here is education and, hence, the school, it is appropriate here to examine the kinds of patterns of behavior he exhibits in the school, and the kinds of responses his behavior evokes.

DISADVANTAGED YOUTH AND THE SCHOOL

The language which the disadvantaged child learns in the home, content as well as patterns of speech, is reinforced in the neighborhood. It is augmented by patterns of language behavior which they do not permit the children to use in their presence —namely, profanity and obscenity. Language as spoken in the slum neighborhood is profuse with profanity and obscenity. Use of the latter is a mark of maturity, "coming of age," of status. Currently, profanity and obscenity characterize the language of black militants and college protestors generally. In part, their language behavior is a rejection of middle-class and upper-class respectability. For black militants it is a symbol of their identity with their brothers in the black ghetto. In view of the status which black militants have achieved, their language behavior is imitated by the children of the ghetto. In fact, profanity and obscenity are now regarded by many as right and proper.

The disadvantaged child speaks poorly and has a limited vocabulary, because this is characteristic of his world. He is spoken to authoritatively and is expected to obey authority without question. The teacher stands in a position of authority. However, he may rebel against *this* authority even though he may not be permitted to rebel at home. Being sensitive to the fact that his language patterns are different from those of the teacher and of his classmates from middle-class homes, that his experiences are limited, and that he does not read well—if he reads at all—may cause him to become discouraged and withdraw from the formal learning process in the school. His inability to read shows up in his low levels of achievement, even failure, in other subjects.

In the school the disadvantaged child answers questions in one-word sentences. Detailed explanations have to be drawn out through intensive questioning by the teacher. When the disadvantaged child attempts to give more complete answers to questions his sentences are ungrammatical. His knowledge of subject matter is limited by his inability to read and comprehend. Since he reads poorly he learns little. The little reading that he does must be done in school where some help is available, if he needs it. He can expect little or no help at home. Multiply this one child by twenty or thirty in the same classroom, in all grades, and it is not difficult to imagine what both teacher and child are up against. Bel Kaufman did not exaggerate the problem in describing her experiences.[7] The teacher, on the other hand, is likely to experience frustration, impatience, discouragement, even anger. She perceives the failure of the disadvantaged child to learn as a lack of ability; hence, she is likely to regard all, or at least most, disadvantaged children as dumb, low-grade morons, or as retarded. If the child shows resentment at the teacher's anger and fights back, he is regarded as insolent. The teacher forgets that the child comes from a world where anger is a commonly expressed emotion; and one learns to fight anger with resistance. If the child, out of his sensitivity, closes up, retreats and says nothing, he is considered stubborn. The picture that the teacher gets of the disadvantaged child is that he is a slow learner, he is insolent, stubborn and often incorrigible. An interesting thing may happen in this classroom. If a middle-class child exhibits these same characteristics, then that child is defined as *maladjusted* and in need of counseling.

The disadvantaged child, the product of cultural and economic disadvantage, perceives the school and what it stands for, the teachers and the other children, as different from him and as his enemies. The only way he has learned to deal with the enemy is to fight back. This accounts, at least in part, for his insolence toward the teacher, and the fights he has with other students. He becomes discouraged at his academic progress, or lack of it. He may be ashamed that others know so much more than he does. He falls farther and farther behind in his classwork. He becomes a truant, and finally a dropout.

The schools themselves which disadvantaged youth attend are hardly of a kind either to inspire good teaching or to motivate learning. As a general rule, the schools are the oldest in the community; in physical appearance they are drab and unattractive like the neighborhoods in which they are located. They range in age from forty to seventy years or more.[8] Since they were constructed for a considerably smaller population than they now serve, in almost every instance the schools are overcrowded. In order to meet this situation many of these schools operate on a double shift. Hence, this segment of the school population which needs *more* schooling *gets only half as much* as children in middle-class neighborhoods. Few of these schools contain gymnasiums, auditoriums, libraries or cafeterias since it was not customary to include these facilities in school buildings at the time that most of them were constructed. Some of the schools have been renovated to provide these facilities. In no instance, however, do they reach the standards of either utility or beauty of the more recently constructed schools in middle-class neighborhoods.

Schools attended by disadvantaged youth are the last to be equipped with modern teaching equipment and materials. In fact, the outdated physical structures are not always adaptable to the use of modern equipment. Neither disadvantaged children nor their teachers are unaware of the wide differentials in physical quality between their schools and the more modern schools in middle-class neighborhoods. The effect of modern physical facilities and pleasant surroundings on teaching and learning can only be estimated. However, it is the consensus of educators that their contribution is significant.

It is ironic that the only area in which the disadvantaged child can compete on a reasonable basis of equality is in sports, especially football, basketball, baseball and track. These are extracurricular activities; while they contribute to the development of some few students, they are not the basic reason for the school's existence. Schools for disadvantaged children fail in their basic function. Often their success is measured by the kinds of athletic teams they produce. Their trophy cases are filled to overflowing with the evidence of their achievements. It sometimes appears that more of the school's resources are channeled in these activities than in the development of academic programs. In almost every large city the perennial winners of athletic titles are schools from the ghettos rather than the schools which have a reputation for academic excellence.

Although competitive athletics motivate students to remain in school, and even to go to college, only a few students are so motivated; only a small portion of the enrollment can participate in interscholastic athletics. It is true that athletics engender school spirit, and this is important in any school. However, school spirit based on athletic competition is likely to last only during the sport's season. Hence, it is artificial. When the season is over the school loses its holding power, which was already weak. Then the dropout rate rises.

Unfortunately the story does not end here. As a dropout, with no great ambitions or aspirations, no special skills and a woefully inadequate education, the disadvantaged youth enters the job market. Obviously his employment, if and when he finds it, is at a low level. Sooner or later he marries and starts a family. Thus the cycle is begun all over again.

CONCLUSION

Again a word of caution. It is easy to assume that the foregoing description characterizes *all* poor people, and that the overt behavior of the "typical" disadvantaged child is characteristic of all. Many poor parents have high aspirations for their children. They are law-abiding, anxious to improve their own status, and encourage their children to get as much education as possible. These parents make many sacrifices to achieve their goals. They make every effort to instill in their children the approved norms and values of the larger society, both by instruction and example. They take great pride in any recognition that comes to their children as a result of unusual or outstanding achievement. They are sensitive to the conditions under which they live, and they are also aware of the attitudes of the larger community toward them. They try hard to protect their children from the coarse behavior that is prevalent in the neighborhood; they prohibit their children, as much as they can, from associating with the "bad" children in the neighborhood; and they constantly admonish their children to "stay out of trouble." Slum families, in spite of the economic poverty that is common to all, are by no means a homogeneous group. There is a wide range of difference in organization and disorganization.

The reality is that in spite of their efforts, only a small proportion of these families are ever able to improve their lot. In spite of their ambitions for their children only a few can help their children realize their ambitions for educational achievement. Although they are frugal and spend their money wisely, few can ever hope to purchase a better home in a better neighborhood and leave the physical deterioration and social disorganization of the neighborhood in which they have spent a greater part of their lives. Most can expect at best to maintain steady employment and stay off the relief rolls. For many, unemployment and public welfare, sometimes intermittent, often continuous, become a way of life.

As pointed out above, several programs have been established and a number of experiments are being tried in the education of disadvantaged youth. Locally, school systems are giving special attention to teaching children in the inner-city schools. New materials continue to be developed, and new or different techniques of teaching are being tried in an effort to raise the levels of performance of disadvantaged youth. Under Title XI of the National Defense Education Act of 1958, as amended in 1964, the United States Office of Education has supported Institutes for Teachers of Disadvantaged Youth; Title III of the Elementary and Secondary Education Act of 1965 makes provisions for the education of the disadvantaged in rural areas; and the Teachers Corps is designed to provide an additional cadre of teachers whose specialized knowledge will hopefully raise the levels of performance of disadvantaged children. In recognition of the differentials in cultural background of the disadvantaged and the impact which these differentials have on learning, departments of education in our Colleges and Universities are revising their curricula to give special attention to this problem.

However, no program, no matter how well-intentioned or how well-funded, can achieve any real success if it fails to include the parents of the disadvantaged child or if it ignores the neighborhood and its culture, its characteristic patterns of behavior, in which the child functions. What we frequently forget is that the school is only one agency which functions in the educative process. The school has the child for six hours a day, five days a week, for nine months of the year, and this contact begins, at least for most, only after he has reached the age of five or six, long after he has acquired language patterns and many other patterns of behavior. Hence, the impact of the school is limited.

The interdependence of all institutions which contribute to the formal process of education cannot be ignored. Historically, where middle and upper-class children are concerned, this interdependence has been taken for granted. With respect to the disadvantaged child it has been neglected. Obtaining the cooperation of parents of disadvantaged children over any sustained period of time will not be easy. The poor are suspicious of "reformers" or "busybodies" who want to "run their lives." Yet their cooperation and understanding can be achieved. The success of Dr. Sam Shepard with the Banneker Project in St. Louis, and Dr. William F. Brazziel in Norfolk, Virginia is concrete evidence that it can be done. Actually we have no alternative but at least to try, if the education of the conservatively estimated sixteen million disadvantaged youth in American society is to prepare them to compete equitably for employment and for satisfactory status in our culture. If we do not make an honest effort, then we can reconcile ourselves to another generation of increasing relief rolls, delinquency, crime, family and community disorganization.

REFERENCES

1. Jones, C.R.: Urbanization modifies rate of desegregation. *South School News,* IX, July, 1962.
2. Havighurst, R.J.: Who are the socially disadvantaged? In Frost, J.L. and Hawkes, G.R. (Eds.) : *The Disadvantaged Child.* New York, Mifflin Co., 1966.
3. Orshansky, M.: Counting the poor. *Soc Security Bull,* Jan., 1965.
4. Orshansky, M.: Who's who among the poor: A demographic view of poverty. *Soc Security Bull,* July, 1965.
5. Miller, L.: Race, poverty, and the law. In Tenbroek, J.: *The Law of the Poor.* San Francisco, Chandler Publishing Co., 1968.
6. *Report of the National Advisory Commission on Civil Disorders.* New York, Bantam Books, 1968.
7. Kaufman, B.: *Up the Down Staircase.* New Jersey, Prentice-Hall, Inc., 1964.
8. United States Office of Education: *Equality of Educational Opportunity.* Washington, D.C., Government Printing Office, 1966.

Chapter XV

SOME EDUCATIONAL APPROACHES AND TECHNIQUES FOR CHILDREN FROM SOCIALLY DISADVANTAGED BACKGROUNDS

Edmund W. Gordon

R ALPH TYLER, who recently retired as the director of the Center for the Advanced Study of the Behavioral Sciences at Palo Alto, has a tale which I think is appropriate to the issues examined in this book. He tells a story of a chap whom we might call Johnnie who was not too rapid a learner. Johnnie's father decided to take him out of school since he wasn't making much progress, and he tried to find a job for him. He tried several spots and was unsuccessful until he finally went around to the minister of his church to inquire about a job as janitor there. The minister said that since the church had a rather well-educated congregation it would be a mistake to bring as a janitor a fellow who had done as poorly in school as Johnnie had done. Finally he did find a friend who was running a garage-filling station, who took on Johnnie to wash cars, a job he could do reasonably well. After a while he began to help his friend to manage the place. When the friend retired, he took over the business. Sometime later another friend told him that he had a chance to buy an automobile agency down the street and Johnnie said, "You know I don't have the cash to buy it." His friend suggested he go to the bank and borrow it. So Johnnie went over to the bank and talked to the banker about a loan. They looked at Johnnie's own account, which was a substantial one, and Johnnie got his loan to buy the automobile agency. As he finished the transaction Johnnie explained that he would need help in signing the papers since he had never learned to read and write very well. He got the help and as he was about to leave, the banker commented on the fact that Johnnie had done very well for himself, particularly in view of his limited education, and wondered aloud what the opportunities might be if he had

215

gone on to finish school. Johnnie answered him, "Yes, I suppose I'd be janitor over at the church."

Now the likelihood that many of the people we are considering here are going to have the kind of opportunities that Johnnie had is certainly less in the present period since the kinds of skills that we demand of people now, or we claim to be demanding of people now, are considerably more technical. There are few opportunities for movement to the top without academic credentials. There does remain the fact that there is a significant difference between the number of persons who are identified as retarded or mentally subnormal in the school years and the number of such persons who can be identified as adults. There seems to be something about the opportunity to participate and produce that enables people either to compensate for or to circumvent specific conditions which are thought to be handicapping. It is possible that the availability of such opportunity is even more important than some of the more narrowly defined characteristics that we have come to identify when we are trying to determine who has got it and who has not got it in terms of intellect.

I have been asked to write about some of the programs that have been developed under what we call compensatory education, or education for disadvantaged children. No matter what we call it, we are generally talking about education of minority group children and poor children, more specifically, children who are not making it in the present school system. We can review the basic characteristics of these programs briefly, for few of them have been notably successful.

Although the existing programs have a wide variety of forms, it is possible to identify them in several different categories. In the period from about 1955 to about 1963, there were perhaps fifty special programs developed around the country for disadvantaged populations; suddenly, attention was focused on this problem and over the period from 1964 to 1970 something like two or three thousand such programs were developed. This expansion is largely a result of the Elementary and Secondary Education Act of 1964, which has enabled almost every school district in the country which has poor children or minority group children to do something for them.

The feature of these programs most frequently encountered can be identified as some attack on the problems of reading and language development. New reading methods, new reading materials, new efforts at training teachers to use these materials, extensive use of a variety of other specialized personnel in connection with remedial reading, earlier reading instruction, language enrichment and a whole range of activities focused on stimulating language development—all are aimed at enhancing the opportunities of youngsters to learn how to read. This emphasis is natural and quite appropriate since in the present period, at least, language disability or limited ability in reading handicaps the student in all other academic pursuits.

Curriculum innovation is the most appropriate way to categorize a broad group of activities which affect both the structure and the content of school experiences. These have included modified teacher organizations, team-teaching, ungraded classes, some experimentation with individualized instruction, use of extra classroom teachers, use of teachers' aides and sub-professionals in the classroom, increased numbers of specialized personnel in the school and new kinds of materials. At the same time that our concern for the disadvantaged has been growing, we have also become somewhat disillusioned with the old forms of curriculum. Variations of new math, new biology, and new sciences curricula have been introduced. New textbooks emphasizing low reading skill and high interest level have been developed and purchased in various school systems. New emphasis has emerged, particularly in the area of social studies, on tests which recognize minority group contributions. Many of these programs have utilized field trips, guest speakers, and a variety of projects to widen the experiential backgrounds of these youngsters on the assumption that a part of their developmental lag is a function of limited experience. In fact, this is the origin of the term culturally disadvantaged, which I reject since it suggests that there is something wrong with the cultures of the people we seek to serve. I think that many people would argue that there is nothing wrong with the culture of minority groups. They are different cultures, and youngsters coming out of different cultural backgrounds may need to broaden these backgrounds, but it is a disservice to them to identify their cultures as inferior, as disadvantaged, as inappropriate, or in some other negative term.

Some schools have moved in the area that we might label as extracurricular innovations, a kind of umbrella phrase for a number of efforts to extend the school's influence into nonacademic or nonschool time and environments. Some examples are after school or Saturday study centers, often using paid or volunteer tutors, tutorial workshops and homework helper programs. Less strictly academic approaches include organized club activities, emphasizing music, reading for pleasure, sports, arts, science, arts and crafts, cultural events, hobby groups, picnics, camping trips and varieties of other activities.

It should be noted that many of the practices that are taken for granted in more privileged neighborhoods, such things as movable furniture, special art classes, or student government activities, have been introduced as innovations in disadvantaged areas. In other words, many activities, resources and facilities that have not been available to disadvantaged youngsters but which have been routinely available in more privileged areas have simply been added to depressed area schools and *called* compensatory education!

Just about every idea that one can find anywhere in the field of education has come to be represented in some form in compensatory education. Almost every sizable program in compensatory education now includes some increased attention to what we call parental involvement. More and more schools serving disadvantaged children have moved toward breaking down the barrier that has separated home and school and community. Recognizing the need for a more aggressive approach to breaking down this wall than a trumpet call to attend the traditional PTA meeting, these schools have utilized home visits by teachers, social workers and community aides. Frequently these community aides are persons from the community themselves who have been employed by the school to increase or improve the liaison between school and home. In addition to simply getting in touch with families, these home visitors interpret the school's programs, provide information about school events, suggest ways parents may assist the school program, counsel about behavioral and other school problems, and put families in contact with appropriate community assistance agencies. When meetings with parents are held at the school they tend to be small, more social and informal, and are often conducted by staff members who have been recruited from the communities. In other words, the better programs are trying to modify the approach of the school to families, to make the school more reflective of the interest, the needs and the values of the communities served.

A question of community involvement has concerned a number of these projects as they reached beyond the parents into the total surrounding community, both to offer and to seek help. Resources have been shared by other community agencies. School doors have been opened to adult education activities. Various community groups have made use of the school's facilities. In return, schools have benefitted from community volunteer help for tutorial services such as English instruction and remediation, from community financial help for enrichment programs, and from the help of business communities in providing widened vocational opportunities. In many project communities the school has found it useful to employ a school-community agent to organize wide-ranging programs for children and their families. Often such a coordinator functions as a liaison person not only between the school and community but also between the school and such government agencies as the local department of public welfare. The most recent development reflecting community involvement is the current move toward decentralization and community control of schools. Frustrated by the schools' history of failure in achieving any degree of ethnic integration and certainly the failure to meet the needs of many children, many black communities are insisting that parents and other community people have a louder voice, even a controlling voice in the policy decisions of these schools.

Some compensatory education projects have placed primary emphasis on newer approaches to instructional equipment and teacher training. Although much government support has gone into such projects, along with cooperative university direction, they are not among the most confidence-inspiring activities in the compensatory education area so far.

Together with remedial reading, special guidance is an approach almost universally included in these projects for the disadvantaged. While guidance personnel are unfortunately still hampered by their traditional preoccupation with maladjustment, increasing emphasis is being placed on providing counseling and guidance to all children in project schools. In guidance-oriented programs emphasis is placed on changing the student through individual and group counseling designed to increase self-understanding, to enhance self-concept and to improve motivation and attitudes toward school. Little attention is given to the problem of changing the school. In addition to expanding the personal counseling role, guidance has also enlarged the informational role, particularly in regard to vocational interests and aptitudes. A typical compensatory guidance program will combine individual counseling, vocationally oriented group guidance and, not infrequently, extensive enrichment activities designed to broaden the child's view of the world.

These are the areas in which innovation has taken place in current compensatory educational programs. Many of the specific approaches just described function as parts of complex programs covering more than one phase of the relationship between the school, the child and the community. Indeed, where resources permit, school districts have initiated total programs which have aimed at improving the entire school experience of the children involved in them. Sometimes these broad-scale programs, including the whole battery of compensatory practices, service thousands of students. In other instances, a variety of techniques are combined in a small program aimed at a very few youngsters.

The two most familiar total programs currently in existence are the programs directed at very young children, that is, the preschool programs and those programs directed at the school drop-outs. Both of these have received such wide attention that further description of them should be unnecessary here. It is significant, however, that so much of the more informal learning experiences have developed in Project Head Start, a program which operated entirely outside of the public school except where such schools sought Head Start money to run preschool programs. Again, most of the activity in school drop-out programs has been developed outside of the school for youngsters who have already dropped out and who may be persuaded to return to school, or may be given supplementary experiences to compensate for the interrupted formal education. It would appear that these two emphases have been so widely accepted simply because they require the least change in the school itself. All of us know from our respective professional and institutional ties that it is sometimes easier to add on new things than to change things that already exist in institutions. This has certainly been true of education. Very few educators are moving with conviction toward radical reformation of the public school. Yet, if equality of educational opportunity is a serious goal, educational treatments that are radically different from those which prevail seem indicated.

Several conditions seem essential to the equalization of educational opportunity and basic educational achievement. It probably is not by accident that we have been relatively unsuccessful in compensatory education, since so much of this work has been directed at the rather narrowly defined cognitive area of development. We know that there are at least three aspects of human behavior that are involved in social and academic learning. They have to do with those processes which we might define as basic cognitive processes, basic affective processes, and basic conative (skills mastery) processes.[1]

Edward Zigler,[2] working at the Child Development Program at Yale, has suggested that perhaps a part of our problem results from the fact that the cognitive area, in which we concentrate most of our effort, may be the least important, and the affective area may be the most important, the most susceptible to change. From his research, Zigler is able to account for significant upward shifts in intellectual functioning of mildly retarded subjects entirely on the basis of their motivation, their involvement in and attention to the task. Arthur Jensen[3] has suggested that the skills-mastery area may be a more productive area in which to work than the attack upon shifts and changes in basic cognitive processes.

I would argue that in the reformation of the public school, there are several conditions which seem to be essential and which grow out of an analysis of what is involved in the teaching-learning process, what is involved in these three processes that reflect learning. The first of these I would discuss in the context of what I call accountability, the way in which the school is or should be answerable to its primary beneficiaries and to society at large. This is reflected most visibly in the current political concern and demand for decentralization and community control of schools. The public schools are probably the only institutions in our society that have not been required to account to anyone for what they do and how well they do it. The schools may enroll youngsters for twelve or any smaller number of years that the students will stay with them; whether or not they succeed with the students, the schools continue to be financed and the teachers remain employed, continuously protecting their tenure, whether the youngsters pass or fail. Communities are now saying to the schools, "You have done a miserable job, and we want to change the situation so that you are accountable to us, so that we can hold the school responsible for what happens or does not happen to our youngsters in that school." I think that this movement is not unrelated to the affective areas which I have mentioned.

The second area for reform is a need to redress the imbalance in the assigning of responsibility for teaching and learning. In education and even in the fields that have greatly influenced it, psychology and psychiatry, counseling and psychotherapy, where have we placed the responsibility for the failure of the treatment, whether it be education for the student or therapy for the patient? Most often this responsibility has been placed on the patient or the learner. If the student is not learning in school, he is labeled retarded; the assumption is that there is something wrong with him. We seldom look to see if there may be something wrong with the teacher or something wrong with the school materials or the school situation. It must be the youngster who is not learning, not the teacher who is not teaching or the school that is not helping him learn. If the student is in counseling and is not progressing, again something must be wrong with the youngster and not with the guidance counselor or the therapist working with him, or even with the whole field of guidance. When youngsters score low on tests, they are immediately considered to have something wrong with them—they are retarded, they are subnormal. No one thinks to ask whether there may be something wrong with the test or something wrong with the way in which the youngster has been tested. Something must be done to redress this one-sided view of responsibility for teaching and learning, to place a greater portion of that responsibility on the shoulders of professionals, on the shoulders of the school, on the shoulders of teachers.

Successful reform of the schools also demands an increased congruence between the content, style, and values of the school and the relevant aspects of the child's life and future. Mario Fantini and Gerald Weinstein have written a little book on *The Challenge of Education for the Disadvantaged,*[4] suggesting that the school's preoccupation with rote learning may be inappropriate to the styles, to the orientation, to the needs of many of the youngsters on whom we have focused. In the book that Wilkerson and the author wrote on compensatory education it was suggested that it may be now necessary to shift from a focus on content mastery to a focus on skill in the management of information that is available in any general area. Successful professionals in the present time depend less on memory as a store of the information that is relevant to a problem and more and more on skill in problem solving and stating the problem in such a way as to begin the search for answers. Somehow we need to shift the focus of what happens in the school from content mastery and simple rote learning to social coping, to problem solving, to information management, to human problem relations and to self-management in vocational, political and human relations. Certainly we can look back in history and see a wide variety of societies which have achieved a high degree of technical and academic competence but whose success has been paralleled by inhumanitarian activities, from the Roman Empire at the time of Jesus to the German nation during the time of Hitler or even our own nation in the present period when we probably are the most well developed, most technically advanced people in the history of man, yet continue to perpetuate the plight of the disadvantaged and impoverished people in this country, and continue to wage war on the people of Vietnam.

A fourth concern for radical educational reform is an increased congruence between the pupil's style, his temperamental traits, his interests, and his developmental rate, and the learning process, a concern which has been reflected in recent moves in the direction of individually prescribed instruction. Through the years there has been some concern with individual differences in human subjects, but nowhere in education has this concern led to a process of quantitative analysis of learning function, of behavioral function in the learner, leading to the designing, for that learner, of a program of instruction, a set of learning experiences that reflect what is known about him. In J. McVicker Hunt's *Intelligence and Experience,*[5] he suggests that perhaps we can significantly increase the level of intellectual function across the board, not by wiping out the individual differences, but by attacking the problem of a match between learner characteristics and the characteristics of the learning situation. This approach has not been reflected in public education and certainly has not been reflected in compensatory education.

One other potentially significant area of reform is successful economic and ethnic integration. To bring about possibly dramatic improvement in education for disadvantaged children, we certainly need to take advantage of the favorable factors that seem to be contributed by bringing youngsters of lower social and economic status into learning situations where the predominant group comes from the higher status group. Coleman's[6] data have made it clear that when youngsters are involved in economically integrated learning situations where the higher economic group is in the majority, youngsters from the lower economic group improve in their academic achievement and youngsters from the higher economic group show no adverse effects, maintaining their status or even moving ahead. Pettigrew[7] at Harvard has tried to interpret these data to defend racial integration in school, which I also advocate, though for another set of reasons. It is not clear that Coleman's conclusions support racial integration as a cause of improvement, but they do very clearly support economic integration. However, if we intend to provide economic integration for minority group youngsters in this country, there is no way to do it other than through racial integration; there simply are not enough minority groups to integrate economically all of the educational settings without also integrating ethnically.

We are frequently told that compensatory education has not worked. What many people mean by this is that it cannot work, and even more, that poor youngsters from minority groups cannot be taught to handle academic learning efficiently. The latest version of this message is the controversial Harvard Educational Review article by Arthur Jensen[8] of the University of California at Berkeley, a development which carries the unfortunate symbolism of two of our most prestigious institutions joining together to tell us that black and poor people are inherently inferior to white and rich people. Whether or not this is a fair representation of the general beliefs prevailing at those two institutions, the symbolism is still undeniably there.

There are, of course, very real complexities to this question concerning the genetic basis for differences in intellectual function. They are not, for me, primarily questions of fact, but questions of meaning. I would be greatly surprised if some day we discovered that genetic characteristics have nothing to do with the intellectual function. This seems unlikely; more probably some aspects of intellectual development are influenced by genetics just as some aspects of physical development are so influenced. I think individuals and groups do differ with respect to genetic material referrable to intellectual development, but the important question has to do with the ways in which they do differ. What is the meaning of the difference? What is the limitation that these differences impose? What do these differences mean in relation to the specification of environmental encounters necessary to develop certain behaviors or functions or achievements? What is the relevance of individual or group differences for the design of educational programs appropriate to a highly industrialized society? This is one of the central problems of education and the related behavioral sciences. This, strangely enough, is the very problem that receives so little attention in our research and in our practice. Until it is answered we cannot say much about the potential of the variety of groups that make up our society. The debate about these issues can go on interminably. Their solution, however, can only come from serious research studies conducted in a society whose social and economic relations provide the conditions conducive to universal wholesome development. It is a hopeful sign that we are, at least, beginning to ask the questions rather than just advancing positions.

In the final analysis we are left with the crucial questions of how man influences the quality and the content of the behavioral repertoire. Almost three years ago I concluded an article with the statement which follows:[9]

> To honor our commitments to science and professional service we must understand the limitations of our knowledge and of our practice. Much of what we do is based on the hopeful assumption that all human beings with normal neurological endowment can be developed for participation in the mainstream of our society. We believe this because we have seen many people from a great variety of backgrounds participate, and because we want to believe it. But we do not yet have definitive evidence to support our belief. We operate out of an egalitarian faith without knowing whether our goals are really achievable. Yet it must be our aim, not only as scientists and professional workers, but as humanitarians as well, to determine the potential of human beings for equality of achievement. If in the light of our most sophisticated and subtle evaluations we conclude that such equality is not generally achievable, if in spite of the best we can do it seems likely that some of our citizens will remain differentiated by their own biology, then we shall merely have answered a persistent question. We will still have no evidence that group differences per se imply any ability on the part of particular individuals to meet the demands of society. We will then be able to turn our energies to helping individuals meet those demands. And if, on the other hand, as we believe, true equality of opportunity and appropriate learning experiences will result in equality of achievement, then we must so organize our professional services and our society that no person is kept from achieving that potential by our indifference to his condition, by the inadequacy or inappropriateness of our service, or by the impediments society deliberately or accidentally places in his path. It is not an unhopeful paradox that the only way we shall ever know whether equality of human achievement is possible is through providing for all our citizens, privileged and underprivileged alike, the kinds of service and the kind of society that assumes that it is possible and makes adequate provision for the same.

REFERENCES

1. Gordon, Edmund W. and Wilkerson, Doxey A. (Eds.) : *Compensatory Education for the Disadvantaged*. Princeton, New Jersey, College Entrance Examination Board, 1966.
2. Zigler, Edward: Mental retardation: current issues and approaches. *Review of Child Development Research*. L.W. Hoffman and M.L. Hoffman (Eds.) . New York, Russell Sage Foundation, 1966.
3. Jensen, A.R.: Social class and verbal learning. In M. Deutsch, I. Katz and A.R. Jensen. *Social Class, Race, and Psychological Development*. New York, Holt, Rinehart, and Winston, 1968. pp. 115-174.
4. Fantini, Mario D. and Weinstein, Gerald: *The Disadvantaged: Challenge to Education*. New York, Harper and Row, 1968.
5. Hunt, Joseph McVicker: *Intelligence and Experience*. New York, Ronald Press Company, 1961.
6. Coleman, James S. *et al.: Equality of Educational Opportunity*. United States Department of Health, Education and Welfare, Office of Education. Washington, D.C., Superintendent of Documents, Government Printing Office, 1966.
7. Pettigrew, Thomas F.: In United States Commission on Civil Rights, *Racial Isolation in the Public Schools*. United States Department of Health, Education and Welfare, Office of Education. Washington, D.C., Superintendent of Documents, Government Printing Office, 1967.
8. Jensen, A.R.: How much can we boost IQ and scholastic achievement? *Harvard Ed Rev*, 39 (1) , Winter, 1969, pp. 1-123.
9. Gordon, Edmund W.: Statement in American Orthopsychiatric Association. *Am J Orthopsychiatry*, XXXV, No. 3, April, 1965.

Chapter XVI

THE AMELIORATION OF MENTAL DEFICIENCY

Barbara D. Bateman

Some men see things as they are and say why;
I see things as they never were and say why not.
ROBERT F. KENNEDY

OUR nation presently has the resources, but not the commitment, to reduce mental retardation by at least half. The purpose of this chapter is simply to add one more plea to the mounting cry that now is the time to begin in earnest the needed crusade against mental retardation and for better treatment of mental retardates. In 1962, Robert F. Kennedy said, "The long-range cure for mental retardation will be the clearing of the swamps of ignorance, poverty, malnutrition and superstition which breed it. . . . As we reach into space for the moon and the stars, we must reach out also to the children at our feet who need our help." Just a few months later the President's Panel on Mental Retardation reported, "Our greatest hope for a major victory over mental retardation lies in general measures to correct the fundamental social, economic, and cultural conditions with which mental retardation is closely associated."[1]

President John Kennedy, in an address to Congress (Feb., 1963), stated very simply that, "More adequate medical care, nutrition, housing, and educational opportunities can reduce mental retardation to the low incidence which has been achieved in some other nations." Recognizing that other countries have lower rates of maternal deaths, venereal disease, mental retardation, or any other unwanted condition is most unpleasant to many Americans. Often our denial takes the form of insisting that other nations' methods of reporting are different, or that our statistics are just more honest than theirs. At this point in history it seems imperative that we stop such nonsense, agree that much mental retardation in this country can

228

be substantially reduced and start working on how to do it. A reasonable estimate is that from 50 to 80 per cent of the retardation in our country is very closely related to social and economic inequities and injustices.

President Kennedy had only to suggest we might have a man on the moon in this decade. Our response was direct, committed and efficient. With what we like to think of as characteristic American know-how, dedication and ingenuity we set about to put a man on the moon. If there is in our land yet one more leader who possesses that rare ability to make a people believe in a goal and in the worthiness of pursuing that goal, and if he or she were to set our sights on reducing mental retardation in the next decade, could we respond? The case is more urgent than that of landing a man on the moon. If we continue to ignore the hideous deficiencies in our social system, the results will be disastrous.

What are some of the factors which operate in our country to double our rate of mental retardation over that in the Soviet Union, Denmark and Sweden? The President's Panel speculated that three relevant factors might be operating in the Soviet Union and Scandinavia:

Reduced Cultural Deprivation. The other countries have made more progress than we have in eliminating slums and in replacing them with housing occupied by families from a variety of occupational and socioeconomic backgrounds. Physicians, factory workers, educators, street cleaners, lawyers and shopkeepers live next door to each other and their children attend school together, share playground facilities, etc.

Free Medical Care, Especially Prenatal Care for Mothers. In the USSR, for example, the rate of premature births is 4.7/100 compared to a rate of 16/100 in the economically deprived areas of New York City. Maternity leave with pay is standard practice in the Soviet Union. We are by no means deficient in our knowledge of the extreme importance of prenatal care and infant care; we just have not yet implemented our knowledge. The increasing recognition being given to early childhood development suggests that we may soon begin to make major strides in this area.

Legalized Abortion without Stigma. In addition to the highly publicized mental and physical handicaps that result from rubella, thalidomide, etc., perhaps even more retardation is related to unwanted children for whom adequate emotional and financial support are missing.

Whitney Young[2] has specified some of the factors within the economically deprived community which increase the rate of mental retardation. Among these are the higher rates of malnutrition (worldwide, the largest cause of mental retardation) in children and in pregnant women, toxemia, infections, physical hardships, brain damage due to lead poisoning from paint used in slums, infectious diseases, and accidents due to inadequate play facilities and supervision. Additional social and psychological factors which increase the rate of mentally retarded functioning are described by Young as the "by-product of the misery of the few and the prejudice of the many." These include physically or emotionally unavailable mothers, inadequate stimulation, crowded housing, poor sanitation and the frustration, anxiety and stigma of being poor.

In short, much of the mental retardation in this country is currently preventable and is caused by poverty and social injustice. It will be prevented only when, as Robert Kennedy said, we are willing to clear away "the swamps of ignorance, poverty, malnutrition and superstition which breed it." One role of psychologists and educators in preventing mental retardation is that of especially well-informed citizens who can bring facts into light and encourage and lead the public to look at the facts and to act.

A problem related to that of commiting our resources and efforts to reducing and preventing retardation by social action is that of fostering more humane attitudes and behavior toward the mentally retarded. Some might object that we have already taken the retarded out of chains. Have we? On June 9, 1969 a report was filed in a California Superior Court describing current practices. Mentally retarded patients at Sonoma State Hospital, old and young alike, are "herded into huge barn-like wards . . . and are treated like, and consequently behaved like, animals in a zoo. . . . The dignity of the individual is violated when he is stripped of all his clothes, when he has absolutely no vestige of privacy, even a shoe box he can call his own . . . rags are used for drying material after patients' toileting, washing and bathing. . . ."

A fanciful report by an angry parent or discharged ward attendant? Hardly. This report was compiled by Dr. Gunnar Dybwad and colleagues. Blatt and Kaplan's *Christmas in Purgatory*[3] has photographically and verbally documented the details of our treatment of the mentally retarded, with much more graphic detail than most readers want. "We know personally of few institutions for the mentally retarded in the United States completely free of dirt and filth, odors, naked patients groveling in their own feces, children in locked cells, horribly crowded dormitories, and understaffed and improperly staffed facilities. . . . Although our pictures could not even begin to capture the total and overwhelming horror we saw, smelled and felt, they represent a side of America that has rarely been shown to the general public and is little understood by most of us."

The everyday, in-the-community kind of cruelties perpetrated against the mentally retarded were recently highlighted in the award-winning movie *Charley* based on Daniel Keyes' *Flowers for Algernon*.[4] The facts are that a) we have more mental retardation in this country than we need have and b) the treatment afforded the mentally retarded is less than the best current knowledge allows. What can educators and psychologists do to help correct these situations? First, we can disseminate the facts and urge social action and responsibility. This job is one that should be shared by all informed and concerned citizens. The remainder of this discussion concentrates on some actions which are squarely within the professional province of educators and psychologists. The broader application of what is already known but not widely applied would seem a reasonable strategy for those with applied interests.

Specifically, the areas where greater dissemination and application of the facts would seem strikingly helpful include the following:

1. More use of operant techniques.
2. Better and more programmed materials.
3. Systematic teaching of social communication skills by role-playing communication groups, etc.
4. More precise and efficient (e.g. Engelmann) teaching of basic concepts.
5. Improved teaching of reading (many of the myths which

have set inappropriately low expectations for reading achievement by the retarded have not been dispelled).
6. Behavioral approach to diagnosis and rehabilitation of the retarded.

The remainder of this discussion examines the last point in some detail, since behavioral diagnosis and intervention looms as a major contribution educators and psychologists can make to the amelioration of mental retardation.

The only justification for psycho-educational diagnosis of mental retardation is so that some action can be taken. The major diagnostic question is "What can be done?" In some cases we can reduce or eliminate some aspects of the retardation; in other cases we can adjust the environment to better accommodate the retarded; in most cases we can do both.

The mentally retarded do not attend conventions about retardation, they do not write journal articles about retardation, and they do not establish university training programs to prepare professional workers in retardation. This places them in a unique position.

In many parts of the world the poor, the oppressed, and the handicapped and the disenfranchised are beginning to speak for themselves more loudly and clearly than ever. Someday, they will be heard as they must if mankind is to survive. But the retarded will always be represented by the nonretarded. This puts a very special responsibility on those of us who presume to decide and plan what should be done for an almost voiceless minority. This problem is illustrated by the true case of a young woman, mildly retarded who had lived for many years in a state institution for the retarded. She was very capable by institution standards and was given considerable responsibility in her job. Her social position and prestige were high and she gave every indication of being an outstandingly happy and well-adjusted young woman. Consequently, a social worker decided the young woman should be discharged and returned to a community where it seemed possible she could maintain herself. Have we the right to move this young woman from an environment which she has mastered to one which would be continually threatening? This represents the dilemma of making decisions for and about the welfare of another human being. Nevertheless, this is what we must do when we plan educational programs and intervention for the retarded.

The diagnostician approaches the diagnosis of known or suspected mental retardation with certain assumptions, some of which may be hidden. One common, but hidden assumption is that mental retardation is basically similar to an incurable disease —if one "has" it or if one "really" is retarded, there is not much to be done by the diagnostician except note that this is indeed a "case" of mental retardation. This assumption may be partially correct in some cases. Its prevalence and tenacity in spite of great talk about the educability and modifiability of intelligence, causes one to wonder. Definitions which refer to retardation as incurable are no longer accepted, but the doubt lingers on. However, as educators, it is better that we assume improvement is possible when it may not be, than that we assume no change can occur when in fact it might. Learned behavior can be taught, although the teaching might require different and better techniques than we now have—and perhaps more time than we have.

A second assumption widely held is that data about past history and present test performance of a retarded individual are helpful to planning future steps. This is false a great deal of the time. How much "case history and diagnostic report" data is actually *used* by those who work with the retarded? Very little appears useful and that tiny portion that is used is often used against him. He may be labeled and excluded from certain programs and/or locked into others. Does this mean it is not helpful to study the retarded individual before making educational decisions? No. But it does mean we need urgently to look at what kind of information is helpful—to the diagnostician and to the individual. At least two diagnostic questions are useful: What would be most beneficial to teach the individual at this point in time, and how can we best teach him?

Teaching always has as its goal the changing of some behavior. If no behavioral change results, the teaching has failed. Our somewhat limited concern is with behavior that can be changed, not with things that are outside the scope of psychoeducational change, such as damaged brains or chromosomes.

If diagnosticians were to ask those people in closest contact with a retarded person which things about him are most in need of immediate change (specifically, what should he learn to do and not to do, beginning right now), we would probably obtain precise, accurate and relevant information. A mother might tell us, "if only he were toilet trained and wouldn't hit the baby." A public school teacher might describe her desire for improvement as, "If only he would work independently and stop running around the room." An employer might report the retarded employee's need "to stop using foul language when customers are in the shop and pay more attention to personal grooming."

But such simple and direct information hardly appears precise, refined and sophisticated enough (even though it is highly useful!). At least two other approaches seem to have merit. A behavioral checklist could be used. Behaviors may be divided into customary headings such as *mobility* (ranging from holds own head up, through walking unassisted, to travels independently in the community); *language* (ranging from understanding one word commands to expresses self in complete sentences); *self-help* (including dressing, toileting, feeding, etc.). Then the behavioral areas can be plotted in a circle which is divided into as many slices as there are areas. The behaviors in each area are placed in developmental order from the center of the circle out. When a behavior is mastered, the corresponding square is filled in so we can see at a glance the next tasks to be learned.

Decisions must still be made as to which tasks should receive teaching priority. If the employer has reported, e.g. that the retarded employee must be able to tell time in order to hold a certain job and the behavioral checklist shows he cannot count, then we know to teach the skills prerequisite to and culminating in telling time. We will return to how we know what those sub-skills are and how to most efficiently teach them.

A second approach to determine what to teach the retarded has not been widely used yet because it requires observation and recording techniques only recently available. However, it seems possible that we can now analyze settings, situations or environments in terms of those behaviors that are essential, supportive, irrelevant and incompatible with successful maintenance in that context. Then, those behaviors which are essential across a wide variety of contexts would assume top teaching priority for all. A person might then be described in terms of the contexts in which his present behavioral repetoire allows him to function. We would also have a clear picture of what he would need to learn and/or unlearn in order to broaden the range of situations open to him.

Of course we have been doing something like this, but very crudely, for a long time. When we say, "He cannot function in a competitive job, but could be semi-independent in a sheltered workshop" we are making a global judgment, not unlike what we are proposing here. It would be much more helpful to specify what missing behaviors prevented him from holding a competitive job or what present behaviors were incompatible with this goal. Our first step in a psycho-educational diagnosis of mental retardation is to determine in very plain language *what* behaviors are to be taught or eliminated. This we could call determining our instructional objectives. They must be so plain and specific that reasonable people could agree when each had been achieved. The following objectives would be inappropriate because it would be difficult to determine when the retarded individual could perform them.

1. Know number concepts.
2. Improve eye-hand coordination.
3. Spell basic words adequately.
4. Develop more appropriate peer relations.

In contrast, a useful instructional objective reveals exactly what the individual will be doing, the conditions under which he will perform it, and the level of performance to be considered adequate, for example, we could all determine whether or not a child could do the following:

1. Presented with ten sets of objects, each set containing between one and twenty identical objects, correctly state how many objects are in each set.
2. Given twenty objects of many different colors, group together all those of the same colors (red, blue, yellow, white, black and green).
3. Spell these words correctly (a list of thirty words), making errors in no more than two words.

Once specific instructional objectives to be sought in a reasonable time period (maybe a week, a month-long camping session, a school year, etc.) have been established by the two-fold process of assigning priorities to desired behavioral change and specifying them operationally, we are ready to move to the next major consideration: How to teach them. The diagnostician has often neglected this area, even when he has attempted to consider the first.

An important distinction must be made between existing behaviors to be eliminated and new skills or concepts to be acquired, as the diagnostician's role is appreciably different in the two cases. Much of what is currently called behavior modification is most appropriate and efficient in extinguishing unwanted behaviors such as temper tantrums, crying and biting, or for shaping behaviors that are weak or in need of some modification such as rare and tentative social contact approaches. In dealing with behaviors to be eliminated, the diagnostician should first determine the frequency and nature of the specific behavior. If the referral statement is that the retarded individual causes trouble on the ward or in the classroom or wherever, this must first be pinpointed. Exactly what does he do and how often? By inquiry and observation it is determined that on the average of three times a week he throws toys at other children. Only by this specification will reasonable men agree when the behavior has been substantially reduced.

When the behavior has been specified or pinpointed and the baseline frequency is known, plans to change the frequency may be considered. The diagnostician should be prepared to examine both the antecedent and the subsequent events which are controlling the behavior. We all know the story of the mother who very successfully taught her child to throw tantrums in the store by giving him a candy bar every time he did (consequence), or of the new blind child in the school for the blind who wet the bed every night, regardless of frequent spankings, until someone thought to show him the way to the restroom from his bedroom (antecedent).

Once the diagnostician knows what antecedents and subsequents are currently operating, he can recommend the necessary changes. Many of the undesirable behaviors we wish to reduce are operant behaviors. Therefore, we need to insure that the child is not being positively reinforced for them. Often it is possible to arrange to reinforce behaviors which are incompatible with those behaviors we want to eliminate.

Diagnosis, as we see it, includes:

1. Determining precisely which behaviors are to be changed.
2. Determining how frequently and under what circumstances the behaviors presently occur.
3. Recommending environmental manipulations to change the frequency of behavior.
4. Evaluating the effectiveness of the interventions and trying new ones as necessary.

If psycho-educational diagnoses were made as described above, one effect would be the reduction or elimination of the discriminatory labeling now done on the basis of IQs.

Much mental retardation can be prevented by long overdue reordering of values and priorities and by appropriate diagnosis in place of unfair and discriminatory labeling. We must take rapid strides in both directions.

REFERENCES

1. President's Panel on Mental Retardation: *A Proposed Program for National Action to Combat Mental Retardation: A Report to the President*. Washington, D.C., U.S. Government Printing Office, 1962.
2. Young, W.: Poverty, intelligence, and life in the inner city. *Ment Retard*, 7:2, April, 1969.
3. Blatt, B. and Kaplan, F.: *Christmas in Purgatory*. Boston, Allyn and Bacon, 1966.
4. Keyes, D.: *Flowers for Algernon*. New York, Harcourt, Brace and World, 1966.

Chapter XVII

THE MULTIDIMENSIONAL PROBLEMS AND ISSUES OF EDUCATING RETARDED CHILDREN, YOUTHS AND ADULTS

I. Ignacy Goldberg

TO echo Ebbinghaus' famous dictum, mental retardation has a long past and a short history. Vigorous action in the prevention, treatment and amelioration of retardation is all within our recent memory.

The broad scope of our present concerns is indicated by the subject matter of the main recommendations of the President's Panel on Mental Retardation[20] comprising the areas of: research, preventive health measures, strengthened special education programs, more comprehensive clinical and social services, improved methods and facilities, a new legal and social conception of the retarded, overcoming manpower problems and developing programs of education and information to increase public awareness of the problems of mental retardation.

Obviously such an undertaking is extremely complex. It requires careful coordination and thorough cooperation among all involved. Yet such coordination and cooperation is by no means easily achieved.

The organized efforts to educate the mentally retarded in the United States were begun in 1848 with the establishment of residential centers geared primarily toward preparing mentally retarded individuals for a greater contribution to society. Public school special classes for the mentally retarded in this country were started about 1900. In the beginning they accommodated many of the "slow learners" recruited from among the immigrant population, and in addition, became dumping grounds for those children who bothered the regular class teacher. The foundations of modern special education began to emerge from these classes in the early 1920's.

Today, according to Mackie,[17] educational opportunities are available to more retarded children in more parts of the United States and in greater variety than ever before, despite a large gap between the number of those in need and those being served. Mackie[17] points out that the challenge of providing educational opportunities to the mentally retarded is being met especially by local public and private schools, and by public and private residential schools. The state education agencies play a major role by providing professional leadership and by contributing financial assistance. The Federal Government has expanded its previous role as a consultative and information service, and now provides financial assistance to local and state schools, fellowships and training grants, and funds for research and demonstration projects.

The following are excerpts from Mackie's[17] analysis of the present status of educating the mentally retarded:

> More than 540,000 children were enrolled in special education programs for the mentally retarded in 1966. This figure is less than half of the number of such children estimated to need some form of special education.
>
> During the past twenty years, enrollments of mentally retarded children in residential schools expanded by more than 100 per cent. In the same period, enrollments of such children in local public schools expanded by about 400 per cent. Currently, more than 90 per cent of the mentally retarded children enrolled in special education are in local public schools.
>
> In public day school programs, children are being taught through different organizational patterns. Most mentally retarded are taught in full-time special classes. In 1963, about 10 per cent of the educable mentally retarded and 2 per cent of the trainable mentally retarded participated part-time in regular classes. A small number of the children—less than 2 per cent—received home instruction.
>
> Nursery and kindergarten programs for retarded children are beginning to develop in a few public schools, but such programs are relatively rare. Programs for mentally retarded children housed in public high schools have multiplied tenfold since 1948, and served more than 140,000 retarded youth in 1966. Such programs were initiated in response to the clear need for opportunities for prolonged occupational, social and academic training for the retarded so they can be prepared for effective living in the community.

More than 34,000 teachers are currently employed in local public schools and in residential schools for the mentally retarded. The current need is for about 93,000 teachers.

THE HISTORICAL AND PHILOSOPHICAL UNDERPINNINGS

Today, mental retardation is considered to be one of our major social problems. The rationale for this consideration was expressed by the President's Panel on Mental Retardation[20] as follows:

> The untold human anguish and loss of happiness and well-being which result from mental retardation blight the future of millions of families in the United States. An estimated 15 to 20 million people live in families in which there is a mentally retarded individual. Economic costs cannot compare with the misery and frustration and realization that one's child will be incapable of living a normal life or fully contributing to the well-being of himself and to society in later life.

It is interesting to note that fifty years ago mental retardation was also considered a major social problem, but for completely different reasons. The following quotation from a speech made in 1912 by Dr. Walter E. Fernald, one of the pioneers of psychiatry in the United States, illustrates the thoughts of those concerned with the problem at that time:

> The past few years have witnessed a striking awakening of professional and popular consciousness of the widespread prevalence of feeblemindedness and its influence as a source of wretchedness to the patient himself and to his family, and as a causative factor in the production of crime, prostitution, pauperism, illegitimacy, intemperance, and other complex social diseases.[5]

As the reasons for declaring mental retardation to be a major problem in 1912 were different from the reasons in 1963, so were the recommendations for remediation of the problem. In 1912 a subcommittee appointed by the Research Committee of the Eugenics Section of the American Breeders' Association suggested, inter alia:

1. Life segregation (or segregation during the reproductive period).

2. Sterilization.*
3. Restrictive marriage law.
4. Euthanasia.⁵

The suggested solutions by the President of the United States in 1963 included the following:

1. Prevention of mental retardation through more adequate medical care, nutrition, housing and educational opportunities.
2. Community resources that will provide a coordinated range of timely diagnostic, health, educational, training, rehabilitation, employment, welfare, and legal protection services.
3. Research in the discovery of the causes of mental retardation as well as in appropriate treatment of the retarded.[16]

Today, we tend to dichotomize retarded individuals into "culturally disadvantaged" and "culturally nondisadvantaged." It was reported by the President's Committee on Mental Retardation[22] that "three-fourths of the nation's mentally retarded are to be found in the isolated and impoverished urban and rural slums" and that "a child in a low income rural or urban family is fifteen times more likely to be diagnosed as retarded than is a child from a higher income family."

It is hoped that the 1910-1920 myth of the menace of the mentally retarded will not recur. This myth originated in the belief that heredity was the major cause of mental retardation and that a large proportion of America's juvenile delinquents, criminals, prostitutes, tramps and paupers were mentally retarded.

According to sociologists, society consists of a population settled within a more or less defined territory, whose members depend on each other for survival and for the realization of common goals. Society establishes criteria for categorizing its members. It specifies what is appropriate. It provides mutual expectations about how people ought to behave. Those who de-

---

* It is interesting to note that in spite of Justice Oliver Wendell Holmes' Supreme Court decision in the Virginia case on May 2, 1927, that "the principle that sustains compulsory vaccination is broad enough to cover the cutting of the Fallopian tubes . . . (and that) three generations of imbeciles are enough," sterilization did not become a widespread means of prevention of mental retardation.

viate markedly from these expected norms are singled out through various labels and thus become stigmatized. The stigma terms used by society to describe its retarded members include: mentally retarded, mentally deficient, trainable, educable, slow learner, idiot, imbecile, moron, feebleminded, feeblegifted, stupid, defective, etc. These words often are used to "explain" the individual's inferiority and sometimes even account for the danger he represents.

The most obvious technique for measuring the seriousness of a social problem would seem to be a numerical count of the people who are affected by such a problem. Most students of social problems add the stipulation that a social problem exists only when influential groups believe that they can do something to resolve or remedy the condition. Therefore one might consider mental retardation as a national social problem not only because of the number of people affected but mainly because our contemporary society has failed to provide optimal facilities for treatment, training, education, recreation and counseling. It is a major national social problem because we are unable culturally, socially, and technologically to exorcise it. A society has either to eradicate mental retardation effectively or to learn how to endure it.

THE EDUCATIONAL CONCEPT OF RETARDATION

There seems to be no operational definition of mental retardation for educators of retarded children to work from in developing programs for diagnosis, placement, evaluation and prognosis, and in deciding on goals, methodology and other aspects of curriculum for these children.

In fact, mental retardation is a term that is often ambiguous in meaning, frustrating, semantically inadequate and at times its use is actually incorrect. What mental retardation is, and who the mentally retarded are may depend on who defines them and for what purpose.

Physicians might be more interested in looking at mental retardation from an etiological standpoint; they might use classifications which attempt to attribute the condition to a variety of causes such as infections, metabolic disorders, psychiatric disorders and sensory dysfunctions. The psychologist might be interested in classification based on the behavior of the individual, his ability to learn, or simply on his measured intelligence. The vocational rehabilitation counselor might classify his clients as directly placeable, deferred placeable, sheltered employable or nonself-supporting.

The educator's main interest is in the degree of educability of an individual or in determining whether the individual is manageable or not manageable in a classroom situation. One educational classification describes three major groups of retarded children and youth: the trainable, the educable and the slow learner. It should be emphasized that these are educational terms and the special classroom teacher should be the key person on the evaluative team to make such a diagnosis. This diagnosis may or may not coincide with medical, psychological or other diagnoses. For example, not all mongoloids are automatically trainable and not all children within the IQ ranges of 50 to 75 should be automatically considered educable. The child with a medical diagnosis of blindness, deafness or cerebral palsy may be educationally gifted, normal, a slow learner, educable, trainable, or nontrainable. The various degrees of retardation (trainable, educable, slow learners) as viewed by the educator are measured according to the cognitive, sensorimotor and affective functioning of an individual of *school age* in a *school set-up*. Thus it is rather a misdiagnosis when one refers to a two-year-old child as educable mentally retarded, or to a twenty-five-year-old adult as trainable.

Our schools are becoming more skillful at identifying children with learning difficulties. Tests have improved and, in general, more effective use is being made of test results. It is widely accepted that an IQ should not be an absolute and final label, since the score is apt to vary with the test and the age and condition of the child. Further, educators are asking pertinent questions: Do we measure enough variables? Are our measures broad enough to gauge abilities of the mentally retarded? To gauge educability?

One of the most fundamental beliefs in American democracy is that the good society results when each individual is given the opportunity to develop with the aid of a universally supported school system. Thus the public school holds as its main objective the provision of education for *all* children. The obligation of the public school is to accept all who fall within a certain age range, to provide an environment that is friendly to all, and to offer experiences which will be useful to each. One of the main functions of special education is to see that this objective is implemented. Special educators resist decisions to reject individuals with disabilities and handicaps, and are busy developing resources within the schools to deal with those individuals who might so easily be rejected and who, in the past, often were rejected.

The development of Special Education as a discipline emphasized the responsibility of schools to allocate children to programs likely to be best for them. Traditionally, the only criterion for placement in a given program was the paramount handicap of the child. It could be physical disability such as deafness, blindness, a crippling condition or an impaired heart. It could be the IQ of the individual. Thus those with IQs below 50 were placed in one program; those with IQs between 50 and 75 in another program, and those above 75 found themselves in regular school classes. Many school systems considered "emotional disturbance" or "delinquency" as the only variable for which to create a special class. Some schools opened special classes for the so-called brain-injured. The paradox of this arrangement is that a discipline such as Special Education, which has as its principal aim provisions for individual differences among school children, should mistakenly assume that all children with deafness, blindness, IQ 50, or other handicaps are the same and need the same educational programs. The result is that in special classes are found children who vary greatly in their abilities, interests and handicaps in every imaginable dimension. Educators have only begun to realize this, and are searching for better methods of allocating children to appropriate special classes.

We came to *assume* that because of the nature of their disabilities and handicaps, mentally retarded children need a special program in a special class. We came to believe that if retarded children are to develop their limited potentialities, they should not be subjected to the more rapid pace of the regular classroom. We also came to assume that if the normal pupils are to progress at their optimum rates, the teacher should not be handicapped by having to make provisions for such slow pupils. In this way special classes for the retarded have been based from the beginning on a "relief" philosophy—relieving the normal child from the "dragging anchor" effect of the retarded child; relieving the teacher of her most discouraging teaching and behavior problems. But what have we done for the retarded child? According to Blackman,[2] we have placed the retarded child in an educational environment which immediately assumes the inexorable fact of his mental retardation—past, present and future. The methods used in most of the special classes are geared toward the *assumed* low-level ability of the child.

Research until very recently neglected to evaluate the possibility of accelerating the intellectual development of retarded children through specific training. Studies indicate that intellectual development of retarded children is not as static as formerly believed. The pessimism regarding changes, especially with young children, is gradually disappearing.

On the basis of information obtained from the literature in the past decade it might be suggested that *mental retardation should be considered by educators as referring to individuals of various chronological ages who manifest, or are perceived as manifesting, a wide range of marked difficulties in effective coping with demands and tasks of their household, school, work and other life situations. The origin of the difficulties can be traced to dysfunctions of the individual's intellectual, sensorimotor and affective abilities caused by interactions among biological, environmental and psychosocial factors.*

As it can be seen the stress is placed on the adaptive behavior of an individual rather than on his IQ.

EDUCATIONAL NEEDS OF THE MENTALLY RETARDED

One of the major objectives of special education is to help the mentally retarded individual develop mechanisms through which he will satisfy his basic psychological, biological, sociological, educational, vocational and recreational needs in ways accepted and approved by the society in which he lives. All these needs intermix so that it becomes impossible to meet adequately the individual's educational needs and ignore his psychological, biological or sociological needs.

In the broad sense of the word, education refers to all those experiences which an individual encounters that affect in any way his development and by which he acquires the ways, beliefs and standards of society.

Educational needs, for the purpose of this discussion, can be defined as the lack of some attitudes, knowledges, skills and information that it can be assumed the individual should have, or that are enjoyed by most members of society. This lack is experienced or felt within the organism and leads somehow to energizing and directing activity toward what is perceived as satisfying the needs.

This definition implies the two types of educational needs mentioned by Stratemeyer *et al.*:[25] a) felt needs or expressed needs—referring to those needs of which the learner himself is conscious, or to his request for help in solving problems or meeting situations, and b) societal needs—referring to those attitudes, knowledges and skills that society demands of its citizens, whether or not the learner is aware of these demands.

Ideally, the special class should develop educational objectives for its students which take into consideration the basic needs of the individual and those of society. However, in practice one notices two diametrically opposed approaches: a) the society-centered position and b) the child-centered position. Advocates of the former hold that the objectives of special education are primarily social. According to them, the purpose of the school is to prepare the individual to live in a certain kind of society. It is, therefore, important that the individual become the kind of person desired by that society and that he acquire the outlooks, knowledges and skills demanded by it.

On the other hand, proponents of the child-centered approach argue that the ultimate purpose of special education is the development of an individual. In other words, it is preparing the individual to achieve maximum social and economic success. The advocates of this position also hold that education, in both purpose and content, must be based on individual needs, capacities and interests.

According to Doll,[7] it has become popular to declare that the educational needs of the exceptional child and his educational management are essentially the same as those for normal children. "This true," he states, "if emphasis is on the essential, because the special child is essentially a child. But his identification as special is *based* on his *deviant* attributes and needs."

The paramount educational need of a mentally retarded child is what Doll calls "adultation." He defines adultation as "the process of becoming, or assisting someone to become, an adult, and by implication a mature, competent person who will be relatively self-sufficient and a contributing member of his family and his social community."

INSTRUCTION

Curriculum is usually defined as the total school program. This definition includes physical facilities, learning activities, interaction of learners and teachers, learners and learners, etc. Curriculum development for the mentally retarded is regarded as the systematic effort of individuals and groups to help children, adolescents, and adults with mental, physical, emotional and social dysfunctions to improve the level of their current mental, physical, emotional and social functioning in our society. It is a continuous process which takes the following into consideration:

1. The nature of our society.
2. The nature of the learner.
3. Educational methods.
4. Research findings.

Ideally, curriculum development should include teachers and school administrators, psychologists, social workers, physicians, vocational counselors, parents, civic and church leaders, occupational, physical and speech therapists among its practitioners. By helping the individual to improve his physical, mental, emotional and social level of functioning, we are helping him to occupy a contributing place in the society in which he lives. This enables him to be an individual who has achieved the following objectives:

1. Understands his own strengths and limitations—self-realization.
2. Can play, work and live with others—human relationship.
3. Can contribute his share of work and responsibility to the social group in which he lives—economic efficiency.
4. Is able to act as a responsible member of the social group in which he lives—civic responsibility.

Curriculum is the way to achieve these objectives and ultimate goals, and will vary in different age groups and in different educational classifications.

Preschool age might be considered a diagnostic period. There is very little division between the trainable and educable. Curriculum for both groups consists mainly of self-help, communication skills, and socialization activities. For the teacher this period of time is the best opportunity to discover the various functions and dysfunctions of individuals as well as the rate of their learning. Concrete materials which stimulate and motivate the child should be used. Optimum opportunities should be provided for the child to explore, for self-expression and for stimulating spontaneous language. Careful anecdotal records kept by the teacher will help to discover trends in functioning and dysfunctioning of the child. The teacher should have an opportunity to contribute his observation to physicians, psychologists, social workers and others, who in turn should share their evaluations and assessments of the child and his environment. If this is done in the preschool period, the teacher, with the help of the rest of the team, could predict the trainability or educability of the child and place him on the proper track.

During school age, the curriculum for trainable children consists of activities revolving around self-help, communication and socialization. The curriculum for the educable involves a gradual increase of skills in concrete as well as abstract areas, but all based on real life situations and realistic preparation.

The post-school age trainable may be directly placeable in a sheltered workshop. Some will be placeable after additional training while some will never become placeable at all. The educable may be directly placeable in sheltered workshops and some will be nonplaceable.

THE TEACHER

We usually say that a teacher of the retarded should be a well-trained person. What constitutes a well-trained teacher for the mentally retarded is a matter of opinion, and opinions vary widely on this subject. To me the successful teacher is one who has the capacity for reaching students as individuals. The architect, the lawyer, the physician usually serves his client or patient by doing something *to* him or *for* him; the teacher, when he performs his work best, does it *with* his student. I believe that the teacher is a practitioner, an artist, an engineer who strives to help children learn. If he is to work effectively with children whose intelligence levels differ markedly from his own, the teacher must know something of the ways in which children mature, how they learn, what motivates them, and how physical, emotional and social factors influence learning and teaching. The teacher must know as much as possible about the nature of learning, the ways of motivating students and about which teaching techniques are suitable for them.

Just as a civil, chemical, or electrical engineer who is concerned with building bridges, streets, and machines must base his procedures on mathematics and basic sciences of physics and chemistry, so a teacher should direct his methods and procedures according to principles and laws that are psychologically sound. We make a distinction between an engineer and a mechanic. A mechanic may be only a tinkerer who tunes up engines by rule of thumb methods, without understanding the basic principles that govern them. An engineer, on the other hand, having studied the sciences basic to his art, is able to meet new situations and to adapt his materials to them.

The teacher does not do his job alone. He is complemented by teacher educators, supervisors and administrators who, we assume, understand the intricate and intertwining elements of special education. He needs aids from the various disciplines concerned—persons to whom he can refer pupils and by whom he will be challenged through "give and take" discussion to promote professional perspective in his efforts to help children grow.

THE FAMILY

The mentally retarded individual should be viewed in terms of the environment and atmosphere provided him by his immediate social group—his family. It is important that educational provisions for the mentally retarded should begin to consider this point of view more seriously. The retarded child is an integral part of the nuclear family, or the primary family unit, composed of a married couple and their offspring. The nuclear family is a union of interacting personalities. The clustered relationships among these personalities are at least eight in number: husband-wife; father-son; father-daughter; mother-son; mother-daughter; brother-brother; sister-sister; brother-sister.

It can be hypothesized that the mentally retarded child in the midst of this primary family unit, because of his multiple handicaps, impairs the development of healthy relationships among the members of this unit and inevitably the whole family unit becomes handicapped. The handicaps of the family unit may lie in the same areas as those of the child, i.e. communication, self-concept, etc. Any educational treatment given only to the child does not necessarily remedy the family's handicap.

FOLLOW-UP STUDIES

One of the reasons for the dramatic growth of special educational facilities and programs for mentally retarded children and youth is the assumed potential of these children for adult adjustment. This assumption could well be expressed in the words of the President's Panel on Mental Retardation:[20]

> Every human being has potential for useful activity. . . . The true goal of education and rehabilitation of the handicapped is to help every individual to make the most of his potential for participation in all the affairs of our society, including work, no matter how great or small his potential may be.

After reviewing follow-up studies of the mentally retarded done in the past seventy-five years, the question arises as to whether the educational retardationists realize that "for the mentally retarded adulthood is often a longer, more painful, and more uncertain process than for others. Their image of themselves often becomes warped and confused. They are not always accepted, treated, and respected as adults."[19] Mayer[18] reminds us that "of all of this nation's disadvantaged groups, the mentally retarded are the most disadvantaged; of all handicapped groups, the mentally retarded are the most handicapped; of all competing groups, the mentally retarded are least equipped to compete."

Gallagher[10] comments that two major identifiable forces that possess unfavorable potential for the adult adjustment of the retarded are the narrowing job market in our growing urban technology and the decline of family influence. He poses the following challenging questions:

> If the means for self-support is reduced and the supportive function of the family is also reduced, then the role of the *benefactor* needs special attention. What other agencies in our society should take greater responsibility in this regard? Should the schools or social agencies prepare for an increased role, as a *benefactor* for mentally retarded youths and adults?

Attempts to determine the fate of retarded children have resulted in a number of longitudinal studies of varying intensity and duration. Tizard,[16] after reviewing most of the studies, concludes that despite restricted opportunities, mentally retarded persons generally made satisfactory occupational adjustment after leaving school. Goldstein,[12] on the other hand, after reviewing most of the same studies points out that the occupational picture for the retarded is far from encouraging. He was able to draw four main conclusions from his review of these follow-up studies. They are the following: a) most of the mildly retarded will make an adjustment to their communities as adults, b) these mildly retarded persons are more often adversely affected by economic depressions than are nonretarded persons, c) prevailing economic conditions largely determine whether or not retarded persons are able to join the ranks of home owners and acquire other of the usual material assets of families, and d) retarded persons inevitably tend to be on the lower end of occupational scales.

According to Heber and Dever,[15] if one were to generalize from an extensive literature up to about 1960 dealing with the social and occupational adjustment of educable mentally retarded adults, the following might be stated:

1. A considerable percentage of the retarded achieved employment. Their job success appeared to be more closely related to attitudinal and personality factors than to IQ, and they performed and retained these jobs about as well as nonretarded persons doing the same work. The jobs, with few exceptions, were mainly in the unskilled category.

2. In contrast to popular opinion, there was little evidence to indicate that they did especially well on repetitive, boring tasks and they were found just as deficient in skills requiring manual dexterity as they were in skills requiring mental dexterity. The retardate was more likely to attain an adequate job adjustment in the late 20's than in the teens. Many were found to hold unrealistic occupational aspirations. The studies showed that close family or professional supervision was better than occupational skill training which was not particularly relevant to the nature of the retardate's employment.

3. In the community they were found to participate less in civic, social and recreational activities, to demand more social services and to demonstrate a greater tendency to commit minor legal infractions, than did the general population.

The same authors point out that follow-up studies since 1960 have been more sophisticated and challenge some of the optimistic interpretations of the earlier work. Studies reported by Windle[23] and Edgerton[9] on institution residents are particularly relevant to this discussion. The purpose of Windle's study was to determine why mentally retarded residents failed to remain in the community. Residents (356) who had spent time in the community but who could not be discharged from the institution were clustered into four groups: a) placed on vocational leave, b) placed on home leave, c) placed on home care and d) on unauthorized absence. With the exception of the family care group all residents fell into the range of mild retardation.

Out of the 356 patients in the four groups, 211 were failures, or about two-thirds of the total group. The reasons for the high incidence of failure were interesting. Those who escaped failed because they were caught; this is to be expected. The other two groups (vocational leave and home leave), presumably selected for their inferred ability to get along on the outside, also failed in large numbers. The vocational leave patients returned mostly because of inadequate interpersonal relations, inadequate vocational performance, or a voluntary return to the institution. Those on home leave failed mainly because of their antisocial behavior (crimes, sexual misbehavior, pregnancy and minor antisocial actions).

Edgerton[9] followed up intensively on 110 persons who were discharged from the institution. He found that they were employed for the most part, but they were marginal economically. Most had major debts; few had any job security and even fewer had any marketable skills. The most dramatic finding of his study was the extent to which the adults depended on various social agencies to help them maintain: a) their self-percept; b) their ability to cope with the world; c) their efforts to "pass" for normal and deny the mental retardation. The dependency of the adults was so great that Edgerton estimated that only three out of the forty-eight persons could be called independent. Edgerton concludes by saying that life in what happens to be a progressive institution did not prepare the subjects for life in the community. Once in the outside world, the stigma of having been convicted of mental incompetence was so great that it had to be denied constantly in order to obtain a sense of personal worth. This was a task impossible for most without added support.

Cobb[3] says that descriptive and comparative accounts of the adult adjustments of the retarded reflect in considerable measure differences in the populations sampled, in the geographical and other environmental loci, and in the period of social history in which the investigation occurred. The adjustment process appears to be strongly influenced, not only by characteristics of the person and by the types of training and other experience he may have had, but also by the characteristics of the social scene in which the attempt to adjust takes place. Consequently, the predictive variables that prove significant in excellently designed research investigations may have little value when applied in the rehabilitation procedures at later times and in other places.

Sparks and Younie[24] reviewed eighteen follow-up studies and concluded that the term "adult adjustment" customarily is used in a very restricted fashion when applied to the educable mentally retarded. According to them, traditionally, adjustment has been considered "good" if the retarded adult is employed, has remained law abiding and has not become dependent on others for primary sustenance. Conversely, poor adjustment has been said to exist when the retarded person is unemployed, unnecessarily underemployed, dependent upon family or public funds for major economic support, or guilty of serious infractions of the law.

PROBLEMS BESETTING ADULT ADJUSTMENT OF THE MENTALLY RETARDED

The recent position statement of the American Psychological Association[1] emphasized that despite abundant resources directed toward resolution of the problem of mental retardation, millions of human beings called the mentally retarded are still in unproductive or custodial situations for most of their lives. It continues to stress the fact that "mental retardation is primarily a psychosocial and psychoeducational problem—a deficit in adaptation to the demands and expectations of society evidenced by the individual's relative difficulty in learning, problem solving, adapting to a new situation, and abstract thinking." The position statement also called for concerted efforts toward classifying those of below average capacity in ways departing from the traditionally stigmatizing influence of the labels "deficient," "defective," or "retardate."

According to Edgerton,[9] one might speculate that no other stigma is as basic as mental retardation in the sense that a person so labeled is thought to be completely lacking in basic competence. "Other stigmatized persons typically retain some competencies, limited though they may be, but the retarded person has none left to him. He is, by definition, incompetent to manage any of his affairs." Is it then possible for a stigmatized adult to "adjust"? According to Goffman:[11]

> The nature of a "good adjustment" requires that the stigmatized individual cheerfully and unselfconsciously accept himself as essentially the same as normals, while at the same time he voluntarily withhold himself from those situations in which normals would find it difficult to give lip-service to their similar acceptance of him. . . . It means that the unfairness and pain of having to carry a stigma will never be presented to (normals) ; it means that normals will not have to admit to themselves how limited their tactfulness and tolerance is; and it means that normals can remain relatively uncontaminated by intimate contact with the stigmatized, relatively unthreatened in their identity beliefs.
> . . . The stigmatized individual is asked to act so as to imply neither that his burden is heavy nor that bearing it has made him different from us; at the same time he must keep himself at that remove from us which ensures our painlessly being able to confirm this belief about him. . . . A *phantom acceptance* is thus allowed to provide the base for a *phantom normalcy*.

Edgerton[9] suggests that another explanation, another word, must be found and the word must avoid the stigma. "Call the condition an 'adjustment deficiency' or 'educational deprivation,' or provide a medical neologism." He emphasizes that whatever the euphemism, it must suggest that the affliction is a partial one—not an all-encompassing "mental" deficit, and that it is amenable to treatment and training. "If a nonstigmatizing label can be found which can be employed consistently, then it may be possible to enlist the mildly retarded as willing participants in their own improvement." He also stresses the fact that if we wish mildly retarded adults to live in a largely independent way, then we must understand and deal with the stigma that they now face.

Guskin,[14] after reviewing a variety of theoretical approaches and empirical studies relevant to social psychologies of mental retardation, presents hypotheses which might emphasize further the difficulties of adult adjustment:

1. In a normal group, the mentally retarded is likely to be seen as deviant in ability. As a consequence the other

    group members may stop comparing themselves with him and may stop associating with him.

2. The behavior of persons interacting with the mentally retarded may be seen as a function of their expectations concerning the defective's behavior and the actual behavior shown by the defective in that situation.

3. Popular attitudes and stereotypes may to some extent influence the way the mentally retarded individual is evaluated by others.

4. The presence of a mentally retarded individual in the family may lead to disruption in family relationships, unfavorable attitudes toward the defective member, and modification in the parents' child-rearing practices.

To repeat after Crow,[4] human adjustment is a complex process. The making of desirable adjustments to the various demands of life is influenced by differing inherited characteristics and varying environmental conditions and situations to which an individual is exposed. Adjustment is an active process that occurs as the individual lives in his family situation, advances educationally, pursues vocational outlets and engages in social relationships. A mentally retarded adult probably is, or at some time in his life has been, motivated by the desire to marry, rear children, experience a happy home life, and earn success in a chosen vocation. In addition, he desires to enjoy the companionship of friends and associates of his choice, and to spend his leisure time in interesting and relaxing activities. He also is entitled to achieve a position of respect among his associates, to enjoy democratic rights, and to establish the foundation of an economically and socially secure old age.

    Many of the desires and needs of retarded adults are hampered by legal restrictions. As was pointed out by the Report of the Task Force on Law of the President's Panel on Mental Retardation,[21] only eight of our states are entirely silent on the subject of marriage of the mentally retarded. Forty-two states passed laws qualifying the right of the retarded to marry. Statutes prohibiting the marriage of "idiots and imbeciles" are common. A few states disqualify the "feeble-minded," although it is not always clear how they are supposed to be identified. It is sometimes impossible to qualify for the statutory exceptions to the pro-hibitions. For instance, a "feeble-minded" person would or-dinarily be unable to show that he had been "cured," as one state requires. The Report suggests that there are three ques-tions to be answered: a) Can the retarded prospective spouse assume the responsibilities of marriage? b) Will the minimum expectations for care and nurture of any children be realized? and c) Will the genetic risks be so small that society can permit them to be taken? "There are no general answers to these questions," says the report, "for the answers do not necessarily depend on the degree of retardation. We merely point out that the rights and dignity of the retarded, their access to permissible activities, and to the comforts, companionship and protection of marriage, must be considered."

Tindall,[26] after reviewing representative writings dealing with the concept of adjustment, delineated seven characteristics or facets of adjustment:

1. Maintaining an integrated personality.
2. Conforming to social demands.
3. Adapting to reality conditions.
4. Maintaining consistency.
5. Maturing with age.
6. Maintaining an optimal emotional tone.
7. Contributing optimally to society through an increasing efficiency.

Doll[8] argued that too little is known about the retarded adult to be able to discuss his adjustment. According to him, "there is almost no information regarding the extent to which the re-tarded adult continues to progress or decline in those direc-tions which have been such a concern to us during his pre-adult years."

A specific area of adult adjustment of the mentally retarded which needs much more careful and systematic investigation deals with work adjustment. Dawis, England and Lofquist[6] indi-cate that work in contemporary society is behavior which is re-inforced in several ways, most characteristically by the payment of wages. This behavior takes place in a locus called the work environment. The longer an individual stays in a given work environment, the more probable it is that the individual has arrived at some adequate adjustment with the environment. When the individual leaves a given work environment, one may infer that the adjustment was inadequate. Work adjustment, according to these three authors, is inferred from two primary sets of indicators: "satisfaction" and "satisfactoriness." "Satisfaction" consists of those variables which represent the individual's view of his "work adjustment." These variables reflect the individual's evaluation of his work situation in terms of how satisfied he is with the many aspects of work, e.g. the type of work activity he engages in, the people he works for and with, the conditions under which he works and the compensation he receives for his work. These variables might then be considered as reflecting the extent to which the individual's expectations concerning work have been fulfilled.

"Satisfactoriness" includes those variables which represent the employer's view of the individual's work adjustment. The employer presumably is concerned with the individual primarily as an employee. He views the individual's "work adjustment" mainly in terms of how well he performs his job. Thus the employer's view provides an organizational criterion while the employee's view represents an individual criterion.

Work adjustment occurs over a period of time. "Satisfaction" and "satisfactoriness" may differ in the same individual for different periods of time. There may be cycles of satisfaction and dissatisfaction, and cycles of satisfactoriness and unsatisfactoriness in the work history of the individual.

CONCLUSION

The term "mental retardation" is extremely negative in our society. It refers to an array of human deviations. The 1960's saw the United States embark, for the first time, on a large scale, comprehensive attempt to confront and cope with the problem of mental retardation. This effort has attracted people from all segments of our national society, representing among them the entire spectrum of opinion on what action the problem requires and how best to effect it. This growing concern has been manifest in Washington, and four successive presidents have expressed enough personal interest in the matter to use their power and prestige to involve both government, on all levels, and private organizations in creative action aimed at overcoming retardation. Consequently, local, state and federal participation in the securing of improved services and opportunities for the retarded increased steadily throughout the decade.

"Retardationists," "retardationologists," and "retardationaries" should be proud indeed of their individual and collective efforts. However, on entering the new decade of the 1970's much more consideration should be given to the educated, trained, habilitated and rehabilitated mentally retarded alumni of the 1960's. Their adjustment difficulties are tremendous, and the tendency among such individuals is to feel that "I am invisible. . . . I am a man of substance, of flesh and bone, fiber and liquids, and I might even be said to possess a mind. I am invisible, understand, simply because people refuse to see me. . . ." (Ralph Ellison's *Invisible Man*, as quoted in Greene.[13]

The declaration of general and special rights of the mentally retarded adopted by the International League of Societies for the Mentally Handicapped in 1968 spells out the basic principles underlying the *modus operandi* of an effective life planning for the mentally retarded in our society:

1. The mentally retarded person has the same basic rights as other citizens of the same country and same age.

2. The mentally retarded person has a right to proper medical care and physical restoration and to such education, training, habilitation and guidance as will enable him to develop his ability and potential to the fullest possible extent, no matter how severe his degree of disability. No mentally handicapped person should be deprived of such services by reason of the costs involved.

3. The mentally retarded person has a right to protection from exploitation, abuse and degrading treatment.

Above all the mentally retarded person has the right to respect.

REFERENCES

1. American Psychological Association: Psychology and mental retardation. *Am Psychol*, 25:267-268, March, 1970.
2. Blackman, Leonard S.: Research in mental retardation: A point of view. *Except Child*, 26:12-14, Sept., 1959.

3. Cobb, Henry V.: Predictive studies of vocational adjustment. In DiMichael, S.G. (Ed.) : *New Vocational Pathways for the Mentally Retarded*. Washington, D.C., American Personnel and Guidance Association, 1966, pp. 5-19.

4. Crow, Lester D.: *Psychology of Human Adjustment*. New York, Alfred A. Knopf, 1967.

5. Davies, S.P.: *Social Control of the Mentally Deficient*. New York, Thomas Y. Crowell, 1930.

6. Dawis, Rene V., England, George W. and Lofquist, Lloyd H.: *A Theory of Work Adjustment*. University of Minnesota, Minnesota Studies in Vocational Rehabilitation, Bulletin 38, January, 1964.

7. Doll, Edgar A.: Adultation of the special child. *Except Child,* 29:275-280, February, 1963.

8. Doll, Edgar A.: Programs for the adult retarded. *Ment Retard,* 6:19-21, February, 1968.

9. Edgerton, Robert B.: *The Cloak of Competence: Stigma in the Lives of the Mentally Retarded*. Los Angeles, University of California Press, 1967.

10. Gallagher, James J.: Comments on Paper: Education and Habilitation of the Mentally Retarded. Presented at the International Conference on Social-Cultural Aspects of Mental Retardation, George Peabody College, Nashville, Tennessee, 1968, mineographed.

11. Goffman, Erving: *Stigma*. Englewood Cliffs, New Jersey, Prentice-Hall, Inc., 1963.

12. Goldstein, Herbert: Social and occupational adjustment. In Stevens, H.A. and Heber, R. (Eds.) : *Mental Retardation: A Review of Research*. Chicago, University of Chicago Press, 1964, pp. 214-258.

13. Greene, Maxine: Existentialism and education. *Phi Delta Kappa—Beta Data,* 1:4, February to March, 1969.

14. Guskin, Samuel: Social psychologies of mental deficiency. In Ellis, Norman R. (Ed.) : *Handbook of Mental Deficiency*. New York, McGraw-Hill Book Co., Inc., 1963, pp. 325-352

15. Heber, Rick R. and Dever, Richard B.: Education and Habilitation of the Mentally Retarded. Presented at the International Conference on Social-Cultural Aspects of Mental Retardation, George Peabody College, Nashville, Tennessee, 1968. Mimeographed.

16. Tizard, J.: Longitudinal and follow-up studies. In Clarke, Ann M. and Clarke, A.D.B. (Eds.) : *Mental Deficiency: The Changing Outlook* (2nd ed.) . London, Methuen and Co. Ltd., 1965, pp. 482-509.

17. Mackie, Romaine P.: *Special Education in the United States: Statistics 1948-1966*. New York, Teachers College Press, 1969.

18. Mayer, Sondra M.: Selected Job Opportunity Areas for the Mentally Retarded in the Borough of Manhattan, the City of New York, in View of Recent Technological Change: A Descriptive Analysis. Unpub-

lished Doctor of Education Dissertation, Teachers College, Columbia University, New York, 1968.

19. Nirje, Bengt: The Normalization Principle and Its Human Management Implications. In Wolfensberger, W. and Kugel, R.B. (Eds.) : *Changing Patterns in Residential Services for the Mentally Retarded.* Washington, D.C., President's Committee on Mental Retardation, 1969.

20. The President's Panel on Mental Retardation: *A Proposed Program for National Action to Combat Mental Retardation.* A Report to the President. Washington, D.C., Government Printing Office, 1962.

21. The President's Panel on Mental Retardation: *Report of the Task Force on Law.* Washington, D.C., U.S. Government Printing Office, 1963.

22. The President's Committee on Mental Retardation: *MR 68: The Edge of Change.* Washington, D.C., U.S. Government Printing Office, 1968.

23. Windle, Charles: *Prognosis of Mental Subnormals. Monogr Suppl Am J Ment Defic,* 66:1-180, March, 1962

24. Sparks, Howard L. and Younie, William J.: Adult adjustment of the mentally retarded: Implications for teacher education. *Except Child,* 36:13-18, September, 1969.

25. Stratemeyer, Florence B. *et al.: Developing a Curriculum for Modern Living.* New York, Teachers College Press, 1957

26. Tindall, Ralph H.: Relationships among measures of adjustment. In Gorlow, L. and Katkovsky, W. (Eds.) : *Readings in the Psychology of Adjustment.* New York, McGraw-Hill Book Co., Inc., 1959, pp. 107-115.

Chapter XVIII

THE USE OF LEARNING PRINCIPLES IN THE EDUCATION AND MANAGEMENT OF RETARDED CHILDREN

C. B. FERSTER

FIRST, I should explain how it is that an experimental psychologist, like myself, who has done so much work in the animal field particularly with pigeons, and so little work with retarded children, or clinically, is called on to talk about clinical matters. An account of my own professional history, typical of others in the field, will give some insight into how and why operant reinforcement concepts are playing such a large part in the activities of many people in the field of mental retardation and in other clinical fields.

Operant conditioning, from a technical and theoretical view, is not really conditioning at all. Technically, conditioning refers to reflexes, like the jerk of the knee when the patellar tendon is tapped, or vasoconstriction elicited by a loud noise, or saliva secretion elicited by food in the mouth. In a reflex there is an internal response, usually physiological, elicited by an outside stimulus. The relationship between the stimulus and the response is fixed and stereotyped. Operant behavior has the reverse direction. The body's long muscles, in activities such as walking, talking, grasping or moving various objects, act on and change the environment external to the person. Reflex conditioning and operant reinforcement tend to be confused because they both bring to mind behavior which is predictable, orderly, controlled in the laboratory or described scientifically. The two kinds of behaviors have very different characteristics. For the technical psychologist, operant conditioning means simply altering the frequency of operant behavior, whether in the laboratory or in the infinite variety and complexity of the natural environment. Control in the context of reflex behavior refers to the one-to-one relation between the stimulus and the response. In operant behavior, no matter how complex or multiply caused, control refers to the technical description of how the performance is related to the environment that generated it. The primary fact of operant reinforcement is frequently demonstrated in a classroom experiment. A hungry pigeon, in a small space, eats whenever a tray of food is raised so it can be reached. The demonstrator increases the frequency of an observed performance by allowing the bird to eat just after it is emitted. The performances followed by eating increases in frequency dramatically. Further, the topography of the performance is exactly the one that the food follows. Complex forms of behavior are reinforced in successive approximations, by increasing the frequency of a variation in the desired direction. Here is control in almost every sense of the word.

Yet the pigeon demonstration shows many of the features of clinical situations. First, there is only one organism, not the average of a group. Second, there is an adjustment and interaction between the person operating the feeder and the pigeon. Finally, what is done at every stage cannot be anticipated but depends on what went before. On the other hand, the repertoire that the bird develops may not be as clinically useful as it is a powerful reinforcer for the person who pushes the button. The novice who carries out such a demonstration gains a conviction that the behavior of the organism is plastic and unlimited if a properly reactive environment can be arranged. If behavior can be altered so precisely and rationally in this prototype environment can we not proceed to apply the same approach to more complex situations and solve some of the pressing social problems we face? The faith that the power to change behavior can be used to better the human condition appears to be similar to that experienced by other mental health professionals such as Freudian psychologists, the group therapists and nursery school teachers who discover an effective technique. My own first steps out of the animal laboratory were experiments with psychotic children, mostly autistic and very primitive, considered untreatable at that time. The differential diagnosis between autistic and retarded children was difficult and many found their way to custodial care in schools for the retarded. Observing these children, as an experimental psychologist, suggested the hypothesis that their repertoire could be augmented significantly if a properly reactive environment could be arranged. My first experience with an autistic child confirmed the conviction that the child would be labile to an environment that was uniquely reactive to him. While making observations in a hospital ward I observed one autistic child who walked around continuously, occasionally passing in front of me. Every time he came in my vicinity, I said, "Hi, Tommy" and those performances which got me to speak increased in frequency until he paced back and forth in front of me. When I stopped speaking he drifted off to other parts of the ward. Strictly speaking, to prove that the exact contingency between the performance and my action was responsible for the changed behavior it would have been necessary to speak to the boy at a distance. Nevertheless, the increase in the frequency of the boy's performance, under control of the environment I had arranged, reinforced my inclination to extend the repertoire of autistic children by reinforcement procedures.

Over a period of several years an automatic environment emerged which could with proper programming and guidance build many complex repertoires in these children.[6, 7] At the start of the experiment the children engaged in only the simplest and most primitive activities, both in the experimental room and out. When we finished they were earning pennies to use in a device which would deliver a towel with which they could go swimming later; they were matching to sample with complex stimuli; they were saving money to use after it was earned; and engaging in other tasks which required paying attention to a host of stimuli and conforming to complicated procedures. Furthermore, the children sustained these complex activities for two and three hours at a time even though they were not able to do so for as long as five minutes elsewhere. Obviously, the main achievement in these experiments was not the literal repertoires that emerged. The experiments did demonstrate, however, that we could develop complex repertoires by arranging an environment to interact with the child's repertoire delicately and in small steps. All the basic processes that we know of from the laboratory to create and sustain behavior operated in the development of the repertoire. The limit appeared to be the patient, cumulative construction of a reactive environment and the skill of the experimenter rather than in any inherent limitations of the child.

If so much behavior representing so many basic learning processes could be generated experimentally in the laboratory, it seemed obvious to extend the same techniques to the development of a normal repertoire. Why could not the same kind of objective and rational program be used in the natural environment to develop social activities and emotional reactivity. With this recognition, and in all fairness to my clinical skills, I lost interest in experiments with autistic children until such time as I could experiment with aspects of their repertoire directly relevant to normal life. At the same time, this same spirit which led me to extend laboratory experience into work with the autistic children led many others into similar work with emotionally disturbed and retarded children.

A comment needs to be made about the use of food as reinforcement in behavioral experiments of this kind. Food has been used often as a means of contacting a child who does not appear sensitive to ordinary social influence. Even when social interactions are possible, food appears to be a quicker and easier route. Food reinforcement has been used with very good effect in many experiments with retarded children who otherwise did not appear teachable.[3, 4] Yet the undesirable aspects of food motivation as a teaching or developmental device are obvious. The repertoire, without food reinforcement, may not persist later when it is supported only with a natural reinforcer. Also, food procedures give the therapist arbitrary power because of the deprivation required to make the reinforcer effective. On the other hand, it is obviously desirable to reinforce with natural events which are part of the children's normal life.[8]

Alternatives to food as a way to motivate and make contact with a child are not always very visible to an experimental psychologist, particularly one without extensive clinical training. Arbitrary reinforcement by food can be rejected only if there is a practical and effective alternative. Fortunately, as an experimental psychologist, I could observe experienced clinicians objectively enough to describe their therapy in detail and behaviorally. Many clinicians could only describe what they did intuitively even when I could observe the behavioral principles which were responsible for the success of their therapeutic procedures. Such observation taught me that clinicians indeed reinforced behavior even though they talked differently than behaviorists about what they did.

The first behavioral description of clinical work at the Linwood Children's Center occurred when I gave Miss Simmons notes I had made of her therapy with a child on a rocking horse after several months of observation. She recognized that the objective description of her therapy was accurate and valid despite her amazement that therapeutic interactions, which she communicated to other clinicians only with the greatest difficulty, were being described by an experimental psychologist. I think it was precisely because I was an experimental psychologist that I could see what she did. The observations I could make of the therapeutic interaction benefited me because I discovered behavioral procedures and reinforcers far more powerful than anything I had seen before. Large changes occurred in the child's behavior, both in its frequency of occurrence and its content. I began to see that experimental psychology could contribute to clinical work by providing a language and theoretical framework that conveys what actually happens in therapy besides applying new techniques. I began to observe that not all clinicians had Miss Simmon's consummate skill and that clinical training programs frequently involved years of training. Even when the programs were successful, there was no real conviction about what part of the training was responsible for what part of the therapist's clinical skill. If experimental psychology can provide tools to identify the effective elements of the therapist's interaction with the child, and if therapy could be described objectively, then clinicians could become sure, quick and more frequent in their effectiveness with the child.

Clinically skilled people who work with children are in particular short supply. Part of the problem is economic because pay levels and, correspondingly, the educational levels of those who work with children are so low. More distressing, however, is the possibility that persons with clinical skill who are in daily contact with the children would not be available even if pay scales were higher. This shortage of clinically trained people is a vacuum into which operant conditioning has stepped. Many procedures have been developed to conform a child's conduct to daily routines administered by the custodial staff.[12] These are simple procedures usually requiring very little training. They frequently involved tokens which the child could cash in later for privileges, food or an opportunity for an outing. Often, the target behaviors of the reinforcement procedures were the day-to-day items of conduct required to manage the children in custodial care such as using the toilet, eating with utensils or dressing. When the children were capable of self-care, the procedures were designed to sustain them at a high enough frequency.

Token systems have also been used in the classroom, as exemplified by the work of Professor Bijou at the University of Illinois, who pioneered in the development of programmed classrooms. Reinforcement procedures in the classroom also involved an analysis of the educational repertoire so that reinforcement could be delivered in a step-by-step program which developed complex repertoires in small, rationally designed increments. The work of Bijou and others who experimented in the classroom, as with the experiments with autistic children, showed that the limits of educability seemed to lie in the limits of our skills and knowledge about how to arrange an effective classroom environment rather than the limits inherent in the child. When tokens and the teacher's reactivity met the student's existing repertoire, when each task set for the child was a small increment from what he already knew how to do, there was always a corresponding increase in the child's competence.

Tokens, of course, are only a step removed from food and they share some of the same problems. Like food, they have the advantage that they can be applied objectively and that the procedure is visible to all who look including the person who applied them. They direct the teacher's attention to small increments in the child's behavior if for no other reason than the increments have to be seen before a token can be delivered. The increase in the child's behavior reinforces the teacher's behavior, increasing the frequency of teaching. Once a teacher can identify the items of behavior to reinforce, their increased frequency, if the teacher is successful, reinforces the teacher for observing and for acting. The clinician's task is often a continuous development over a week, a month, three months and even a year. The ability to sustain such continuous procedures would, as a matter of course, depend on being able to observe the constituent details. Neophyte clinicians frequently become discouraged because global changes in behavior happen slowly. Reinforcement procedures visualize tiny changes in the child's behavior which in turn sustain the therapy along the way to larger changes. Theoretically, at least, we can expect behavioral training to develop the student's ability to see the small step-by-step, moment-to-moment, changes in behavior which the experienced, sensitive clinician reacts to so intuitively.

Even though many token procedures and programmed environments appear to be unusually successful practically,[1, 2, 5, 11, 14] they raise puzzling questions because there are theoretical reasons why they should not work. There is something unreasonable, for example, about a child learning to read in order to get food or candy. Later in the real world reading will have to occur because of its natural consequences, the other repertoires in the child's life it makes possible, rather than from the arbitrary intervention of a "feeder." Or to put the matter in the reverse direction, the inclination to interact with the social environment by reading appears to be more crucial than the components or content of the reading behavior. A child who learns to read because of food may stop reading as soon as it is withdrawn. A child who is inclined to read because it makes possible experiences which are important to his life will sustain and enlarge his repertoire. Yet, token procedures backed up by food often seem to be quite effective. Possibly the result is a by-product of the token procedure, rather than the result of token procedure and of the immediate control. A teacher who as a result of token procedures observes small details of conduct may become personally reactive to these same features of the student's conduct.

In a word, she reinforces more frequently, more selectively and more to the point. The teacher who can give a token selectively to produce small increments in the child's behavior is also becoming more observant and hence more sensitive to the child. If the teacher is watching the child carefully and reactive to it, not only will she give a token, but she will also give attention, prompt the child, indicate the next step the child might consider, and react to the child's immediate concerns.

Such objective definition of small units of the child's repertoire is essential for programming and for successive approximation of a large repertoire in small increments. The token may also have the same purpose for the child as for the teacher. It is not only backed up with food but it also amplifies the child's conduct making his progress and competence visible. When the child can visualize his own competence and accomplishment in directions relevant to his own needs, then natural reinforcers will take precedence over the tokens.

In the course of my work with clinical psychologists I have discovered that the natural consequences of a child's behavior in a normal environment may be as effective and durable a reinforcer as food or other concrete things. In order to teach a child to dress itself, for example, an obvious procedure would be to use food to build the repertoire in successive approximations, beginning, say, with just touching or picking up the coat. At each step, reinforcement shifts to a performance which is a small variation in desired direction. The procedure is little different than that used to shape a complex repertoire with an animal and the result would be equally predictable. The same performance could also be developed with natural reinforcers. If we begin with a child who is inclined to go outside and play on a cold day we have two natural events, the outside play activity and the outside temperature, as the ultimate reinforcers to sustain the performance. To start with, reinforcement occurs when the child is intercepted at a time when he is inclined to go outside to play. His arm is put into one sleeve of the coat and his other arm put half way in the other sleeve. All the while the child is kept loosely and good naturedly in the vicinity of the therapist by the crook of the arm and the position of the body. With enough sensitivity to the situation, the child will push his hand the remaining distance, perhaps three inches, into   the coat sleeve. As the coat goes on, the therapist says, "Fine, Timmy, let's go outside" and he is out in a flash. The reinforcer is immediate, natural and effective. On the next occasion for going outside, the child's hand is only started into the sleeve so that this time he has to extend it further in order to get the coat on. Step by step less of the activity is supplied by the therapist and more is controlled by its contribution to getting the coat on until the child eventually takes full responsibility for dressing reinforced by getting the coat on which is in turn reinforcing because it is an occasion when he can go to the playground.

The objectivity and specific application of reinforcement principles is the same with the natural consequences of putting on a coat and going out as with food and tokens as reinforcers. The main difference is that the natural reinforcer has to be discovered by observing the individual child while food and tokens can usually be applied arbitrarily. The control of the behavior by the outside temperature is a little more complicated because the consequences are not so immediate as with going through a door, but the principles are similar.

The autistic child shares with the retarded a minimal repertoire often ineffective in dealing with simplest social and physical environments. A therapeutic exchange between Miss Simmons and an autistic child, which I have described elsewhere, illustrates how a detailed objective description of therapy reveals an educational program which increases the child's competence.[9] Miss Simmons' singing, patterned with the child's rocking on the horse, increased the frequency of rocking. A doll which the child held compulsively was dropped during a tantrum, was used as a reinforcer to teach the child how to climb off and then back onto the horse. In each of the activities that Miss Simmons helped the child to learn, she provided as much collateral support for the child's behavior as possible by programming the task into component parts, only one of which was taught at a time. To start, for example, Miss Simmons offered her hands so close that Karen had simply to lay her hands on Miss Simmons. Only when Miss Simmons felt Karen's hands touch did Miss Simmons grasp Karen's hand and wait for muscular pressure in the direction of raising off the horse. As soon as the pressure was felt, Miss Simmons lifted Karen to support her full weight. To get the child's right leg across the saddle, Miss Simmons lifted her just high enough so that the child had only to lift her leg a few inches. Miss Simmons prompted the movement of the right leg by hesitating first for a moment while the child was held in position. It took some judgment and experience to gauge how long to pause and how much to require of the child so that the performance could occur and be reinforced. If she were wrong she would have lifted the child off without participation or held the child in the air for a long time without anything happening. As incidents like this recurred Karen was able in successive steps to get on and off the horse without help.

The expanded repertoire on the horse was a rewarding activity itself which provided an additional reinforcer in the total play environment. Progressions of activities in which one activity makes possible the next can be deliberately arranged in the classroom in the same way as going outside follows putting on a coat, picking up a doll follows climbing off the horse and standing on the floor follows lifting the second foot over the saddle. To make the classroom reactive to the child in the same way that Miss Simmons and the rocking horse were reactive to Karen's behavior, it is necessary to have a behavioral syllabus so that a complex repertoire may be analyzed or observed as component activities, some of which are in the student's current repertoire. The teacher's role, in such a capacity, is that of an advisor. The child performs (motivation) because his behavior produces a consequence (is reinforced) which is inherent in the child's current activity. The teacher can "program" the educational environment using reinforcers already maintaining the child's behavior by creating an environment which visualizes for the child what he does and what is accomplished by it. If a second task is better accomplished as a result of a residue from a preceding one, then it is a potential reinforcer.

The picture that emerges, when we combine the views of the experimental psychologist who emphasizes the frequency of identifiable performances occurring because they are reinforced, and the clinician who deals with natural events basic to the child's immediate life, is that of a classroom in which ordinary events are molded and energized into a highly reactive environment. All of the advantages of reinforcement procedures are preserved because objective behaviors are identified and reinforced. Performances which are endogenous in the child's life and related enough to his past provide natural reinforcement because each performance makes possible another one that has an important place in the child's life. Seemingly innocent events may be substantial reinforcers if used effectively. A change in location, the child's clear view of his own activity, an increase in repertoire, or one event enabling the next can contribute to maintaining and expanding a repertoire. Instead of "making the child learn" the teacher reacts to performances which achieve the child's goals rather than those which annoy the teacher.

An important contribution that a functional analysis of behavior brings to clinical subject matters is communicability and the possibility of teaching others. Traditionally the master teacher and the intuitive clinician just "grew like Topsy." Training programs for clinicians are uncertain and the supply is short. The structure and design of a classroom in which the main events are visible can provide support for a teacher to operate at a higher level of technical skill than would be otherwise possible. Furthermore, training of teachers and clinicians in the functional analysis of behavior could provide a tool which would give them access to the knowledge of the skilled clinician and the skill to function adequately in a properly structured environment while they are gaining the long experience required to be an effective intuitive clinician.

REFERENCES

1. Atthowe, J.M., Jr., and Krasner, L.: A preliminary report on the application of contingent reinforcement procedures (token economy) on a "chronic" psychiatric ward. *J Abnorm Psychol,* 73:37-43, 1968.
2. Ayllon, T. and Azrin, N.H.: The measurement and reinforcement of behavior of psychotics. *J Exp Anal Behav,* 8:357-383, 1965.
3. Bijou, S.W.: Application of operant principles to the teaching of reading, writing and arithmetic to retarded children. *New Frontiers in Special Education,* NEA, 1965.

4. Bijou, S.W., Birnbrauer, J.S., Kidder, J.D. and Tague, C.: Programmed instruction as an approach to teaching of reading, writing and arithmetic to retarded children. *Psychol Rec,* 16:505-522, 1966.

5. Fairweather, G.W.: *Methods for Experimental Social Innovation.* New York, Wiley, 1967.

6. Ferster, C.B. and De Myer, M.K.: The development of performances in autistic children in an automatically controlled environment. *J Chronic Dis,* 13:312-345, 1961.

7. Ferster, C.B.: A method for the experimental analysis of the behavior of autistic children. *Am J Orthopsychiatry,* 32:89-98, 1962.

8. Ferster, C.B.: Arbitrary and natural reinforcement. *Psychol Rec,* 17:341-347, 1967.

9. Ferster, C.B.: Transition from the animal laboratory to the clinic. *Psychol Rec,* 17:145-150, 1967.

10. Ferster, C.B. and Perrot, M.C.: *Behavior Principles.* New York, Appleton-Century-Crofts, 1968.

11. Liberman, R.: A view of behavior modification projects in California. *Behav Res Ther,* 6:331-341, 1968.

12. Parsons State Hospital. Detailed Progress Report. A demonstration program for intensive training of institutionalized mentally retarded girls. January, 1967.

13. Rogers, C.: *Client Centered Therapy.* Cambridge, Houghton-Mifflin, 1957.

14. Schaefer, H.H. and Martin, P.L.: *Behavioral Therapy.* New York, McGraw-Hill, 1969.

15. Skinner, B.F.: *Science and Human Behavior.* New York, Macmillan Co., 1957.

Chapter XIX

DIAGNOSTIC TEACHING OF THE RETARDED PRESCHOOL CHILD

JENNY W. KLEIN

THE sixties will be remembered by many as the decade when preschool education came of age. The growing awareness of the importance of the preschool years to the development of the child has been dramatically reflected in efforts focused on the disadvantaged as well as new concepts in educating the mentally retarded. The proliferation of programs for children with special needs is an outgrowth of evidence accumulated by behavioral scientists indicating that the development of all children is determined by the interaction of genetic factors and environmental influences.

For many years, educators largely influenced by Gesell[1] assumed that early intellectual growth occurs in a fixed pattern and at a biologically predetermined rate. This was frequently interpreted to mean that intervention procedures were not only futile but could, indeed, be harmful.

For the mentally retarded child, the relative unimportance attributed to the preschool years was reinforced by the theory that the retarded must achieve a certain maturity or "readiness for learning." Adhering to the readiness concept, many special education programs did not admit children before their eighth birthday and preschool education for the retarded was virtually unknown.[2] As recently as 1958 a group of Montgomery County, Maryland parents contemplating establishment of a nursery school for the retarded in the greater Washington, D.C. area, had difficulty in convincing professionals as well as laymen that very young mentally handicapped youngsters might benefit from such a program.[3]

The recent expansion of early educational opportunities for mentally retarded children stems from the environmental emphasis promoted by the Swiss psychologist, Jean Piaget.[4-6] While accepting the thesis of sequential development of the child,

274

Piaget hypothesized that intellectual growth results from both assimilation of new information and the subsequent accommodation of behavior which results from new learning. Further impetus to early educational or intervention efforts was given by the writings of Hunt,[7] who saw the environment as affecting both the occurrence and sequence of specific development, and Bloom[8] whose review and analysis of many research studies culminated in his well-known conclusion that approximately 50 per cent of the development of intelligence takes place during the first four years of life.

The merits of the environmental emphasis for children with special learning problems has been widely heralded. However, the danger of what Zigler[9] calls the "environmental mystique" has received less consideration. While intervention efforts can help a child achieve his full capabilities, it is important to remember that we can neither alter a child's genetic make-up nor cure his handicap. But we can offer him support, stimulation and training which will enhance his inborn potential and help him perform at his maximum level.

Unfortunately, many retarded children never encounter early opportunities which lay the groundwork for optimum growth. When confronted with a retarded child, some parents seek solutions in early institutionalization. Others choose to keep their handicapped children at home, cloistering them in sterile environments which stifle curiosity and may actually accelerate retardation. Even in homes which appear to offer possibilities for broadening the child's horizon, retardation may be reinforced by subtle reactions set in force when retarded babies fail to respond to early attempts of parents and other adults to provide interchanges. Many discouraged parents, anticipating the child's lack of response, stop trying to communicate with the child; while other parents push children beyond their capabilities causing them to recoil from new experiences.

For such children a well-planned preschool curriculum grounded in socialization for competence and individualization of instruction can provide a rich and stimulating environment.

A specialized remedial program rests on many of the assumptions which underlie preschool education for children without learning disabilities. Among these are the precepts that:

1. Learning is an active process that must involve the child.
2. Children learn through the serious business of play.
3. Patterns of learning proceed from the simple to the complex and from the concrete to the abstract.
4. IQ is not constant.
5. The preschool years are vital to the child's total development.

In terms of program design, the basic assumption is that all children can learn, although the rate, potential and style of each learner differs. This notion underlies the diagnostic teaching approach utilized in schools for preschool retarded children.

Diagnostic teaching is a flexible, remedial method based on continuous evaluation of the total needs and capabilities of each child. Although it considers medical, psychological and social data, diagnosis in the medical sense is not implied.

In dealing with the whole child, diagnostic teaching is not only concerned with mastering of specific skills but also with a configuration of attitudes and motivational factors. This orientation is important for teachers of all preschoolers, but it is critical for the retarded child. The personality of the retarded child is often influenced by an early perception of himself as a nonlearner which has been nurtured by the concerns and fears of his parents into a self-fulfilling prophecy.

In its concern with the total development of the child, diagnostic teaching requires an orchestration of effort. The teamwork approach includes all staff members of the nursery school (i.e. teachers, aides, volunteers, psychologist, speech therapist) as well as parents, physicians and other professionals having contact with the retarded child.

Diagnostic teaching avoids "pigeon holing" of children according to etiology, IQ, prognosis or other labels. Instead of categorizing children in terms of such factors as specific syndromes or severity of retardation, an attempt is made to assess the strengths and weaknesses of each child. Individual cognitive and learning patterns are noted in evaluating the specific accomplishments and failures of each child and in analyzing why the child has succeeded or failed.

Of course the staff should be advised as to the medical and

psychological diagnosis, intelligence quotients, and etiology of retardation. However, they must also be made aware of the limitations of early testing, diagnosis and prognostication, and of the role of adult expectations in molding the subsequent behavior of children.

The diagnostic teacher determines the child's level of performance and gently leads him through sequential steps. In assessing the child's readiness to move ahead, observation is the basic tool. Children with similar diagnosis may arrive at the nursery school at seemingly parallel stages of development and still vary in their abilities to adjust, to relate to adults and/or children, and to learn new skills.

In a well-conceived program children should be able to move from individual play, to parallel play and ultimately, group play. These varied experiences help children to learn to delay gratification, to initiate activities, and to care for themselves and their materials. Group activities give youngsters a chance to learn to relate and communicate with each other and to share materials and adult attention.

Mentally retarded children need opportunities to work on a variety of perceptual and discriminatory tasks according to their own rates and styles. Many simple materials are available which serve the multiple goals of enhancing curiosity and positive affect toward learning while developing skills.

Provision for large muscle activities is vital not only for physical development but for demonstrating that the child can have an effect on his environment. Effectance motivation[10] is especially important for the retarded child who is apt to perceive himself as ineffectual.

Concept and language development should be an integral part of each day's experiences. Such development can be effected during both energetic and sedentary activities. Story time is especially well suited to language and concept development and facilitates diagnostic teaching. Some children may be able to look at simple picture books and learn to identify and label objects while others may listen quietly to a story individually or in a small group. Still other youngsters may require the use of concrete materials or pictures drawn by a teacher which can be related to their actual experiences.

Providing an individualized approach and curriculum is difficult and time consuming, but it is a necessary and rewarding aspect of diagnostic teaching. Educators have long given lip service to individual differences. Early childhood education, with a high staff ratio and an emphasis on the environment can capitalize on individual differences during the child's most vulnerable years.

Research results are accumulating which indicate that the early years have developmental effects which are difficult to reverse. New modes of teaching very young children are being developed constantly.

What is the best way to teach young, retarded children? The final answer is still not known. However, we are aware of the valuable contributions that diagnostic teaching can make—not only in fostering the growth of the mentally retarded but in providing insights which will lead educators to more definite answers.

REFERENCES

1. Gesell, A. and Amatrudo, C.: Developmental diagnosis in normal and abnormal child development. In *Clinical Methods and Pediatric Application.* 2nd ed., New York, Hoeber Co., 1947.
2. Kirk, S.A.: *Early Education of the Mentally Retarded.* Urbana, University of Illinois, 1958.
3. Klein, J.: Co-op for retarded children. In *Learning Together.* An Anthology. Parent Cooperative Pre-school International, Quebec, Canada, 1969.
4. Piaget, J.: *Judgement and Reasoning in the Child.* New York, Harcourt, Brace, 1928.
5. Piaget, J.: *The Child's Conception of the World.* New York, Harcourt, Brace, 1929.
6. Piaget, J.: *The Construction of Reality in the Child.* New York, Basic Books, 1954.
7. Hunt, J. McV.: *Intelligence and Experience.* New York, Ronald, 1964.
8. Bloom, B.: *Stability and Change in Human Characteristics.* New York, John Wiley and Sons, 1964.
9. Zigler, E.: The environmental mystique: Training of the intellect versus development of the child. *Childhood Education,* May, 1970.
10. White, R.W.: Motivation reconsidered: The concept of confidence. *Psychol Rev,* 66:297-333.

Chapter XX

EARLY EDUCATION OF MODERATELY MENTALLY RETARDED CHILDREN

MAURICE H. FOURACRE

THE early education of moderately mentally retarded children, as for all children, should begin in the home. Unfortunately, the birth of a retarded child often produces an unnatural and frequently an abnormal type of family situation—many times one of complete rejection. Ordinarily, the birth of a child is the fulfillment of a dream of having a normal, healthy child to carry on one's heritage. To the mother of a newborn defective child this dream becomes a nightmare, the euphoria is shattered, the long time planning comes to a sudden halt. The parent is now confronted with immediate problems for which she has had no training or experience, nor did she anticipate that an abnormal child would be born into the family. In the case where the diagnosis of mental retardation is delayed several months or longer, the mother may begin to question her own ability as a parent, a family crisis may now arise which is similar to the one previously mentioned when the pediatrician confirms what the mother has secretly suspected for some time. The feelings of guilt begin to mount, the shame attached to not having provided better postnatal care may weigh heavily.

The realization that retardation may be the reason for the child's slow development can cause the mother to expect less of the youngster and thereby begin to overprotect her child and expect little from him. The father's degree of acceptance or rejection of the child identified many months after birth may be quite different from the acceptance or rejection of the child identified soon after birth. In the postnatal period the retarded child may have developed a personality and the father's relation to his son or daughter may have begun to blossom until the diagnosis was made. Now, the father absents himself from the home

279

as the child is not an adequate sample of the progeny he thought should have been produced.

The home environment or the environment for teaching and learning has become seriously impaired. Attitudes of the parents toward the defective child, although they may appear to be wholesome on the surface, are colored internally by such thoughts as, "How will the child's grandparents accept this condition?" "What will the neighbors think?" "What will my child look like when he grows up?" "How will he fit into our present way of life?" "Will he ever be able to get a job?" to list but a few.

The attitudes are likely to affect child rearing practices unless the primary physician or the counselor is alert to the need for emphasizing certain positive aspects. There is research evidence which indicates that when teachers have low expectations for their students the latter will conform to these lower expectations in behavior and performance. This evidence lends weight to the need for positively oriented classroom teachers. The same conclusion can apply to parents who expect too little and consequently do things for their child which he could learn to do if allowed to imitate and practice.

Two studies, neither designed to study the retarded, have direct implications for the early education of mentally defective children. One study indicated that the best time for compensatory education is before a child is three. A three-year project[1] was conducted to raise the intellectual functioning level of lower socioeconomic status Negro infants in Washington, through home tutoring beginning at fifteen months and continuing to three years of age. The results of this project confirm the importance of verbal development during the second and third years of life for the intellectual development of the child. This development is highly related to the amount of intellectual stimulation, particularly verbal stimulation, that the child receives.

The second study also has possible implications for the education of infant retardates. At the University of California in Berkeley the findings of a study[2] using rats reinforces the idea that early stimulation of an animal causes it to respond to stimuli and to become actively involved with its environment. The stimulation produces a subject morphologically superior and better adapted to learning than animals placed in unstimulating environments.

The purpose of an educational program is to assist a child developmentally to function as close to his mental, physical, social and emotional potential as possible. If a good training program can be started and continued by the parents at home, the more capable the child will be when he enters the nursery school, the more capable he will be in the special class and undoubtedly the more successful he will be in the future when he enters the competitive work world, the sheltered workshop or the residential institution.

The parent education program in the home may be on a tutorial basis, conducted by an empathic teacher, public health nurse or social worker. However, at our school, St. John's Child Development Center, the staff decided to approach parent education through visits of the mothers and their babies at the Center.

The project began in October, 1966 with two mothers and their moderately retarded children. Since that time twenty-six mothers have been enrolled. It has become necessary to limit the number of participants because of the lack of staff time. This project has been undertaken as an extracurricular activity by the staff and at no expense to the mothers except the cost of transportation from the home to the Center and return. All of the children at the time of their first visit were under three years of age. One mother attended her first meeting when her daughter was ten days old. Eight children who have participated in the program are now enrolled in nursery school programs.

The monthly meetings were scheduled for the mothers to meet with a person or persons knowledgeable in the areas of child growth and development and parent counseling. While the mothers met to discuss specific problems related to the care and training of their children, other members of the staff including the psychologist, the speech and language developmentalists and the nursery school teaching staff observed and cared for the children, making records of changes in behavior, growth and development each month.

The last half hour of each session, the mothers had an opportunity to observe their own children in peer relationship situations and to discuss with staff members progress and recommendations. Frequently the mothers were taken to the Nursery Building to observe children somewhat older than their own who were participating in a full day nursery education program. It was believed that such an observation benefitted mothers, as they could observe other moderately retarded children functioning quite capably in a group situation, exhibiting acceptable social characteristics which were commensurate with the individual child's mental ability. The visits helped the mothers to project their own child's future behavior.

The primary goal of the parent education project was to modify the child-rearing practices of the group of mothers, however as the meetings progressed it became apparent that other objectives had to be incorporated. Behavior modification in parent-child relationships remained the prime objective, with teaching the child to learn new skills running a close second. It was often necessary to give the mothers specific suggestions and professional support in their own ability to teach new skills to their child.

A third objective of the program was to develop the problem-solving approach through group interaction. It was found that the group functioned best when there was group interaction directed toward solving their own problems. The group leader did not attempt to approach the group in a dogmatic fashion, but served as a catalyst, summarizing and concluding when the discussion about a problem seemed to be exhausted.

The format of the meetings continued to be flexible and specific attempts were made to meet the needs of all members. New members were given child development charts which were helpful in assessing the child's present functioning level and what immediate goals could be established for each individual. The importance of keeping an ongoing log, a careful record of growth and development, was stressed.

Discussions were primarily centered on child development (physical, mental, social and emotional growth), language and speech development, activities of daily living, self-help skills (particularly feeding and toileting training), child management or discipline, sibling relationships, coping with families, relatives and neighbors, involving the husband in appropriate child-rearing practices, relationship with professionals (primarily medical) and the need for parental recreation, rest (vacations) and outside interests.

Parenthetically, I would like to take this opportunity to expand one of the topics discussed in our group meetings. The topic deals with the physician and his relationship with parents of a defective child at the time of birth or soon after. Sometimes it is helpful to have an outsider ask the profession to take a look at itself.

Many parents have been very frank to admit that the physician handled the problem badly and caused mental anguish which could have been tactfully avoided. Parents who have good intelligence and great respect for the medical profession have asked such questions as: "Why can't the pediatrician or family doctor recognize the child's condition sooner?" "Why does he say 'wait and see'?" "Why do they recommend institutionalization before I become attached to the child? I became attached to the child when I first felt life." "All parents have to face separation from their child, why can't this be done at a later date when all involved are emotionally more settled?" "Why aren't physicians aware and knowledgeable about this type of child and the need for early services?" "Why does the physician refer the case to a fellow physician who is no more knowledgeable about the condition than he?" Although these questions which have come from parents are directed to physicians, some parents have indicated that nurses have given misinformation which has been equally devastating. There is no intent here to imply that the medical profession has been the only profession criticized. Education and psychology are not blameless and members of those professions have been justifiably criticized for their poor handling of parents and their retarded child.

Now returning to the early education of the moderately retarded child, most special educators believe that the retarded can profit from nursery school participation providing the staff is empathic and aware of the specific needs of these children.

Children coming to the St. John's nursery for the first time may require gradual emergence into the program by first attending an hour and gradually building up to a full five-hour day. The five-hour day has appropriate rest time, snack breaks and a lunch period. The latter period is regarded as an important part of the total, as here the child not only learns to eat in a socially acceptable manner for his functioning age, but also to regard mealtime as a pleasant social situation with verbal interaction with adults and children.

The importance of early education in nursery school for retarded children is borne out of research reported by Kirk[3] at the University of Illinois and Fouracre, Connor and Goldberg[4] at Teachers College, Columbia University.

Conclusions from the Kirk study will be sufficient here to support the contention that early education is imperative if the child is to grow to the near-maximum of his potential in all attributes.

Kirk's study involves thirty-one children and the following conclusions were formulated:

1. Children from psychosocially deprived homes can accelerate their rate of mental and social growth if placed in foster homes and given preschool education.
2. Children who remain in their psychosocially deprived homes but are given preschool education tend to increase in rate of development, but not to the extent of those placed in foster homes and offered preschool education.
3. Children who remain in their psychosocially disadvantaged homes without preschool experience but who attend school after the age of six tend either to retain their rate of growth or to drop in rate of growth.

The St. John's parent counseling program attempts to diminish the psychosocial deprivation in the home prior to children entering the nursery program and requires the nursery mothers to attend monthly meetings after their child's entrance into the preschool program. The second phase of the counseling program is extremely important as the mothers are now made aware of their responsibility of putting into practice in the home those skills the child has acquired in school. If similar standards of behavior and management are expected in the home the child begins to develop an acceptable habit pattern. If the standards between the school and home are dissimilar, the child becomes confused and frequently sets up a double standard of behavior, one for the home, one for the school.

The general objectives of the nursery school program are incorporated into the educational philosophy of the St. John's Child Development Center which is briefly:

1. To understand each individual child who is enrolled in the school program through intensive study of educational and psychological test results, observations of physical, social and emotional behavior in individual and group situations and through parent interviews.

2. To provide an educational environment which is commensurate to each child's mental, physical, social, emotional and communicative level of functioning.

3. To provide children with experiences which will lead them to become better adjusted socially and emotionally.

4. To provide experiences for the children to achieve personal satisfaction from living, learning, working and playing with others.

5. To provide activities which will develop those skills and abilities, including functional symbolic learning, which will serve them in every step of childhood and youth as contributing members in school, in the home and the community.

6. To provide opportunities for the inculcation of moral values and ethical practices.

The specific objectives at the nursery school level are basic to the development of more complex skills learned by the children in school later. The more specific goals are the following:

1. Sensory development. To have each child develop the five senses (vision, audition, tactile, taste and smell) to the maximum of his potential in each area.

2. Motor development. To provide through adapted physical education and play, opportunities for the child to develop both large and small muscles, so that they will become better coordinated and less likely to draw attention to himself and his retardation because of ungainliness.

3. Communication. To provide the opportunity to develop oral communication skills, both expressive and receptive, as they will be important means of relating to his parents, superiors and peers.

4. Self-care. To have each retarded child learn to care for his

own personal needs, toileting, dressing, personal cleanliness and grooming, and eating.

5. Socialization. To provide the opportunity for each child to develop a degree of social adjustment commensurate with his mental, physical and emotional ability. To learn to behave in a socially acceptable manner to peers and adults at school, at home and in the community.

6. Useful home and community living. To follow directions and take responsibility which may make a contribution to home and family life.

The education of moderately mentally retarded children must start early in the child's life if it is to be effective. Psychologists report[5] that 50 per cent of one's total mentality is reached by the age of five. Therefore, the parent of a retarded child has a great responsibility to provide an environment in which learning can take place. The retarded child's apathy and lack of response to visual, auditory and tactile motivation often causes the mother to unconsciously reduce the amount of stimulation, thereby depriving the child of the needed prolonged experience that is necessary for him to acquire any proficiency. Further, the parent of a retarded child is required to teach simple concepts to his child which are acquired in the child of normal intelligence vicariously.

The nursery school program supplements the parents' teaching and adds the element of socialization, thus giving the child wider experience in learning to live with others. Nursery school enrollment also has a value which is often overlooked as it affects the child indirectly, but nevertheless it aids him in his growth and development. A mother of a young handicapped child frequently must provide constant supervision of her child during the day. The mother's life is regulated by the child's dependency and lack of ability to entertain himself for any period of time. It is understandable why mothers feel frustrated and unhappy about their own lives, and many times become irritable and discouraged as they see nothing but a dim future. Nursery school placement often does much for the mother's mental health as she is now free of the child for five hours, and may pursue some of her own interests or satisfy her "nesting instinct" which could not be done with the child under foot. The child returns at the close of the school day to a mother whose mental attitude is quite different and an environment which could be more conducive to the establishment of good child rearing practices.

Education of the mentally retarded begins at the "mother's knee" and must continue more formally in a group situation when the child reaches nursery school age. Any attempt to postpone this learning will undoubtedly impede the child later in life. Itard,[6] seventy-five years ago, thought that he had failed as a teacher because Victor, his "Wild Boy of Aveyron" exposed to the most progressive teaching techniques at age twelve for the first time, did not progress academically. What Itard did prove was that education without motivation starting as late as twelve years of age will produce little improvement in the child.

REFERENCES

1. Schaefer, Earl S.: A home tutoring program. *Children,* 16:2, March-April, 1969.
2. Krech, David: Department of Psychology, University of California at Berkeley. Reported in *The Nation's Schools,* 81:2, 63-64, February, 1968.
3. Kirk, Samuel A.: Diagnostic, cultural and remedial factors in mental retardation. *The Biosocial Basis of Mental Retardation.* Osler, Sonia F. and Cooke, Robert E. (Eds.). Baltimore, Maryland, The Johns Hopkins Press, 1965.
4. Fouracre, M.H., Connor, Frances P. and Goldberg, I. Ignacy: The Effects of a Pre-school Program Upon Young Educable Retarded Children, Volumes I and II. Research Reported Pursuant to a Contract with the U.S. Office of Education, Department of Health, Education and Welfare No. SAE6444, 1962.
5. Watson, Goodwin: *What Psychology Can We Trust?* Bureau of Publications, New York, Teachers College, Columbia University, 1961.
6. Itard, J.M.G.: *The Wild Boy of Aveyron.* 1894. Translation by G. and Muriel Humphrey, 1932 (reprint), New York, Appleton-Century-Crofts, 1962.

Chapter XX1

A THEORETICAL LOOK AT LEARNING IN THE MENTALLY RETARDED

E. Paul Benoit

A FEW years ago, a theoretical article appeared over my signa-
ture on the application of Hebb's theory[1] to the education
of the retarded person. The paper focused on how the retarded
mind functions in the light of neurological theory. It presented
only suggestions of usefulness. The international literature has
since incorporated these thoughts to the extent that they appear
in most technical publications on mental retardation and its
psychological and educational implications.

There is need of further elucidation on what the theory means
practically. This relevance can be brought out in a number of
ways.

First, Hebb's system recommends the study of graduality and
continuity in the expansion of thought content in the retarded
mind. The progressive factor is crucial. The degree of differentiation between concepts when there is impaired (or immature)
neurology must not be great. The more extensive the common
features between successive percepts and concepts, the greater
the probability of successful and easy progression. This point
stems from the basic cell assemblies as well as from the superordinate structures that result from the temporal overlapping of
related cognitive elements. The higher the degree of association,
the more marked the facility with which the mind can proceed
from subordinate to superordinate perceptual and conceptual
structures.

Learning, in this frame of reference, may be defined as a development that occurs when two or three percepts concur in a
person's consciousness with a strong feature of similarity and a
relatively secondary element of differentiation. When difference
is not marked, it is possible for attention to absorb the common
features, to abstract these, and, as a result, awareness moves into

a superordinate percept or concept, depending on the level of subtlety in the content. A high degree of facility would be associated with presenting the individuals of a species, namely, a series of pictures, say, of horses, in order to enable the person to grasp the notion of horse. But then, one can appreciate that the commonness of elements can become more deeply embedded in stimulus complexes in which differences can be quite considerable. In these situations it takes much more intellect to grasp the common elements and abstract the superordinate content. Thus, in the realm of analogy, it is much more difficult to see the sun, the moon, a burning electric bulb, and a cigarette lighter as sources of light. For that matter, one can become even more subtle and see light in the sheer experience of understanding. When one deals with an impaired neurology, it is important to pay attention to the necessity of moving with great progressiveness and not work on common elements that are too heavily covered over with individualities that hinder the process of abstraction and association.

One may say that, for the mentally retarded person, teaching will succeed according as one is successful in staying close to the principle of common elements and not requiring the extraction of thought elements that are markedly characterized by irrelevance. This is a general principle which emerges from the theory; its application is likely to guarantee successful learning.

A corroboration of the significance of this principle is illustrated in Piaget's research,[2] in which he delineates the evolution of content in a child's mind. He is careful to note variability in rate of progression and in capacity to detect common features in a wide variety of objects. The fundamental point is that Piaget proceeded empirically in uncovering the manner in which the thought content matures in children.

Hebb's point of view is that he strives to illuminate how thought evolves and how its evolution can be facilitated or obstructed, depending on the degree of similarity or dissimilarity in the elements presented to the child's consideration, depending on the visibility and simplicity of the common features that the child is expected to draw out of his experience; depending also on the degree of obfuscation that irrelevance can bring to bear on the thought process. He derived this approach from the neurological correlates of learning in his frame of reference. Hebb's approach is intended to facilitate the emergence of mind in the child through a gradual presentation of thought. What is true of this formulation is likewise true of action, since motoric patterns are learned in much the same way as units of cognition are acquired. A child cannot move too rapidly in acquiring motor patterns. This point must be understood in the broadest sense so as to include even speech, which can only evolve at a rate in keeping with the basic capabilities inherent in the person's neurology.

Hebb provided a theoretical basis for inferring that both knowledge and art (involving motion of various patterns) require progressive differentiation. The implications of this principle in regard to motor learning are virtually limitless. What is needed is a breakdown into steps in which common elements are maximized in order to secure progression. This process necessarily entails careful analysis of learning material and strategy, but most of all a great deal of time.

Hebb's theory, among other things, points out the enormous importance of the prolonged involvement of the retarded child in the learning situation in order to elicit his optimal reaction at all levels of psychic reaction. The retarded child needs time to go through a far greater number of steps than the normal child, and there must be at every step the opportunity to practice sufficiently until appropriate insight or a reasonable degree of facility is generated.

The theory provides an answer to a phenomenon that fairly frequently appears in the verbal behavior of retarded adolescents and adults. This behavior was characterized recently by the parent of a child in these words: "She behaves like a mountain goat which bounces from peak to peak." The implication was that the child was capable of isolated thought units of some complexity but then the child moved in a disconnected manner from one thought to another. One may be inclined to believe that this behavior is simply one of the many characteristics of retarded mentality—this tendency to manifest islands of intellection which seem to bear no relationship to one another. This behavior is unquestionably found in many retarded persons, but

Hebb's theory indicates that it is not an inherent aspect of mental deficiency. The reason behind the occurrence of this phenomenon is that the mentally retarded child usually does not have opportunity to make progress in the intellectual continuity of discourse. There is implied in the child's development a lack of faith, a lack of interest on the part of the environment, with the result that little effort is made to elicit in the child the cognitive continuity which is in keeping with neurological capacity.

Normally, if people lived in the full cognizance of the theoretical potential of the child, they would strive to make the child progress at following a trend of thought at his level. This tendency of momentum in thought would expand and move into progressively more complex areas and thus make it more possible for the individual to see a thought through.

The same problem of discontinuity applies also to the plane of action. Many retarded children or young people can be observed to change focus in attention with great frequency in a given period of time, as compared to normal persons. A person with a healthy mind is able to stick with a trend of thought and follow it to its natural conclusion, and then there is movement to another trend, and so on. The tendency is to obtain closure. Because the environment pays little attention to the mental habits of the retarded person, early in life the individual learns to flit from one focus of attention to another. There is no follow through; there is no reward for following through; there is no anticipation, and hence there is only a free-flow of associations in the person's consciousness. This condition by no means reflects an intrinsic characteristic of the retarded person; rather it is a result of the environment's inability to adapt to the mental limitations of the child and to move him along at *his* rate.

In this sense, Hebb's theory shows that many of the mental traits that we see in the mentally retarded are traits that are merely empirically found in them, but are not inherent in the basic condition of mental retardation. The limitations are resultants of educational neglect rather than developmental manifestations that are inescapably associated with their individual etiologies.

Another way of understanding the emergence of retardation is to recognize that ability to cope adequately with the environment and one's problems requires a certain amount of information. If the environment is uninforming, the child matures with less input than is needed for him to provide an output that will resolve the issues as he seeks to find his place in society. What is true of a general environmental inadequacy is also true of subjective deficiencies that impede the accession of information to the brain. Serious sensory deficits, as of hearing and vision, definitely can have some bearing on the development of mental subnormality in the sense that an individual who may have started with a healthy nervous system becomes, after a period of years, incapable of coping with environmental processes as a result of being radically unprepared to deal with them. What is mental retardation but a chronic inability to solve one's problems in one's environment, or a social dependency which entails a variety of maladjustments?

A very fruitful area of application for Hebb's theory would be in the general field of curriculum development and also in educational technology.

In curriculum development, rethinking would have to be done on the presentation of symbolic and motoric content to the retarded in all areas of relevance to life. Study would begin with the basic tool subjects and gradually move into the many areas of practical application.

In the field of educational technology, Hebb's theory suggests numerous adaptations in the use of instruments involving facilitation of perception, attention, and association, and providing for practice—particularly independent practice. It would be important to have equipment that the child can handle himself, even away from school. Bombardment must continue as systematically as possible. This kind of scheming to facilitate the development of thought in the child is not unknown to normal children who want to get ahead, for example, some mothers will help a child with a spelling list exhibited over the bathtub, the wash basin, or at table or a bedroom wall. It has been a pity that educational practice for the retarded has concentrated so exclusively on what happens during the school day and has taken for granted that the child is unable to do anything fruitful for himself except under the guidance of the teacher. What the child's needs require, rather, is that there be constant machinating on the part of the teacher to extend the utilization of resources by the child throughout his waking day by means of various instruments or with the help of other people. In other words, the retarded child will get the most out of his impaired neurology if the whole environment cooperates in securing all possible response from him. In this sense, teachers should see their roles as technicians whose advice and methods operate far beyond the school period.

Hebb's theory provides for considerable rethinking in the field of classroom organization, classroom management, in the adaptation of educational technology, and in the organization of the child's whole life, including the time he spends on the bus or at home waiting for dinner and bedtime. Hebb's theory basically recommends the necessity of hustling for the retarded child so as to maximize his thought potential by every possible means.

The theory makes possible the interpretation of a variety of trends, for example, distracted, disorganized or uninhibited behavior. It is not theoretically appropriate to say that a child with a brain injury is inherently disorganized. The neural mass simply is *not* organized and gives rise to random exploratory activity associated with a certain amount of impulsive behavior. Largely, this behavior results from the lack of organization that should have been introduced through the educational process over the years. One might similarly explain sluggishness or apathy. It may very well be that there are biological deficiencies of energy behind relative inactivity, but it is conceivable that in many instances the environment has been so detached that it has failed to create momentum in proportion to the intellectual resources of the child. In other words, the characteristics that were described by A.A. Strauss many years ago, namely, distractibility, impulsiveness, uninhibitedness and all the other related traits, are not clearly true properties of mental retardation but are merely characteristics that are found in children whom the environment has failed to stimulate and organize appropriately.

In short, the retarded psyche has been studied for a long time but actually seldom has an attempt been made to really identify the essential substratum of retarded mentality and truly separate it from the agglomerations that accrue to it as a result of mismanagement and insensitivity on the part of the environment. To a great extent professionals have been including in their definition of the retarded child the results of their inability, and perhaps even their unwillingness, to give him a better chance for self-development.

REFERENCES

1. Benoit, E.P.: Relevance of Hebb's Theory of the Organization of Behavior to Educational Research on the Mentally Retarded. *Amer J Mental Defic*, 61:497, January 1957.
2. Piaget, J.: *The Origins of Intelligence in Children*. New York, International Universities Press, 1952.

Chapter XXII

DEVELOPMENTAL-ENVIRONMENTAL VARIABLES ASSOCIATED WITH MENTAL RETARDATION

JACOB D. GOERING

THE phenomenon of retardation in infants and young children has been gaining increasing attention from several disciplines and professional groups in the past decade. The etiology of some of these conditions has only slowly become less obscure, and effective prevention and amelioration continue to be elusive.

As a first step in approaching this topic it seemed that it might be instructive to consult some standard definitions of retardation. Funk and Wagnalls states the following: "1. A lessening of velocity, gain or progress; a hindrance effected. 2. That which retards; a hindrance. 3. Slowness. 4. In music, a gradual slackening of the time." Webster suggests the following: "Retard; a holding back or slowing down. An abnormal slowness of thought or action. Slowness in development or progress." These statements certainly support the view that retardation is not a fixed or absolute condition, and perhaps most persons are in one form or another somewhat retarded. Yet, the term "mental retardation" has been and continues to be useful in the professions even if it is somewhat general. Because of its generality the causes contributing to the condition are diverse in both nature and intensity.

According to some estimates[1] about one in fifty babies is born with a greater or lesser degree of abnormality inherited from its parents. Only some of them are doomed to some form of mental retardation. This book has focused considerable attention on the role of genetics in mental retardation. In this chapter attention will be called to four clusters of forces or conditions which frequently are associated with the developmental histories of individuals who later function on a retarded level, even though there is no evidence of any genetic defect. No doubt many other variables could be mentioned, but the four categories on which we shall focus briefly are the following:

1. Malnutrition.
2. Sensory deprivation.
3. Inadequate language development.
4. Discontinuities in socialization cues.

These are not offered as discrete categories but rather as a convenient grouping for the purpose of calling attention to some developmental-environmental factors that can be and often are involved in retardation.

MALNUTRITION

The first phenomenon here discussed, apparently contributing to impaired mental functioning, is that of malnutrition in infancy and early childhood. For many years it has been common knowledge that malnutrition in many parts of the world contributed to smaller body size among the poor. Most of the attention, however, was focused on the high mortality rate of malnourished infants and preschool children in the developing countries. In 1967 an International Conference on Malnutrition, Learning and Behavior was held at M.I.T. with more than five hundred medical, biological and social scientists from thirty-seven countries in attendance. Here, much of the research on malnutrition was reviewed with the resulting emphasis on the urgent need for better understanding of the consequences of early malnutrition in man. Since then there has been a considerable amount of publicity giving voice to this concern in scholarly publications, in the popular press and most recently in the Congress. The publication, *Perspectives on Human Deprivation: Biological, Psychological, and Sociological,* by the National Institute of Child Health and Human Development is most informative.[2] Nevin Scrimshaw of M.I.T. in an article in the *Saturday Review* of March 8, 1968, also conveys a picture of what happens when children are malnourished.[1] Scrimshaw relates that as long ago as the 1920's experiments with rats began to show that nutritional deficiencies not only retarded physical growth, but affected the central nervous system as well. He states,

> More recently, early malnutrition sufficient to impair growth in experimental animals has repeatedly and conclusively demonstrated its effect

on their subsequent learning, memory, and adaptive behavior. This has led to the stunning implication that infants and young children whose physical growth is stunted by malnutrition may also be prevented from attaining their full mental capacity and social development.

Two types of disorders associated with undernutrition in infancy are marasmus and kwashiorkor. Again, according to Scrimshaw, marasmus is particularly common in children less than one year of age when the rate of postnatal brain growth is at its peak. It occurs because, under conditions of poverty and ignorance, some children are weaned early in the first year of life, and then are given substitutes for breast milk which are inadequate in both calories and proteins. When children are not weaned until the second or third year of life in such very poor families, they are likely to receive sufficient calories but inadequate dietary protein. This can result in kwashiorkor, a condition which is due primarily to protein deficiency and is often fatal.

SENSORY DEPRIVATION

A second factor or set of factors which we shall consider here and which, it is believed, contributes to impaired performance on learning tasks and adaptive behavior, is what is sometimes referred to as sensory deprivation. Again, it is most likely to occur in families from low-income communities. Numerous studies with animals indicate that self-induced movement in dependable and stable surroundings is necessary for adequate development as well as for maintenance of stable visual-motor behavior. Other studies have reported remarkable effects of postnatal handling on the subsequent development of laboratory-reared animals.[3-6] Mice, kittens and dogs given small amounts of extra early handling grew up to be "better" animals as measured by a wide variety of tests. They were superior in many physical and adaptive respects. Sylvia Brody in her book, *Patterns of Mothering*,[7] noted that infants who received moderate handling were consistently more visually attentive than those receiving minimal handling. White and Held[8] did some experimentation and observation of some human infants born and reared in an institution. They were particularly interested in the role of contact with the environment, and in the development of sensorimotor coordination. Their first major conclusion is that the age range from 1½ to 5 months is a time of enormous importance for early perceptual-motor development. Their studies also demonstrated that aspects of early visual-motor development are remarkably plastic, although the limits of this plasticity are not yet known.

The failure to thrive syndrome, sometimes also known as dwarfism or deprivation dwarfism, is a very dramatic manifestation of what we are talking about. A rather interesting study reported in *The Sciences*[9] was conducted by Dr. Powell at Duke and two associates at Johns Hopkins. They evaluated thirteen children who ranged in age from three to eleven years. Each had attained a height of a normal child half his age. The eleven-year-old had a height age of five years, three months, and a bone age of six years. The three-year-old had a height age of one year, eight months, and a bone age of one year.

> These children were first believed to have growth failure as a result of idiopathic hypopituitarism, pathologically diminished activity of the pituitary body. Further examination of the children's histories suggested emotional disturbance and abnormal home environments, factors that were not common to the histories of patients with idiopathic hypopituitarism. In virtually all the sets of parents there existed either divorce, extramarital affairs, day-to-day hostility or excessive drinking. Few of the parents had finished high school, and only one had entered college. Among the aberrations demonstrated by the children when they were placed in a convalescent home was a bizarre type of polydipsia, or abnormal thirst. When left unobserved, the children would drink from toilet bowls, from glasses filled with dish water, puddles, old beer cans full of stagnant water, and from the hot-water faucet. Patients were also known to have eaten jars of mustard, mayonnaise, a loaf of bread, or a box of corn flour at one sitting. In addition, all the children were extremely withdrawn and manifested a variety of behavioral problems.

While the study group considered the possibility that nutritional factors may have played a part in the children's growth retardation, the conclusion was that emotional disturbance and abnormal home environment was the major cause. According to the investigator's report,

> The behavior of the children appears to be an aberration of the normal developmental patterns which usually make their appearance at one or two years of age—that is, speech, feeding oneself, toilet train-

ing, and initiation of interpersonal relations. In the present study, onset of symptoms and growth retardation began at the same time. The
first two years appear to be the most critical in establishing a proper
parent-child relationship. Such factors as personal vulnerability and
degree or length of disturbance may account for the fact that certain
children suffer growth retardation, whereas others, including their siblings, do not. These factors need more detailed study!

This report goes on to relate the subsequent progress of the
children, and the findings tend to support the authors' earlier
impressions. Once the children were placed in a convalescent
hospital they began to grow again, as much as 1.2 inches per
month, even though they received neither HGH nor psychiatric
help. One child who spent forty-five months in a hospital grew
eight inches in the first year. His total increase during that time
was 17.4 inches for an overall rate of 0.39 inches per month.

Another interesting speculative but provocative view in this
whole area is given us by George Crile, Jr., in his little book
A Naturalistic View of Man,[10] the main thesis of which is contained in the following quotation, ". . . there is a critical time in
the life of each cell, each organ, each animal, each society and perhaps even in the ecology of the world, at which the organism in
question is particularly sensitive to its environment and best
able to make an adaptive change. Before or after that time, stimulation may be ineffective." Crile is impressed with the work of
Konrad Lorenz, and with the importance of imprinting in the
development of many animals, and thinks it is probably so in
human beings also. This is a fascinating notion worth studying
and being aware of in the years ahead.

INADEQUATE LANGUAGE DEVELOPMENT

A third factor or perhaps more accurately—cluster of factors—
that is highly relevant to the child's development of the necessary competencies to enable him to take a full share in social participation is the development of language. Western culture is
highly literate and verbal, so much so that in many circumstances
we seem to assume that if a thing is not articulated in either
written or oral form it does not exist. Affect, for example, is still
not highly regarded in some circles.

If a child is to become a full participant in this society, he must learn its symbol system, and must be rather facile in its use. Thus the adequacy of the structure of the language a child learns, as well as the timing and sequence of such learning may have a good deal to do with how well a youngster is equipped to cope with society's expectations. Both linguists and psychologists have been interested in studies of language development, and a certain body of data has accumulated. The existing studies represent attacks on various aspects of the subject from many different angles. While some very valuable observations have been made, Hoffman and Hoffman in their *Review of Child Development Research,* make this statement: "The basis for the child's most important and complex achievement still remains unknown."[11]

Since language acquisition will likely receive further elaboration elsewhere, we shall discuss it here only briefly. Certain aspects of language acquisition can impair functioning in certain circumstances. Social class variations in this area have been widely observed. Why this might be so is suggested by those who hold that there is a contrast between "restricted" and "elaborated" codes. The former are associated with closed communication networks where the assumptions are familiar and the communication is more likely to be solidarity-supporting such as in families and in in-groups of various kinds. This code is typical of lower socioeconomic classes. Elaborated codes are needed for specification of meanings such as one would have to use when discussing topics with strangers. The middle class uses both forms (code-switching). Class differences in speech have been seen in children as young as age 5 years. By age 12 to 15 years the speech differences tend to increase.

Other studies suggest how learning accuracy in labeling may influence later performance. It appears that finer labeling categories, the kind more likely to be contained in the language and vocabulary available to the middle class child, produce more accurate recognition. To quote from Smart and Smart:[12]

> The more words (a child) learns, the more readily he stores his experiences as memories. The more memories he stores, the more available is past experience for use in thinking and problem solving. Hence the acquisition of language is an integral part of cognitive growth. The child who does not acquire adequate verbal symbols and who does not use them in thinking becomes retarded intellectually.

DISCONTINUITIES IN SOCIALIZATION CUES

Finally, discontinuities and conflicts in socialization cues seem to be involved in some children's inability to function at expected levels. The supporting data here may be less firm, but it does seem something worth calling to attention. Some work has been done in studying the conflict between the family and the school in such matters as language, values, attitudes, conflict resolution and others. Such inter-class conflicts, and especially if a bilingual factor is included, have taken a severe toll in the energies and sense of self-esteem of children of immigrant and other ethnic groups. On a visit to some of the Indian Reservations in the Dakotas last year the author was told a story which aptly illustrates this point. Among the Sioux, some families spoke LaKota at home. A few years ago when the children came to school many were unable to speak English, but they were also forbidden to speak LaKota. Needless to say, the alienation of the child from the school and its culture is rather quickly firmed up in such instances. In the case of one family, about six weeks after the children had started school, the father heard of some seasonal work in a neighboring state. Thereupon the family was loaded into the old car, and they all proceeded to the source of employment without notifying anyone, and especially not the school. After the children had been absent from school for about two weeks, the social worker was notified and asked to investigate. She found the home abandoned. Another four weeks later with the beet harvest over the family returned, and the children again showed up in school. What they encountered was further rejection and hostility perhaps for so cavalierly disregarding the rights and prerogatives of the school and what it stands for. The distance between the child and the school widened. To the child it seemed, these were two irreconcilable worlds. Of course his academic learning under these circumstances were very minimal and never really took hold, and the outcome is rather easy to predict. Unfortunately, we are told, this is by no means a rare or isolated case among the American Indians.

But a similar pattern of experience has existed for many members of other minority sub-cultural groups in our society with tremendous cost in social isolation, and in underdeveloped human resources. In their widely publicized study on the role of teacher expectation in the performance of school children, *Pygmalion in the Classroom,* Jacobson and Rosenthal[12] help to illumine this problem. The potency of the teacher's expectation resulting in the self-fulfilling prophecy phenomenon appears to be more than many children can cope with. When this is directed toward impeding a child's progress the result can be most unfortunate. Similar discrepancies and conflicts in demands and expectations can and often do exist entirely within the family, and clinicians and others are abundantly aware of the impaired function which results.

Our culture is an exceedingly complex one, and is in many respects in the process of rapid change. It is, therefore, not surprising that many of our children seem to get "hung-up" and find themselves unable to sufficiently integrate or harmonize the disparate cues for successful functioning.

These then are some of the many developmental and environmental forces which in certain combination may conspire to prevent a child from functioning at a level both he and society have a right to expect.

REFERENCES

1. Scrimshaw, N.S.: Infant malnutrition and adult learning. *The Saturday Review,* March 16, 1968.
2. U.S. Dept. of Health, Education and Welfare: Perspectives on Human Deprivation: Biological, Psychological and Sociological. Public Health Service, National Institutes of Health, The National Institute of Child Health and Human Development, 1968
3. Denenberg, V.H. and Karas, G.G.: Effects of differential infantile handling upon weight gain and mortality in the rat and mouse. *Science,* 130:629-630, 1959.
4. Held, R. and Hein, A.: Movement-produced stimulation in the development of visually-guided behavior. *J Comp Physiol Psychol,* 56:872-876, 1963.
5. Levine, S.: Infantile experience and resistance to physiological stress. *Science,* 126:405, 1957.
6. Meier, G.W.: Infantile handling and development in Siamese kittens. *J Comp Physiol Psychol,* 54:284-286, 1961.
7. Brody, S.: *Patterns of Mothering.* New York, International Univ. Press, Inc., 1951.

8. White, B.L. and Held, R.: Plasticity of sensorimotor development. In Rosenblith and Allinsmith (Eds.) : *The Causes of Behavior II*, Boston, Allyn and Bacon, 1966.

9. *The Sciences.* Vol. 7, No. 3, August, 1967, Published by the New York Academy of Sciences.

10. Crile, G., Jr.: *A Naturalistic View of Man, Early Training in Learning, Living and the Organization of Society*, World, 1969.

11. Hoffman, L.W. and Hoffman, M.L.: *Review of Child Development Research*, Vol. II, New York, Russell Sage Foundation, 1966.

12. Smart, M.S. and Smart, R.C.: *Child Development and Relationships.* New York, Macmillan, 1967.

13. Rosenthal, R. and Jacobson, L.: *Pygmalion in the Classroom.* New York, Holt, Reinhart and Winston, 1967.

Chapter XXIII

SOME FINDINGS ON THE IMPACT OF EARLY STIMULATION PROGRAMS ON ASPECTS OF COGNITIVE AND SOCIAL-EMOTIONAL DEVELOPMENT

LOIS-ELLIN DATTA

ON her deathbed, Gertrude Stein said, "What is the answer?" And then she said, "What is the question?"

There are some questions that have been asked time and again throughout recorded history. The existence and nature of evil may be the most compelling question. It is compelling as an area of philosophical inquiry and it is compelling for the consequences on our lives of the answers we give as a society and as individuals. Perhaps less compelling but no less enduring is the question of the extent of the influence that environments may exert and the manner in which this influence is expressed. For the adult, this is the central question of psychotherapeutic intervention. For the child, this is the central question of educational intervention.

We are concerned with the manner and extent of environmental impact. We are concerned further with evidence that environment may retard, and that environment may then accelerate, developmental processes. At this time we are particularly concerned with retardation and intervention in those whose environment is shaped by poverty. And since I am most familiar with preschool programs, I will be concerned with those who are impoverished and who are young—with the impact of preschool programs on the development of children from low-income families.

In thinking about this, I found myself asking four questions. I reached some answers to the first three questions but for the fourth question there was only the itching in my toes that tells me that I do not understand.

The first question was, "Are children from low-income families cognitively and social-emotionally retarded?" The answer I found was that there are some behavioral differences between poor children and less poor children, but to describe these as retardation implies a process limitation that can mislead us into dark valleys. Considering first affective development; Jesser and Richardson[1] have completed a monumental integration of research papers on psychosocial deprivation and personality development. They conclude that there appears to be a syndrome quality to what is meant by deprivation and to its consequences for personal-social development. This deprived personality syndrome includes low achievement orientation, low perception of opportunity, low sense of control, poor imaginative capacity, poor social role development and interpersonal skills, low self-esteem and little ability to delay gratification.

The studies on which this description is based are limited in ways that include subcultural representativeness of the samples, restricted age ranges, and problems of measures and measurement contexts. Grotberg[2] reviewing the research on Head Start children found no evidence of social class differences in emotional pathology. This is consistent with data from a national study of Head Start programs. Teacher ratings of the social-emotional adjustment of sixty-five children selected for extreme deprivation and twenty-three children from privileged backgrounds did not differ reliably, nor, it should be added, were the deprived children less likely than the privileged children to gain in rated social responsiveness, emotional stability, self-confidence and task orientation.

Grotberg emphasizes dependency conflict as a differentiating characteristic of economically deprived children. She cites the work of Beller in particular in identifying the difficulty that children from low-income families experience in accepting dependency needs and in permitting themselves to turn to a protective environment for emotional, intellectual and physical support. Does dependency conflict develop, then, into the deprived personality syndrome? Or does the syndrome arise from the children's school experiences more than from their home experiences? If it is the former, how focused are preschool intervention efforts on dependency? How successful in preventing the "deprived personality syndrome" are such programs as Sprigle's which would seem likely to foster the child's willingness and ability to rely on adults and to use adults as sources of information? If it is primarily a post-school event, what about the environment of the school-age child may catalyze the development of the deprived personality syndrome? And finally, what are the behaviors and attitudes one would substitute for the syndrome and on what psychodynamic basis? If there is a "privileged personality syndrome," I suppose the individual would tend to be high on self-esteem, sense of control and achievement orientation. Yet what may be a reality-oriented response in the one individual's life circumstances might be pathological in other circumstances, however much we might wish self-esteem, confidence and a belief that the individual can achieve through skills and effort to be universally good.

What about the children's cognitive development? Birren and Hess[3] have summarized reviews of the influences of deprivation on learning and performance. They conclude that it has been repeatedly demonstrated that children from low income families are likely to have lower scores on global estimates of cognitive ability, on profiles of cognitive operations and on measures of educational achievement. Inhibition of the development of the abstract and categorical use of language is considered to be a common denominator in this retardation and the period from eighteen months to three years particularly critical to the acquisition of linguistic skills.

Again, problems of measurement may cloud inference from behavior to process. Zigler and Butterfield[4] suggest that the frequently reported deficit on global measures such as the Stanford-Binet Intelligence test may primarily reflect such factors as a general wariness of adults. These writers conclude that changes in the intellectual performance of deprived children who have attended preschool may be more related to positive changes in motivation and emotional reactions than to increased knowledge. Grotberg[2] has pointed out that careful analysis of test items and comparisons among various tests suggest wide variation in performance within groups and between sub-populations. She further points out that the language behavior of parents tends to be a more reliable predictor of children's language patterns than socioeconomic status per se.

Perhaps one of the most important studies on this topic was a comparison of test performance and rate of learning. Usually, that is in middle-class children, intelligence test performance predicts rate of learning with some accuracy. Sonia Osler[5] reported that while children from low income families have lower scores on standardized tests, they have showed no impairment in rate of learning in a variety of laboratory situations. Her interpretations of this finding centered about the distinction between learning ability and test performance. Osler concluded that there was little evidence for a deficit in basic learning processes, and that motivational factors were probably central in test performance data.

This argument probably holds only up to the point where specific content and information are weighted in test scores. It does, however, indicate the need for clearer identification of process variables implicated in the deficits on cognitive tasks. Such information might be a surer guide to the development intervention programs than more straightforward interpretations of the test scores.

The second question was, "Suppose I assume—for the sake of argument—that these behavioral differences should be taken at face value, and the performance deficits in children from low-income families should be prevented or remedied. What evidence is there that intervention programs can have a substantial immediate or more enduring impact?" The answer I found was that there is ample evidence that intervention programs can have an immediate impact on cognitive growth in children from low-income families. The evidence on social-emotional development is sparse, possibly due to the state of the art in measurement, and possibly due to a looser conceptual relationship among locus of intervention, mode of intervention and criterion measurement.

I will consider a few of the experimental programs, and for brevity's sake, only one measure, the Stanford-Binet IQ.

Strodbeck[6] found in thirteen weeks a six-point gain for his experimental subjects as compared to a one-point gain for traditional nursery controls. Weikart[7] has reported gains of from ten to fourteen points for the children in his experimental program as compared to gains from zero to seven points for the controls. In the Sprigle study (Van de Reit and Van de Reit[8]), the children in the experimental program gained fourteen points over a year while the controls lost five points. Hodges, McCandless and Spicker[9] reported seventeen-point gains for the children in their diagnostically based curriculum as contrasted to a four-point gain for controls. Di Lorenzo and his colleagues[10] found gains of zero to four points for a large sample of disadvantaged children enrolled in preschool programs as contrasted to a three-point loss for controls. Karnes[11] comparing seven different approaches found gains of from four to seventeen points for the children receiving various treatments contrasted to a one-point gain and a three-point loss for two control groups.

Almost all research-scale studies of Head Start programs have reported a significant gain for both Summer and Full-Year programs. Cross-sectional data from a national study of Full-Year Head Start programs indicate a ten-point difference between children initially tested in the first two weeks of the program and children initially tested in the 19 to 20th weeks of the program. The cross-sectional data also indicate a ten-point difference at the time of the final test between children tested for the second time after seventeen weeks in the program and children tested for the second time after forty-two weeks in the program. The average IQ for the sixty-seven children who received the second test at week seventeen was 93.7; for forty children who received the second test at week forty-two, the average IQ was 103. Cross-sectional data are, quite properly, considered suspect when the children are not assigned at random to different times of testing. The comparisons here were fortuitous, capitalizing on variation due to administrative factors. The data may be suggestive, however, of what a true before and after study of program-new children might show, and we expect to conduct in the future a carefully designed investigation of changes over time.

What about the impact of preschool programs on affective development? The data here are difficult to compare, since there are few commonly used measures of social-emotional development, and the most extensive data are available for studies which do not have control groups. Such data as we have indicate changes in the direction of greater self-confidence, task orientation, and extraversion, and of an increased responsiveness to the social initiations of other children and of adults. In one of the best designed and most comprehensive studies, Hodges and his colleagues[9] found greater intensivity of involvement in teacher-directed tasks for the experimental than for the traditional nursery school children. At the end of the first grade, the children who attended the diagnostically based preschool were rated by their teachers as higher in sound growth and personal adjustment. The experimental children as judged by their peers were also somewhat more popular. Weikart[7] has reported that the children who had been enrolled in preschool programs generally were seen by their kindergarten teachers as behaving in a more socially desirable manner. Interestingly, in view of Grotberg's comments, Weikart writes,

"Possessive of the teacher" is usually considered to be an undesirable characteristic. However this characteristic can also be viewed as an attempt toward a more positive relationship with the teacher. For a group of disadvantaged children, seeking to establish a close relationship with a middle-class socializing agent may be a necessary step in internalizing the values which are held in high regard by the school and in achieving academic success.

On the "no difference" side, Klaus and Gray[12] found little evidence that the early training project had positive influence on the children's self-concept, reputation among peers, ability to delay gratification, achievement motivation as measured by a project technique, or social schema as measured by Kuethe's technique. They find some encouragement in that the findings did not indicate any aversive effects from the early training effort.

As I mentioned earlier, the conceptual basis for intervention and measurement in the affective domain appears to be looser than for language development or conceptualization. This may, in part, account for the greater inconsistencies among findings in the affective than in the cognitive domain.

In the balance, preschool programs have a substantial immediate impact on global test scores and achievement test scores. Miller[13] writes,

> . . . we have found it is not much of a trick to obtain an average Binet IQ score gain of fifteen to twenty points over a year of intervention. . . . The real trick is to maintain these gains over a period of time so that the usual picture of progressive decline does not emerge. . . .

There is also evidence, as Miller indicates, that the intermediate and longer range impact of even high-powered programs is inadequate protection against all that being poor can mean if the children go from the programs into most public schools under most circumstances. While time precludes a review of follow-up studies, I will mention some findings, again for the Stanford-Binet IQ.

Kirk[14] found a catch-up effect with no loss for the community children over a year in public school, but an eleven-point gain for the controls. Weikart[7] reports a two-point loss for experimental children and a three-point gain for controls in Perry preschool program Wave 0; Wave 1 retained the post program difference between experimental and controls. For Sprigle's program, Van de Reit and Van de Reit[8] report a three-point loss for first grade, and a loss of five more points at the end of the second grade for the experimentals. The controls had gained ten points by the end of the second grade. What was a twenty-point difference after the preschool program decreased to a two-point difference after two years in public school, due to both control group gains and experimental group losses. Hodges and his colleagues[9] found a two-point gain for the experimental and a five-point gain for the controls after a year in public school. Karnes[11] reported a three-point loss without continued programmatic support. A national follow-up study of Head Start children[15] showed an advantage in academic readiness, particularly for children who were Black, from the South, or from inner cities, over children who did not attend Head Start. This advantage was found in the first, but not the second or third grade data for children who attended full-year Head Start programs.

There are as yet few studies in which all or some elements of the program are continued. The studies of which I know offer grounds for optimism that the rate of the change during preschool programs may be continued if there is continued support. Karnes,[11] for example, has reported a nine-point gain, from an average IQ of 100 to an average IQ of 109 when public school kindergarten was supplemented by a special one-hour tutoring program. When another group of children were continued in Karnes' special program, the fifteen-point IQ gain of 93 to 108 reported for the six months program was followed by a gain of 12 points, from 108 to 120 after the second year.

Karnes' findings may lend additional weight to Klaus and Gray's[12] conclusion:

> Intervention programs for preschool children of the most effective sort that could possibly be conceived may not be considered as a form of inoculation whereby the child forever afterward is immune to the effects of a low-income home and of a school not appropriate to his needs. Certainly the evidence of human performance is overwhelming in indicating that such performance results from the continual interaction of the organism with its environment. Intervention programs, well conceived and executed, may be expected to make some relatively lasting changes. Such programs, however, cannot be expected to carry the whole burden of providing adequate schooling for children from deprived circumstances; they can only provide a basis for future progress in schools and homes that can build upon that early intervention.

A national study, Planned Variation, will explore the effects of continued experience in Head Start and Follow-Through of participation in eleven different curricular models.

My third question was, "Suppose we agree that many preschool programs have a meaningful impact on the child. What is it that somebody is doing right so that we can have more of this educational good news? What is it that somebody may be doing wrong so we can avoid it?"

For preschool programs, there are some answers here, too. The first is in what the program brings to the family. The second is in what the program brings directly to the child. The family, in most studies, means the mother. Although most low-income families have a father and a mother, the father is usually out working, and he may be less accessible to researchers. The family of the low-income child typically has four children competing for the attention of two adults. The adult-at-home, particularly one confronted with a struggle for physical survival, may not be a reliable emotional or intellectual resource for the child. As mentioned previously, a recent review of the literature has indicated that dependency conflict is marked in the low-income child and that increased demands for attention by the child on the public school teacher may distinguish the child who has attended preschool programs. Anecdotal evidence suggests that this may be regarded by some public school teachers as a nuisance so that the children who have been rewarded in preschool for seeking adult contacts may be punished in public school for the same behavior.

The mother typically presents a linguistic world that is restricted in mode to orders and to linguistically simple, noncontingent forms. The content is typically structured to obedience to a world over which the child has little control, and Grotberg's review of the Head Start literature has indicated that conceptual and elaborative test performance is most markedly retarded in the low-income child. Hess and his colleagues[3] have recently completed an elegant series of studies documenting the relationships among maternal linguistic and conceptual style, her teaching patterns and child performance.

Time precludes as detailed a review of the literature here as I gave for the other two questions; briefly, programmatic intervention with families has included training mothers to teach a preplanned language curriculum, on-the-job training of mothers as teacher aides, home visitor services, weekly meetings at the Centers, and intensive efforts to provide meaningful parental involvement in program decisions and policies.

Among the most extensive and successful parent programs is that of Susan Gray[12] and her colleagues, who report not only an impact on the target child but also vertical diffusion to siblings and horizontal diffusion to neighbors.

What the program brings to the child has been more systematically investigated. In general, the principles to which most educators would subscribe seem to apply to preschool education: the children gain more the more clearly stated are the teacher's goals, the more reliably she receives feedback on how successful she is at reaching these goals, the more she believes that she can have an impact, the more she is responsive, perceptive, and accepting without lowering her expectations for the child or smothering him, and the more she is an open, growing, generalizing person. Most studies compare the experimental program against the "traditional" nursery school; most experimental programs have a preplanned or structured curriculum. It would be easy to conclude that prestructured or prepackaged programs are the essence of the good news we have been seeking. This may be so—or at least it may be so for some situations.[16] Preliminary observations on a study of the Buchanan program currently being conducted at the University of South Carolina, Tulane University and the University of Texas suggest that relatively inexperienced teachers find this prepackaged program a structure within which they can elaborate while more experienced teachers may chafe at the constraints. Some early child development specialists have felt these programs put the accent on the wrong or cognitive syllable or are worried about the implications of extrapolations from the powerful behavior modification techniques. The critical studies comparing social and cognitive development in exemplar Bank Street, exemplar preacademic and exemplar behavior modification programs are yet to be completed. And so a conservative answer to the question, "What is good news?" seems to be first an eclectic approach to specific materials or patterns such as Sprigle's games for two children and one teacher. Second, what successful programs seem to have in common is clear and detailed goal specification, belief in the child's ability to flourish, and the perceptiveness that sees something is not working and invents something that does. I would expect that the role of the program coordinator is crucial here— someone who is vitally concerned with each child and who provides through whatever techniques are available to her, frequent opportunity for the teacher to assess her progress and to explore, verbally, new approaches and new possibilities.

The fourth question—the one for which I had no answers— was preschool for what? We seem to assume that preschool programs should prepare a child for a world where adults are to be trusted, where they care about him, where they are wise and fair. Perhaps we can by the follow-through programs and efforts continually to upgrade schools make this world a real world, and prepare children to continue to grow in it beautifully and openly. But this is not the real world I see now. In the real world I see now the poorest children attend the worst schools, where there are thirty or more children to one teacher, who is given little of the social, medical and other supports of the preschool programs, who is burdened with administrative demands, who often has inadequate materials and is inadequately prepared to meet changing community expectations. The children are not making it in this world. When they reach early adolescence, they have learned the survival skills to protect themselves against the enemy. What should the early education program be to prepare children for the schools Jonathan Kozol[17] has described? I am not worried about whether preschool programs can have an impact on affective and cognitive development. They can. But can we move our world, the world of public education, fast enough and far enough to keep faith with the children whom we have dared to teach to trust adults, to rejoice, to be curious? Can we move fast enough to keep faith with the parents to whom we have offered help in their efforts to survive, and the respect of partnership in their children's education? I do not know. I can only hope that those who have data to show what is possible will speak loudly and clearly. It is true that the data are not all in and I should like to make clear that my optimism is by extrapolation. Only the negative side, the cumulative decrement seems well documented. The study demonstrating the cumulative increment of coordinated infant, preschool and primary school programs is yet to be conducted. Yet, in the long history of the nature/nurture controversy, rarely has nurture seemed to have so good a case.

REFERENCES

1. Jessor, R. and Richardson, S.: Psychosocial deprivation and personality development. Chapter I in *Perspectives on Human Deprivation: Biological, Psychological, and Sociological.* National Institute of Child Health and Human Development, mimeo, 1968.
2. Grotberg, E.: *Review of Research 1965-1968.* mimeo, 1969.
3. Birren, J. and Hess, R.: Influences of biological, psychological and social

deprivations upon learning and performance. Chapter II in *Perspectives on Human Deprivation: Biological, Psychological and Sociological*. National Institute of Child Health and Human Development, mimeo, 1968.

4. Zigler, E. and Butterfield, E.: Motivational aspects of changes in IQ test performance of culturally deprived nursery school children. *Child Dev*, 38:1-14, 1968.

5. Osler, S. and Cooke, R.: *The Biosocial Basis of Mental Retardation*. Baltimore, The Johns Hopkins Press, 1965

6. Strodbeck, F.: Progress report: the reading readiness nursery. *The Social Psychology Laboratory*. University of Chicago, 1963, mimeo (cited by Weikart, 1969).

7. Weikart, D.: *Preschool Intervention: A Preliminary of the Perry Preschool Project*. Ann Arbor, Campus Publishers, 1969.

8. Van de Reit, V. and Van de Reit, H.: A follow-up evaluation of the effects of a unique sequential learning program, a traditional preschool program, and a no treatment program on culturally deprived children. Evaluation Report, OEO Contract B89-4425, November, 1968, mimeo.

9. Hodges, W., McCandless, B. and Spicker, H.: The development of and evaluation of a diagnostically based curriculum for preschool psychosocially deprived children. Final Report, Grant No. OEG-32-24-0210-100, December, 1967.

10. DiLorenzo, L., Salter, R. and Brady, J.: Prekindergarten Programs for the Disadvantaged. University of the State of New York, The State Education Department, Office of Research and Evaluation, December, 1968, mimeo.

11. Karnes, M.: A research program to determine the effects of various preschool intervention programs on the development of disadvantaged children and the strategic age for such intervention. Paper presented at the American Educational Research Association meeting, February 10, 1968.

12. Klaus, R. and Gray, S.: The Early Training Project for Disadvantaged Children: A Report after Five Years. Mimeo, 1967.

13. Miller, J.: *Diffusion of Intervention Effects in Disadvantaged Families*. Urbana, Illinois, University of Illinois Press, 1968.

14. Kirk, S.: *Early Education of the Mentally Retarded*. Urbana, University of Illinois Press, 1958 (cited by Weikart, 1969).

15. Smith, M. and Bissell, J.: Report analysis: the impact of Head Start. *Harvard Ed Rev*, 40:51, February, 1970.

16. Bissell, J.: Impact of Head Start: An evaluation of the effects of Head Start on children's cognitive and affective development. *Childhood Education*, 46:449, May, 1970.

17. Kozol, J.: In Roxbury: Way out of a fortress. *Education Digest*, 35:12, May, 1970.

Chapter XXIV

PROBLEMS OF DELINQUENCY IN THE MILDLY RETARDED CHILD

WILLIAM W. BARR

THERE is a considerable amount of ferment today in the District of Columbia metropolitan area regarding the alarming rate of crime and delinquency, which, it seems to us, makes it quite timely to include a discussion of "problems of delinquency in the mildly retarded child." It is with zest that we enter into this discussion because of our belief that practitioners, as well as the general public, may not be as aware as they need be of what happens in the delinquency control system to the mildly retarded child who becomes an adjudicated delinquent. We are excluding a most enlightening period of the child's history—the pre-delinquency interval—in order to concentrate on the involvement of police, courts, institutions and aftercare programs.

Our effort here is to explore the reality of the child's experience with correctional (or rehabilitative) services in terms of whether his problems of mental retardation or those of delinquency are paramount in the estimation of those who: a) apprehend and arrest him; b) make the judicial decision; and c) plan the rehabilitative program. Our personal experience, gained by participation in many formal and informal discussions of the subject in and around the District, as well as in other geographic areas, seems to indicate the existence of a belief in the minds of many that the official handling of this type of offender is precise and distinctive and that mental retardation is separated out from delinquency with special services being extended promptly from the beginning of court intervention. What is the truth? Is the problem of mental retardation clearly identified and, if so, is it the main determinant in making the judicial decision and planning rehabilitation? What is the child likely to receive in the way of services while he passes through the delinquency control system? Is there a problem at all? Perhaps we will see as we move along.

It seems pertinent at this point to relay some of our experiences with the Mental Retardation Committee of the Public Health Advisory Council, which Committee developed a comprehensive plan for mental retardation in the District of Columbia.[1] We had the pleasure of chairing the Working Party on the Retarded Offender, which was one of 15 subcommittees. This working party, made up of professionals from the control system and universities, struggled for months (during 1965 and 1966) with the foregoing questions and arrived finally at some definite conclusions.

We should further round out our perspective by defining what we mean by "mildly retarded child." We are talking about a child with an IQ range from 60 to 89, bridging a variety of behavior problems. Our concepts are described quite precisely in the writings of G. Orville Johnson[2] of the School of Education, Syracuse University:

> The slow learners are the highest intellectual group of retarded children and are largest in number. They form the 15 to 17 per cent of the school population that can not quite "keep up" and are usually doing the poorest work in the regular classroom. Slow learners are essentially normal in their emotional social, physical and motor development. Even in intellectual development the slow learners are at the lower fringe or range of the normal group. Thus, while they are retarded and consequently have difficulty in "keeping up" with the rest of the class, their deviation is not so great that they cannot be adequately educated in a regular classroom situation.

> The mentally handicapped are defined as those children who are so intellectually retarded that it is impossible for them to be adequately educated in the regular classroom. They are, however, educable in the sense that they can acquire sufficient knowledge and ability in the academic areas that the skills can and will become useful and usable tools. Further, they have a prognosis of social adequacy and occupational or economic self-sufficiency as adults. They will be able to apply the skills learned during the years of their formal education toward maintaining an independent social and economic existence as adults.

An additional identifying factor is the legal age of being adjudicated as a delinquent in the District of Columbia. The lower limit is age seven and the upper limit is age eighteen. Jurisdiction may be waived at age sixteen.

It seems to us that it might further set the tone for our discourse if we were to share with you some of the material developed for the Working Party on the Retarded Offender by Elyce Zenoff Ferster,[3] who is Associate Professor of Law at George Washington University with the Institute of Law, Psychiatry and Criminology. This report states:

> Although insufficient data exists about the mentally retarded offender to enable this Working Party to offer specific recommendations about changes in laws and procedures for determining their guilt or rehabilitating them, there is enough data to indicate that these offenders present unique problems to the administration of justice which to date have not been dealt with adequately. Estimates of the percentages of prisoners who are retarded has varied through the years depending on the theory of criminology which was dominant at the time. Before the development of psychological tests, the premise was that vast majority of criminals were inferior in the noncriminal period. They were thought to be inherently defective physically and mentally. In the early 1900's Goddard began testing intelligence tests in prisons and training schools and reported that a large percentage of the inmates were retarded and predicted that as the skill of the testers improved a higher percentage of prisoners would be found retarded. However, as more refined tests were developed and control groups were used, many researchers reported that the criminal and noncriminal population had approximately the same intelligence. Variations in intelligence were attributed to cultural, economic conditions and school systems. The result was that not only mental retardation's relation to crime was ignored for several decades but also the special problems of the retarded offender.

Much of what develops for juveniles in the way of correctional services follows the patterns of the adult programs, e.g. work-release and half-way houses. The mentally retarded child is no exception. Let us travel with the child through the maze of the delinquency control system from the time he is apprehended for an act of delinquency or brought into court on a complaint such as truancy.

POLICE INTERVENTION

The primary role of the police officer is to apprehend an offender and place him in secure custody if he so decides. He has no way to determine the existence of mental retardation unless he knows the individual's background from having been stationed in a neighborhood over a period of time. While it is true that he might handle a minor act or misdemeanor in such known cases by turning the child over to parents or guardians rather than placing him in the Receiving Home for Children, he has no choice but to incarcerate the child as having committed an unlawful act if he elects to detain him. There are no facilities available to police officers in the District, nor any diagnostic services working with them, to determine the existence of mental retardation at the point of arrest. This diagnosis, and study, then becomes the responsibility of the court after the child has been placed in detention.

THE COURT PROCESS

The Juvenile Court of the District of Columbia has jurisdiction over children under eighteen, hears complaints involving law violations, habitual truancy, beyond parental control, being without parental care or being in a situation harmful to themselves or others.

An Intake Officer screens and evaluates complaints concerning juveniles referred to the Court by parents, school attendance officers or law enforcement officials alleging various offenses, ranging from misdemeanors to capital offenses. The preliminary investigation includes interviews with the child, parents or guardians, and other adults when appropriate; contacts with other agencies to whom the family and child are known; and evaluations from all schools attended by the child. Need for referral is determined on the basis of data collected, as well as what step should be taken by the Court legally.

If an arraignment occurs, it is determined whether or not the child is involved. In most cases where the child is found involved, the case is continued for ninety days and assigned to a Probation Officer for a social study and recommendation for disposition. It is at this point of service that the question of retardation might be raised and the child referred to the Child Guidance Clinic at the Court for additional study. The Court estimates that 10 percent of children seen in the Clinic fall into the mentally defective range (0-65); 30 per cent into the borderline group (66-79); 30 per cent into the dull normal category (80-89); 27 per cent into the average classification (90-110); and 3 per cent into the "above average" area. The great majority of those who fall into the mentally retarded group are likely to be committed to the Department of Public Welfare for institutional services.

The Court considers the nature of the act, resources in the family and community, and the need for institutional care when making the decision for disposition. Where function and potential are very low, the Court is likely to recommend further legal processing for ultimate placement in the District Training School even though the child will be placed initially in an institution for delinquents.

INSTITUTIONAL CARE

The Children's Center at Laurel, Maryland, administered by the D.C. Department of Human Resources (formerly the Department of Public Welfare), includes four component institutions, three of which house delinquents and one of which cares for mentally retarded persons.

Maple Glen School has a capacity for 241 younger, less aggressive, delinquent boys (age 7 to 14½). Cedar Knoll School has a capacity for 352 older, more aggressive boys (age 14½ to 18) and 200 girls (age 7 to 18). The new Juvenile Facility, which is the fenced replacement for National Training School for Boys, has a capacity of 150 and houses older, recidivistic boys who need secure custody while being involved in a program of rehabilitation. Forest Haven, also known as District Training School, houses approximately 1,230 mentally retarded persons ranging from infancy to old age.

When a child is placed at any of the delinquency facilities for the first time, a study is done by Social Service and Psychology to determine whether special treatment services are needed. All previous diagnostic material is reviewed and any specific recommendations of the Court (especially regarding children who seem retarded or severely emotionally disturbed) are picked up for further handling.

Assume that we are following the child with an IQ of 60 or below through the institutional services. The Orientation Committee (a multidiscipline team) will plan a program of remedial academics and (in Cedar Knoll and the new Juvenile Facility) vocational education. Counseling by Department of Vocational Rehabilitation employees based at Children's Center may well be a part of this program, with ultimate job training at Help for Retarded Children or Goodwill Industries. If, in a period of nine months to a year, the child's level of functioning rises and he achieves a stable personality adjustment, he most likely will not be referred to U.S. District Court through the Mental Deficiency Clinic at D.C. General Hospital. If he is referred, based on poor adjustment and low level of functioning, diagnosis and study by the Clinic and Children's Center material will be presented at Court to secure a commitment to District Training School.

Following are the number of children committed to District Training School over a five-year period, who originally came to the Children's Center as committed delinquents:

Fiscal Year 1964 13
Fiscal Year 1965 11
Fiscal Year 1966 16
Fiscal Year 1967 12
Fiscal Year 1968 19
Fiscal Year 1969 (referrals) .... 3 (as of 3/28/69)

It is worth noting the sharp drop in the current fiscal year as we head into the last fiscal quarter. The figure of three represents referrals only and no more are pending as of that report. Initial information indicates that community-related programming at the delinquency facilities, plus intensified special programming within those institutions, is partly responsible for this dramatic drop.

PROFILE OF THE MILDLY RETARDED CHILD WITHIN THE INSTITUTION

In the Delinquency Facility

The child may have the potential to function at least in the dull, normal range but be functioning at a lower level of retardation. If his personality has been damaged, he may behave poorly in classrooms or during group activities, which tends to enhance the picture of "mental retardation." On the other hand, if his personality is quite intact, he may behave well enough to learn at a simple level in school, especially in the vocational area, and be trained for employment in fairly routinized jobs. Most likely, he will be a follower in the fast moving crowd of delinquent children and probably will be "low man on the totem pole." Nonetheless, he may well pass through this facility and be returned to the community without being referred for placement at District Training School. Much depends on the actual level of his functioning and the stability of his behavior.

In the District Training School

Here, he will likely rise to the top of the group and constitute part of the peer leadership. He is programmed for training in remedial academics and vocational training. He may well gain employment out in the community and, if his behavior is stable, gain much status in all of his relationships. Employers in the Laurel, Maryland area are quite vocal in praising the work and behavior of these students who generally work in simple jobs. Some of them develop their potential to the point that they can be somewhat deceptive in giving responses, but most are quite open and frank.

Generally, except for cases of assault with weapons or physical assault, the delinquency complaint rarely becomes a consideration in rehabilitation and will not hinder placement in the community. Having been committed to District Training School, however, the release will continue to have Social Service available for years after he is returned to the community to help him over any hurdles encountered.

A clear fact is that, throughout the correctional process, there is a limited focus on the problem of retardation until the child is placed in an institution. He is few in numbers and it may require regional planning to set up adequate diagnostic and rehabilitative facilities *based in the community*. He may well be included with other handicapped persons so served who have not run afoul of the law. He does need our closest attention so that he does not become lost in the doldrums of sweeping yards and picking up paper as a part of his rehabilitation.

REFERENCES

1. D.C. Public Health Advisory Committee: Report of mental retardation planning committee. D.C. Dept. of Public Health, 1968.
2. Johnson, G.O.: The education of mentally handicapped children. In Cruickshank, W.M. and Johnson, G.O. (Eds.) : *Education of Exceptional Children and Youth*. Englewood Cliffs, Prentice Hall, Inc., 1958.
3. D.C. Public Health Advisory Committee: Report of working party on the retarded offender; mental retardation planning committee. D.C. Dept. of Public Health, 1966.

Chapter XXV

THE IMPORTANCE OF AN EARLY DEFINITIVE EDUCATIONAL EVALUATION OF THE CHILD WITH LEARNING DISABILITIES

WRETHA K. PETERSEN

BEFORE discussing the educational evaluation of the child who has learning disabilities it is important to identify what we mean by the term "learning disabilities." Certainly there is no prototype. However, a child who has the following cluster of characteristics is frequently considered to be the prototype. This child seems to be constantly on the move, flitting from one activity to another. He is easily diverted by surrounding sights and sounds. He finds it difficult to attend to the spoken word and to respond to it. He has few impulse controls, is compulsive and aggressive. He is clumsy and awkward. He has poor interpersonal relationships with both his peers and adults.

Certainly, a child with learning disabilities may show some or all of the above characteristics. However, a child with learning disabilities can show very different characteristics. He may be a quiet, retiring child, refraining from involvement with people and things, especially people. Rather than flitting from one thing to another, he may continue at an activity long after it has ceased to be meaningful. He may appear to be attending closely to the spoken word, but may not respond appropriately. And he may be well developed in gross and fine motor control.

There may be auditory and/or visual perceptual problems including foreground/background confusion, reversals, sequencing problems and inability to get the Gestalt. If perception is impaired, the processing of the input and the response to it would be inaccurate. It is also possible that problems may be present in the processing act or in the area of response. Memory, auditory and/or visual, may be effected; as well as immediate recall, or delayed recall, or both. Thinking may be extremely concrete. Organizational ability may be poor.

324

Learning disabilities may be present in various combinations and in different degrees of severity. No two children will show the same pattern. Again, there is no prototype.

The term "learning disabilities," as used by many people working in the field, refers to the disabilities as seen in children with at least average intellectual capacity. This does not exclude the existence of learning disabilities in children below average. However, the lower intellectual ability complicates the problem. There is a very important precaution to be kept in mind, however; that is, that learning disabilities may be the cause of a depressed IQ score.

Although it is difficult, if not impossible, to define the term learning disabilities in a universally accepted manner, Kirk's[1] definition seems most inclusive and appropriate. This definition states that "a learning disability refers to a specific retardation or disorder in one or more of the processes of speech, language perception, behavior, reading, spelling, writing or arithmetic."

Although there is no prototype for the learning disabled child, a few characteristics are shared by all children identified as having learning disabilities. McCarthy[2] describes these as follows:

1. All are retarded or disordered in school subjects, speech or language and/or manifest behavior problems.
2. None are assignable to major categories of exceptionality such as mental retardation or deafness.
3. All have some presumed neurologic basis (cerebral dysfunction) for their manifest disability or disabilities.

In order to plan an effective educational program for the child with learning disabilities, it is necessary that the teacher know as early as possible, and in educational terms, the areas wherein problems lie. Through the use of educational media and techniques the teacher seeks not only to identify learning disabilities which may be present in any given child but also to determine functioning levels in the various areas affecting academic and social behavior.

Since success in education depends on communication skills, communication is assessed throughout the period of time the child is being evaluated. The teacher checks the child's knowledge about himself and his ability to communicate it. Such knowledge, depending on the child's age and home environment, may include knowing his own full name, his age and birthdate (month and date), his father's and mother's surnames, his address and his telephone number. Other communication areas checked include knowledge of labels, ability to follow directions (simple and complex), ability to formulate and use language both in response to the teacher and in initiating communication, and ability to tell a personal story about a past event logically and in proper sequence.

The teacher also needs to know the following things about a child because his ability, or lack of ability, in these areas affects his performance in the program usually provided:

1. Can he sort colors and forms.
2. Can he match pictures, letters, words.
3. Can he work puzzles and at what level of difficulty.
4. Can he color within lines.
5. Can he make the scissors cut paper; can he cut on a line.
6. Can he reproduce a block design and at what level of difficulty.
7. Can he write his own name; can he do other writing.
8. Does he have sequencing skills; for example, can he do such things as arrange two to four pictures in order.
9. Does he have a feel for the meaning of numbers; can he count.

Throughout the period of time the teacher works with a child, the following observations are being made:

1. Is he work oriented; that is, does he tend to stay with a task until completed.
2. Is he able to leave an activity when completed or must he continue after it has long since lost its meaningfulness.
3. Is he able to keep in mind the directions given by the teacher.
4. Can he remember new materials learned.
5. Are frequent visual reversals present, such as seeing and placing or writing letters and numbers backwards or in reverse order, in seeing the printed letters "f" and "t" as identical, in seeing "on" as "no," and so forth.
6. Are auditory confusions present such as hearing "enemy"

as "emeny," or in sounding a word in sequential order but pronouncing it out of order as, for example, the word "stop" being sounded and then pronounced "tops" or even reversed to become "pots."

7. Does he catch and use the rhythmic patterns presented in speaking, or is his speech pattern jerky and accented incorrectly.
8. Does he seem to perceive spatial relationships as they relate to his maneuvering his body about the room, as he handles and arranges materials with which he is working, or as he arranges work on a paper. Is he aware of positional relationships such as before/after and first/last.
9. Do the clock and the calendar have meaning for him.
10. Can he organize an activity; if not, what seems to get in his way.
11. Can he think abstractly or is he dependent upon the concrete.
12. Can he integrate and use that which he learns.
13. What about his overall motor coordination.
14. What hand does he seem to prefer.
15. Does he tire quickly.
16. Does he seem to need to move about frequently.
17. Can he come back to an idea once he has been diverted.
18. How does he relate to other people.

When the teacher has looked definitively at the child, a beginning program is planned. But this is indeed only the beginning. Each segment of the program is presented and thoroughly evaluated in terms of whether it was at the child's functioning level and whether it accomplished that which was intended. The program must not only be at a level where the child can succeed but also be challenging and interesting, appealing both to the child's sense of accomplishment and of moving ahead.

Constantly the teacher looks at the program being presented in terms of what was learned about the child during the educational evaluation paired with what is happening in the here and now. What is succeeding? Why? What is not working? What needs to be changed?

The total child must always be kept in mind. Functioning in any one area must always be in relation to the whole. Many children with learning disabilities will need help in organizing, integrating, generalizing and using that which they learn.

Early identification of learning disabilities cannot be emphasized too strongly. When learning disabilities are recognized at the time of school entry and appropriate programming initiated, the prognosis is good. Earlier identification is even better. Prognosis is poor when identification is later than time of school entry.

REFERENCES

1. Kirk, S.A.: The Illinois test of psycholinguistic abilities: its origin and implications. In Hellmuth, J. (Ed.) : *Learning Disorders*. Vol. III, Seattle, Special Child Publications, 1968.
2. McCarthy, J.J. and McCarthy, J.F.: *Learning Disabilities*. Boston, Allyn and Bacon, Inc., 1969.

GLOSSARY

Note: This is a brief list of many of the essential, frequently used technical terms that occur in this book. It is included to make the book more useful to readers who may be unfamiliar with particular areas of this field. Each term is defined primarily in the context in which it is used in the text of the book.

Allopurinol—A drug used in the treatment of conditions with increased levels of uric acid in the blood. It acts to lower the blood level of uric acid by blocking the conversion of hypoxanthine to uric acid. Xanthine which is very soluble is excreted in the urine.

Amino Acids—A class of essential organic compounds that are the building blocks of proteins.

Aminoacidopathy—An abnormal condition in which there is a defect in amino acid metabolism.

Ankyloglossia—Tonguetie.

Assay—A method of or the act of measuring the amount of a substance.

Asphyxia—Death secondary to a deficiency or absence of oxygen.

Autoradiography—A technique by which the presence of radioactive compound is detected by its exposure of x-ray film.

Autosomal—A trait, character or condition controlled by a gene or an autosome.

Autosome—A chromosome not involved in sex determination. Not a sex chromosome. There are forty-four human autosomes.

Basal Ganglia—Anatomic regions of the brain located within and at the base of the cerebral hemispheres. They play an important role in muscle control. They include the caudate nucleus, the putamen, the globus pallidus, the amygdala and the claustrum.

Bifid Uvula—A uvula divided into two parts.

Biosphere—The totality or total extent of life on, above and below the surface of the earth.

Bossing—Prominent rounded areas (usually of the skull) that look but are not swollen.

Carpal Tunnel Syndrome—A condition characterized by burning or tingling sensations in the hand secondary to compression of the median nerve at the wrist as it passes through a boney, ligamentous tunnel.

Choreoathetosis—A condition characterized by rapid, jerky coordinated movements combined with slow, sinuous, writhing involuntary movements.

Chromatin—Material in the nucleus of the cell staining with dyes that stain DNA.

Clone—A group of individuals or cells originating from a single individual or cell.

Cognitive—Intellective; pertaining to the power of perception; relating to the intellect or higher cerebral capacities.

Consanguinity—A marriage or mating between genetically related individuals.

Corneal Opacification or Clouding—Loss of the normal transparent appearance of the cornea.

Cytomegalic Inclusion Disease—A virally caused, often fatal illness of the newborn characterized by the presence of multinuclear giant cells with both cytoplasmic and intranuclear inclusion bodies in the liver, lungs, brains, kidney and other organs. Symptoms include fever, jaundice, difficulty breathing, ecchymoses and internal hemorrhage.

Deamination—Process in which an amino group is removed from a compound.

Decarboxylate—Process in which CO_2 is removed from a compound.

Dermatoglyphics—The study of the patterns of ridges of the skin of the fingers, palms and soles of the feet.

DNA—Deoxyribose nucleic acid. The primary chemical component of the genetic material in chromosomes. The chemical macromolecule in which the genetic information is encoded and stored.

Dysarthria—Abnormal or defective speech articulation. Usually secondary to cerebral abnormality.

Dyslexia—An abnormality in the ability to read and understand often due to central nervous system involvement.

Dysplasia—Abnormal formation or development.

Endogenous—Originating from within the body.

Epicanthal Folds—A fold of skin covering the inner corner of the eye. It may occur on one or both sides.

Galactoside—A compound containing a carbohydrate which is the sugar galactose.

Genetic Heterogeneity—The concept that conditions with the same or similar description have different genetic bases.

Genotype—The actual genetic makeup of an organism at a given locus or place on a chromosome.

Gibbous—A convex, humped or protuberant deformity of the back.

Gluconeogenesis—The conversion of protein or fat to glucose.

Haptic—Touch or tactile.

Hirsutism—Unusual amount of hairiness when compared to other members of the family or the same ethnic group.

Hydrolase—An enzyme that promotes the cleavage of a compound by the addition of water.

Hyperkinesthetic—A heightening of the sense by which muscle movement and position are perceived.

Hypertelorism—Abnormal increase in the distance between the orbits of the eyes.

Hyperuricemia—Increased levels of uric acid in the blood.

Hyperuricosuria—Increased excretion of uric acid in the urine.

Interphase—The period in the cell cycle between successive mitosis.

Karyotype—Photographs of chromosomes cut out and mounted in a standard sequence according to decreasing size and structural characteristics.

Kernicterus—A serious abnormality of the nervous system presumably due to severe jaundice (high levels of bilirubin in the blood). Usually seen in infants.

Landau Posture—A test to evaluate muscle tone in the newborn. A normal infant will arch his back and raise his head to the level of his back when supported on the abdomen with one hand. The hypotonic infant will not be able to assume this posture when thusly supported.

Lyon Hypothesis—The supposition proposed by Dr. Mary Lyon that in mammalian cells a maternal or paternal X chromosome is inactivated so that most genes on the inactivated X chromosome are nonfunctional and mammalian females are as a result X-chromosomal mosaics.

Lysate—The product of the lysis or disruption of cells.

Lysosome—An ultra microscopic body in many types of cells containing many enzymes most of which split compounds by the addition of water.

Macromolecule—A very large molecule like DNA with a molecular weight in excess of one million.

Macrophage—A large cell with one nucleus coming from the tissue which migrates and devours foreign or dead material.

Metachromatic Staining—Staining of tissues in which different parts of the tissue take on different colors when a certain dye is applied or staining by dyes in which different tissues are stained differently.

Meconium—The dark mucoid intestinal excretion of the fetus. It constitutes the newborn's first normal bowel movement.

Micrognathia—Atypical reduction in size of the lower jaw which usually results in a smaller than normal oral cavity.

Mosaicism—The presence in an individual of cells having differing genetic expression or different chromosomal constitution but of the same genetic origin.

Opisthotonus—A type of extensive muscle spasm in which the back, head and legs are strongly arched backward.

Osmiophilic—Tissues which preferentially stain readily with the metal osmium.

Pedigree—A standard diagram describing the ancestral history of a given individual usually called the proband.

Phenotype—Those characteristics of the organism or individual that are observed; usually a result of the interaction of the genotype and the environment.

Polygenic Trait—An inherited condition determined by two or more genes. It usually varies quantitatively.

Polysomes—A compound structure consisting of ribosomes held together by a molecule of messenger RNA.

Proband—That individual through whom the members of a particular pedigree are found. Propositus is a synonymous term.

Respiratory Distress Syndrome—A condition occurring in the newborn period, particularly in premature infants, characterized by increasing shortness of breath, difficulty breathing and cyanosis. Also known as "hyaline membrane syndrome."

Ribosome—One of the RNA family. It is a ribonucleoprotein particle with two unequal subunits each made up of roughly equal parts of RNA and protein.

RNA—A compound from a family of polynucleotides composed of a sugar, ribose and a purine or pyrimidine base (not thymine). They are single stranded and weigh less than DNA.

Sib—A blood relative, usually a brother or sister.

Sibship—A group of persons all descended from a common ancestor.

Stereognosis—The ability to ascertain the shape and consistency of objects by touch.

Stigmata—Mental or physical marks or peculiarities that assist in diagnosing a condition.

Syndrome—A group of two or more signs and/or symptoms that occur together.

Toluidine Blue—A dye which stains tissues metachromatically.

Tetraploidy—An abnormality of chromosome number in which there are four sets of chromosomes instead of the usual two sets of chromosomes. In man the normal chromosome number is 46 and the tetraploid number is 92.

Toxoplasmosis—A condition produced by infection by a parasite Toxoplasma gondii. The condition can be transmitted from mother to fetus where it may produce cerebral calcification, seizures and mental retardation.

Triploidy—An abnormality of chromosome number in which there are 3 sets of chromosomes rather than two which is normal. In man the triploid chromosome number is 69.

INDEX

A

AMP, 52, 146

Abortions
  due to chromosomal abnormalities, 18-20
  legalized, 229-230
  therapeutic, 72, 91, 96, 180

Adenoidectomy, in MPS, 103

Adenylic acid, *see* AMP

Adult adjustment, 251-258

Aggression
  in disadvantaged, 207-208
  in Lesch-Nyhan syndrome, 61
  in MPS, 97
  in XYY syndrome, 38, 42

AID milk program, 134

Albinism, 48, 49

Albumin turbidity test, 100

Alcaptonuria, 49

Alcian blue stain in MPS, 101

Allopurinol in Lesch-Nyhan syndrome therapy, 54, 59, 60

Amelioration of mental deficiency, 228-237
  abortion, legalized, 229
  cultural deprivation, reduced, 229
  medical care, free, 229

American Association on Mental Deficiency, 160

American Breeders' Association, 240

American Psychological Association, 254

Aminoacidopathies and mental retardation, 45-57
  clinical abnormalities, biochemical basis, 49-56
  deficit index, 46
  histidinemia and deficit index, 46-47
  scope, 45-46
  screening and diagnosis, 47-48
    limitations, 48-49

Amino acids, 54
  aspartic acid, 50, 51

  in histidinemia, 48-49
  in Kwashiorkor, 108, 134
  tryptophan, 26
  see also Glutamine & Glycine

Amniocentesis, 68-72, 91, 173, 179

Amniotic fluid cultures, 179
  enzymes in, 69
  for MPS, 102-103
  for Lesch-Nyhan syndrome, 64-72

Antibiotics, 91

Antisocial behavior: role of the environment, 33-35, 42
  see also Aggression

Anxiety in XYY syndrome, 39

Aperts' syndrome, 151

Aphasic children, 110

Arachnodactyly, 154

Asphyxia, neonatal, 173, 174-176, 179, 180-182

Ataxia-telangiectasia, 18-19, 21-22

Audiogram, 114, 132

Audiometrics, 117

Auditory tracking, 110, 115, 120-123, 126, 128, 130-131

Autistic children, 263-265, 270

Autoradiography, 7, 66, 143-144

Autosomes
  and growth, 17-18
  and intelligence, 5-12
  in recessive mode transmittance, 18-19, 79, 96, 98-99, 164

B

Banneker Project, St. Louis, 199, 214

Barratt Impulsiveness Scale, 41

Basal ganglia and HG-PRTase, 52-53, 63

Behavior
  adaptive, 236-237, 245, 282
  language, 234
  mobility, 234
  self-help, 234

Behavioral and cognitive aspects of the

XYY condition, 30-44
 antisocial behavior: role of the environment, 33-35
 background and characteristic findings,
  30-33
 characteristics, behavioral, 39-42
 characteristics, mental and emotional,
  35-38
 frequency of the condition, 33
Behavioral Sciences, Center for Advanced Study, Palo Alto, 215
"Berry spot test," 99, 155
Biochemical abnormalities, 49, 56
 in histidinemia, 45-47
 in Lesch-Nyhan syndrome, 50, 52
Biochemistry, 49
 applications in training mentally retarded, 138-150
Biopsy
 for gangliosidosis, 90
 renal, 80
 skin, 66, 71, 101
"Black power," 197-198
Bloom's syndrome, 18-19
Brain *see* Cerebral
Buchanan Program, 313

C

Cardozo Project, Washington, D.C., 199
"Carpal tunnel syndrome," 98, 104
Carrier, 18, 75
 detection and inheritance, 64-68
 for gangliosidosis, generalized, 91
 genetic counseling and amniocentesis,
  68-72
Caste, class and intelligence, 185-198
 language codes, 300
 premises, set of, 186-187
 society, caste structure of, 187-190
 stagnation in infancy, prevention of,
  190-198
 see also Disadvantaged child
Cat-cry syndrome, 11
Cedar Knoll School, 320-321
Cellular clones, 68
Central nervous system
 damage at birth, 173, 174-175
  prevention, 178

development, 187-190
 functioning, 28
 in MPS, 95, 103
 scrambling in histidinemia, 110-111
Cerebral
 deficit, prenatal factors, 173-184
 dysfunction, xv, xvi
Cerebral function, xv-xvi, 138-140
 β-galactosidase activity in gray matter,
  86
 response, 146
Cerebral Palsy, 58, 176, 179, 182, 188
Child Development Program, Yale, 221
Child Guidance Clinic at Court, 319, 321
Children's Center, Laurel, Md., 320
Children's Hospital of the District of
  Columbia, 26
Choreoathetosis in Lesch-Nyhan syndrome, 61
Chromosome
 breakage, 18-22
 chromatin positivity study, 13
 defects and abnormalities, xvi, 11-12,
  18, 23, 25, 156-157
 deletion, partial, 11
 extra X, 6-10, 13-14, 23
 extra Y, 30-44
 sex, 12-14, 14-17, 22-23
 sex chromatin surveys of males, 12
 study, controlled, 11
 translocation, 7
 X-chromatin body, 12, 96
 see also Autosome, Chromosome aberrations
Chromosome aberrations, human: correlations with mental and growth retardation, 5-25
 autosomes and growth, 17-18
 autosomes and intelligence, 5-12
 chromosome breakage, intelligence and
  growth, 18-22
 chromosomes and intrauterine growth,
  18
 chromosome variations and normality,
  22
 sex chromosomes and growth, 17-18
 sex chromosomes and intelligence, 12-
  14

sex chromosomes and mental disorder, 22-23

speculations, 23-25

see also Chromosome

Clinicians, 266-268, 272

"Clucking John syndrome," 110

Cognitive and social-emotional development, findings on impact of early stimulation programs, 304-315

Conditioning, operant and reflex, 262, 264

reinforcement, 265-269

Conradi's syndrome, 157

Consanguinity, parental, 162

Corneal clouding, 95, 98

Curriculum

development, 247-248, 292

innovation, 217-218

Cytogenetics, 6, 23-25

Cytomegalic inclusion disease, 173

Cytoplasm

vacuolation in MPS, 101

vacuolation in splenic histiocytes, 79-80, 82

D

Deficit index and histidinemia, 46-47

Definition of mental retardation, 161, 242-243, 295

Deformities *see* Malformations

DeLange, Cornelia, syndrome, 151, 157

Delinquency in mildly retarded children, 316-323

court process, 319-320

institutionalization, 320-321

police intervention, 318-319

Deprivation

cultural, 201, 229

environmental, 166, 190

psycho-social, 190-191, 284

sensory, 297-299

Deprived personality syndrome, 305-306

Developmental aspects of mental retardation, 171-328

Diagnosis

antenatal in Lesch-Nyhan syndrome, 64-68, 72

antenatal in MPS, 102-103

behavioral approach to, 232

etiologic, of mental retardation, 159

of gangliosidosis, generalized, 90-91

in histidinemia, 48-49

prenatal, 173, 179

preschool, 248, 274-278

psycho-educational, 234-237

Diagnostic teaching, 274-278

Dietary control

in Kwashiorkor, 108-114, 127-137

in Lesch-Nyhan disease, 54-56

tube feeding, 91

see also Protein diet

Disadvantaged child

cultural milieu and education, 199-214

conclusion, 212-214

who are disadvantaged, 201, 203

cultural milieu, 204-208

school, 209-212

socially; educational approaches and techniques, 215-227

Disorders of Development and Learning, Dept. of, Chapel Hill, 175-176

District Training School, 320-321, 322

Down's syndrome, 5-10, 22, 155

chromosome, extra, 6-10

5-hydroxytryptophan administration, 26-29

malformations, 8-10

translocation, 7

twins with, 5

see also Trisomy

Dropouts, 200, 210, 212, 220

Dwarfism, 298

E

Educability, 233, 236, 243

limits, 267

see also Education

Education

adult, 219, 281

compensatory, 216-220, 225, 233, 242-245, 280

Dept. of, 199

of disadvantaged child, 199-214, 215-227

early, of moderately mentally retarded, 279-287

and management of retarded child; use of learning principles, 262-273

problems and issues of educating mentally retarded, 240-242

public school reformation, 221-225, 244

school system, 192, 209-212

training school, 322

see also Conditioning

Embryology, 151, 187

Employment, 209, 214, 250-261

Environment and mental retardation, 165-167

antisocial behavior, role in, 33-35

automatic, 264

home, 280, 298

teaching, 280

variables in, 295-363

language development, inadequate, 299-300

malnutrition, 296-297

sensory deprivation, 297-299

socialization cues, discontinuities in, 301-302

Enzyme, 145

demonstrated in amniotic fluid cell cultures, 69

gangliosidosis, generalized, defect in, 84-90

Kwashiorkor, deficiency in, 108

Lesch-Nyhan syndrome, defect in, 51, 54

Estrogen therapy in Turner's syndrome, 14

Euthanasia, 241

Evaluation, educational, of child with learning disabilities, 324-328

F

Family

conflicts with school, 301

retardation in, 163-165, 279

structure, 204, 250

studies, 7

Fanconi's pancytopenia syndrome, 18-19

Federal Government assistance, 199, 239

Ferric chloride urine test, 108-109, 110, 134

Fibroblast culture

in gangliosidosis, generalized, 91

for detection of carriers in Lesch-Nyhan syndrome, 66-68

in MPS, 101-102

mutant culture, 67

Formimino-transferase-deficiency syndrome, 109

Fucosidosis, 104-106

G

GMP, 52, 54, 60

Galactosidase activity, 84-91, 104-106

Ganglioside

GM1, 87-90, 104-106

GM2, 88

Gangliosidosis, generalized; molecular defect and mental retardation, 75-92

chemical findings, 83-84

clinical manifestations, 75-78

diagnosis, 90-91

enzymic defect, 84-90

genetics, 79

pathologic manifestations, 79-83

prevention, 91

radiologic findings, 79

structure, 84

therapy, 91

Gaucher's disease, 84, 87

Genetics

autosomal recessive, 18-19, 79, 96

carriers and detection, 18

in Lesch-Nyhan syndrome, 64-68

chromosome breakage, increased, 19

control of heritability, 160

counseling, 68-72, 91, 96, 99, 180

in gangliosidosis, generalized, 79

and metabolic aspects of mental retardation, 3-169

molecular, 84

MPS, 94

mutant, 64, 75

see also Amniocentesis

Giemsa stain, 6, 67

Glutamine, 50, 51, 55-56

Glycine, 50, 51, 60

Growth
and autosomes, 17-18
brain, postnatal, 297
and chromosome breakage, 18-22
and chromosome, sex, 14-17
intrauterine and chromosomes, 18
in MPS, 95
optimum, 275
Guanylic acid *see* GMP

H

5-HT in Down's syndrome, 26-29
5-HTP
in Down's syndrome, 26-29
in histidinemia, 26
reduced levels, significance, 26
therapy with, 27-28
Hand abnormalities in malformation
syndrome associated with mental retardation, 151-158
arachnodactyly, 154
chromosomal abnormalities, 156-157
hand development, 151-152
MPS, 155
nail abnormalities, 157-158
pseudohypoparathyroidism, 153
Rubenstein-Taybi syndrome, 152-153
short broad hands, 157
Haptic-kinesthesis, 112, 124, 129-130, 132
Head-Start, 134, 199, 220, 305, 308, 310,
311, 312
Hebb's system, 288-292
Hepatomegaly in gangliosidosis, generalized, 76
Heredity and heritability
and carrier detection of Lesch-Nyhan
syndrome, 64-68
chromosome abnormalities, 7
control, 160
genetic counseling and amniocentesis,
68-72
and mental retardation, 241
metabolic defects, 109
modes, usual, 159, 163
recurrence risks, 162-165
X-linked mode, 58-59, 64, 65, 69
Heterozygote
carrier in MPS, 102, 103

detection, 135
lymphocytes, 66
Higher Horizons Program, N.Y.C., 199
Histidinemia, 26, 55
and the Deficit Index, 46-47
-like behavior in Kwashiorkor, 108-137
Homocystinuria, 154
Homozygotes
in Lesch-Nyhan, 64
in MPS, 103
Hunter's syndrome, 94, 96, 102, 103, 155
Hurler's syndrome, 76, 94, 95-96, 103, 155
5-Hydroxytrytophan *see* HTP
Hyperreflexia syndrome, 76
Hyperuricemia in Lesch-Nyhan syndrome, 50-54, 58-59
Hypoglycemia, neonatal, 173-174, 179
Hypoplasia
in gangliosidosis, generalized, 75, 77,
79
in Goltz's syndrome, 157
Hypotonia, 27
in gangliosidosis, generalized, 75, 76
in Lesch-Nyhan syndrome, 53
Hypoxanthine guanine phosphoribosyltransferase *see* PRT

I

IMP, 51-52, 60
IQ
and Deficit Index, 46-47
in mental retardation, 161-163, 166,
243-244, 317
in prematures, 178
tests, 160, 161, 165, 192, 237, 243, 306,
307-308, 310, 325
in Turner's syndrome, 37, 38
in XO subjects, 23
in XYY males, 36, 37
"I-cell disease," 104-106
Infantile hypothyroidism, 26
Infantile spasm syndrome, 26
Infections
in gangliosidosis, generalized, 78
perinatal, 173, 230
Inosinic acid *see* IMP
Institute for Teachers of Disadvantaged
Youth, 213

Institutionalization, 23, 275, 320-321, 321-322
Interactions
  group, 282
  social, adult-infant, 190, 250
  therapeutic, 266
Intelligence
  and autosomes, 5-12
  caste and class, 185-198
  chromosome damage, 18-22
  chromosomes, sex, 12-14
  development of, 275
  modifiability, 233
  see also IQ
International Conference on Malnutrition, Learning and Behavior, 296
International League of Societies for Mentally Handicapped, 259
Intervention programs, 304, 307, 311
  police, 316-323
Isotopic test for purines de novo, 60

K

Kennedy, President John, 228-229
Kernicterus, 173-174
  prevention, 179
Klinefelter's syndrome, 17, 23, 31, 38
Kwashiorkor, 297
  histidinemic-like behavior, 108-137
    historical review, 108-112
    population selection, 112-114
    recovery, 132
    results, 127-132
    significance, 133-135
    testing procedure, 114-117
    test results, 117-127

L

Language and speech
  codes, 300
  development, inadequate, 299-300
  development studies, 111, 300
  histidinemia, disorder in, 109-111
  Kwashiorkor, disorder in, 128
  learning, 192, 217, 277
  patterns, 205-207, 209, 306
  see also Auditory tracking
Law and disadvantaged child, 207

delinquency, 316-323
Lawrence-Moon-Biedl syndrome, 151
Learning
  adaptive, 190, 233
  disabilities, 188, 217
    early educational evaluation, 324-328
  informal, 220
  language, 194, 217
  principles in education and management, 262-273
  processes, 221-222, 265, 276
  rate, 307
Lesch-Nyhan syndrome, 50-56, 58-74
  clinical and biochemical features of, 58-74
Lesion
  glomerular, 80
  hemorrhagic, 174-175
  nuclear, 181
  renal, 80
Lipid storage diseases, 79, 84, 93, 104-106
"Lipomucopolysaccaridosis," 104-106
Loading tests
  in histidinemia, 48
  in Kwashiorkor, 108, 133
Lysosomal structures, 84, 88, 106

M

MPS, 78, 79, 88, 93-107
  antenatal diagnosis, 102-103
  classification, 99
  clinical management, 103-104
  hand abnormalities in, 155
  recognition, 93-99
    Hunter's syndrome, 96
    Hurler's syndrome, 95-96
    Maroteaux-Lamy syndrome, 98-99
    Morquio's syndrome, 97
    Sanfilippo's syndrome, 97-98
    Schie's syndrome, 98
  similar disorders confused with MPS, 104-106
  screening tests for MPS excretion, 99-102
MSG in Lesch-Nyhan syndrome therapy, 54-56
Macromolecules, memory, 139, 140-142, 144-145

Malformation
  in Down's syndrome, 8
  in gangliosidosis, generalized, 75-78, 79
  in Hurler's syndrome, 76
  in MPS, 93-99
  see also Hand abnormalities
Malnutrition, 230, 296-297
  in Kwashiorkor, 108-114, 127-137
    infantile protein, 133-134
  in Lesch-Nyhan syndrome, 53, 55
Mannosidosis, 104-106
Maple Glen School, 320
Maple Syrup Urine Disease, 49, 55
Marasmus, 109, 297
Marfan's syndrome, 154
Maroteaux-Lamy syndrome, 94, 98-99
Marriage of mentally retarded, 241, 256
Medical care, free, 229
Memory, 139
  processes, biochemical studies of, 144-146
  storage, 140-141
Mental Deficiency Clinic at D.C. General Hospital, 321
Mental Retardation Committee of Public Health Advisory Council, 317-318
Mental retardation, moderate, early education of, 279-287
Mental retardation and self-destructive behavior: clinical and biochemical features of Lesch-Nyhan syndrome, *see* Lesch-Nyhan syndrome
Mental retardation, simple, 159-169
  and environment, 165-167
  etiology, polygenic, 160-163
  in families, 163-165
  inheritance, modes of, 159, 163
  prevention, 167-168
Metabolism
  blocks, 49, 88
  glutamine in brain, 56
  hereditary defects, 49-50, 55, 109, 180
  Lesch-Nyhan syndrome, defects in, 58, 62-63
  MPS, defects in, 93, 102
  see also Genetic and metabolic aspects of mental retardation
Metachromatic inclusion, 100-101

Microcephaly, 175-176
Minority, ethnic, 195, 217, 301
  integration, 224-225
  see also Racism
Molecular defect and mental retardation
  see Gangliosidosis, generalized
Mongolism *see* Down's syndrome
Monosodium glutamate *see* MSG
Morquio's syndrome, 94, 97-98
Mortality, infant, 11
Mosaicism, 10, 23, 64-66, 67
  in Down's syndrome, 28
Motor development, 298
Mucopolysaccharidoses *see* MPS

N

Nail abnormalities, 151, 157-158
National Training School, 320
Neurobiology Program of University of North Carolina, 141
Neurological abnormalities, 182, 289
  in Lesch-Nyhan syndrome, 61, 63
Neuronal pathways, 139-141, 145
Neuropsychology, 288
  and Deficit Index, 46
Niemann-Pick disease, 84, 87
Noonan's syndrome, 157
Number series, 114, 118-120
Nursery school, 283-287, 309, 313

O

O.E.O., 199
Oral stereognosis, 116, 123-125, 126, 128, 130-131, 132

P

PKU, 111, 133, 135
  detection, 135
PRPP, 51-52, 60, 62-63
PRT, 52, 58, 60-61, 62-67
Parent counseling programs, 282-285
Pare's high serotonin syndrome, 26
Peptides, 145
Periodic acid Schiff stain, 79
Phenylketonuria, 26, 55-56
5-Phosphoribosyl-1-Pyrophosphate *see* PRPP
Physician of mentally retarded, 283

Poverty and mental retardation, 201-208, 212-214, 230, 305-306
Practice in learning, 290, 292
Prader-Willi syndrome, 157
Prematurity, 174, 177, 178
Preschool programs, 220, 248, 304, 306, 308, 312, 314
  diagnostic teaching, 274-278
  see also Education, early
President's panel on mental retardation, 228-229, 238, 240-241, 250, 256-257
Prevention of mental retardation, 48, 91, 167-168, 178-180, 230
Primary infantile autism, 26
Project Mission, Baltimore, 199
Protein
  deficiency, 166, 188, 297
  diet
    in Kwashiorkor, 108-114, 127-137
    in Lesch-Nylan syndrome, 54-56
  synthesis, 140-141, 144-145
  see also Kwashiorkor
Pseudohypoparathyroidism, 153, 157
Public Welfare, Dept. of, 320
Purine, de novo synthesis
  in histidinemia, 109
  in Lesch-Nyhan syndrome, 50-55, 58-60, 62-63
  pathway diagram, 51
Pyruvic acids, 108-109

R

RNA, 64, 140-146
Racism, 195-197
Radioactivity in RNA, 142-143
Radioautographic studies *see* Autoradiographic studies
Radiology, 79
Receiving Home for Children, 319
Recurrence risks *see* Heredity
Rehabilitation of mentally retarded, 232, 316, 318
Reinforcement, 272
  food, 265-267, 270
  natural, 269-271
  token, 267-269, 270
Renal calculi in Lesch-Nyhan syndrome, 54, 59
Repertoires, 264-265, 270

Respiratory distress syndrome, 179, 181
Ribonucleic acid *see* RNA
Rights of the mentally retarded, 259
Rubenstein-Taybi syndrome, 152-153

S

Sanfilippo's syndrome, 94, 97, 103
Schie's syndrome, 94, 98, 104
Segregation of mentally retarded, 240
Self-destructive behavior, 58-74
  in Lesch-Nyhan syndrome, 50, 55
Serotonin, 26, 55, 111
Simian line, 151, 152, 157
Social-emotional and cognitive development, findings on impact of early stimulation programs on, 304-315
Socialization, 285-286
  discontinuities in cues, 301-302
Society
  caste, class and intelligence, 185-198
  see also Disadvantaged child
Spasticity
  in gangliosidosis, generalized, 76
  in Lesch-Nyhan syndrome, 61
  quadriplegia, 175-176
Splenomegaly in gangliosidosis, generalized, 76
Stanford-Binet Intelligence tests, 306, 307, 310
Sterilization, 167-168, 241
Stigma of mental retardation, 242, 254-255
Stimulation
  programs on aspects of cognitive and social-emotional development, 304-315
  sensory, 141-144
    deficits, 292, 297-299
St. John's Child Development Center, 281, 285
Sulfates, 179
  dermatan, 96, 98, 99
  heparan, 96, 97, 98
  kerato, 88, 97

T

Taylor Manifest Anxiety Scale, 39-40
Tay Sach's disease, 80, 83, 86-88

Teacher's Corps, 199, 213
Teaching the mentally retarded, 233-237,
  247-249
  diagnostic, of preschool child, 274-278
  success, 289
  teacher, 249-250
  see also Education
Tests
  amniocentesis, 68-72
  carrier detection, 64-68
  enzymic, 48
  for gangliosidosis, 91
  isotopic, 60
  for Kwashiorkor, 108, 114-127, 133
    modified sign, 118-120, 128
  loading, 48
  for MPS excretion, 99-102
  WISC, 46, 192
Tetraploidy, 18, 19, 20
Thalidomide, 174
Thought progression, 288-291
Toluidine blue stain for MPS, 99, 101-
  102
Toxoplasmosis, 173, 175, 188, 230
Training of mentally retarded and bio-
    chemical applications, 138-150
  approaches, 141-143
  brain function, ignorance, 138-140
  memory, storage, 140-141
  memory processes, biochemical studies
    of, 144-146
  results, 143-144
Translocation in Down's syndrome, 7, 10
Trauma, birth, 173-174
Triploidy, 18, 19
Trisomy syndromes, 19, 20

13 or *D*, 8, 11, 18, 156
18, 8-12, 18, 156, 157
21, 7, 17, 22
Turner's syndrome, 14-17, 23, 37, 38, 157
  growth spurt chart, 15
  height, correlation of patient to paren-
    tal, 15
  height and sex chromosomes graph, 16
  IQ subtest of female's with, 37
Tyrosinase system, 48

U

Uric acid
  in Lesch-Nyhan syndrome, 51-54, 58-
    60, 62
  molecule, schematic presentation of,
    50

V

Vacuolation, cytoplastic, 79-80, 82
Visual matching, 116, 125
Visual system development, 187
Visual tracking, 110, 114, 117-118, 128,
  132

W

WISC tests, 192
  in histidinemia, 46
Workshop, sheltered for mentally retarded, 248

X

XO Turner's syndrome *see* Turner's syndrome
XYY syndrome, 30-44